Heavy Metal Thunder

Heavy Metal Thunder

by Philip Bashe

Omnibus Press
London/New York/Sydney/Cologne

A Sarah Lazin Book
© Copyright 1985 Philip Bashe and Sarah Lazin.
First published by Dolphin/Doubleday, New York.
This edition © 1986 Omnibus Press, London.
(A Division of Book Sales Limited).

Cover design by Pearce Marchbank Studio, London.

Printed in England by Ebenezer Baylis & Son Ltd.

ISBN 0.7119.0764.1
Order No. OP 43496

Exclusive distributors:
Book Sales Limited
78 Newman Street, London W1P 3LA, UK.
Omnibus Press
GPO Box 3304, Sydney, NSW 2001, Australia.
To the music trade only:
Music Sales Limited
78 Newman Street, London W1P 3LA, UK.

Acknowledgments

⊂⊃⊂⊃⊂⊃

I would like to thank the following people for their contributions to the creation of this book.

First, the performers whose generous cooperation over the years was invaluable: Rob Halford and the members of Judas Priest, AC/DC, Black Sabbath, Def Leppard, Iron Maiden, Motley Crue, Ozzy Osbourne, Quiet Riot, Rush, Scorpions, Van Halen, Eric Bloom of Blue Oyster Cult, Ronnie James Dio, Mark Farner of Grand Funk Railroad, Roger Glover of Deep Purple, Lemmy Kilminster of Motorhead, Mike Levine of Triumph, Michael Schenker, Paul Stanley and Gene Simmons of Kiss, Roger Taylor of Queen, and Link Wray.

Thanks to the photographers, their representatives, and collectors: Ross Marino; Paul Natkin/Photo Reserve; the Michael Ochs Archives; Laurie Paladino; Neal Preston; Jodi Peckman, Tom Vincent, and Walter McBride of Retna Ltd.; Ebet Roberts and Desmond Sullivan; and Mark Weiss.

For their support and assistance, thank you, Janna Allen, Mr. and Mrs. Robert Bashe, Sari Becker, Ron Bienstock, Howard Bloom, Mark Bosch, Jill Buckler, Janis Bultman, Mary Ellen Cantaneo, Patti Conte, Fran DeFeo, Rosemary Diminno, Michael Dinhoffer, Warren Entner, Nancy Farbman, Stephanie Franklin, Steve Futterman, Sherry Ring Ginsberg, Robert Hahn, Dan Hedges, Michael Jensen, Ronni Kairey, Ida Langsam, Marilyn Laverty, Carl Leeds, Steve Mandel, Lisa Markowitz, Rhonda Markowitz, Lois Marino, Bill McIlvaine, Brant Mewborn, Jody Miller, Michelle Miller, Annette Monaco, Linda O'Brien, Maureen O'Conner, Joe Owens, Rob Patterson, Vivian Piazza, George Ploska, Caroline Prutzman, David Reichert, Nancy Rice, Gail Roberts, Melani Rogers, Gerald Rothberg, Mitchell Schneider, Ricki Sellner, Michael Shore, Rhonda Shore, Rod Smallwood, Pat Smith, Michael Smolen, Julie Steigman, Audrey Strahl, Sandy Sawotka, Doug Thayler, Katie Valk, Sharon Weisz, and Anne Weldon.

Special thanks to my editor at Doubleday, Jim Fitzgerald; his assistant, Casey Fuetsch, and Doug Bergstreser. For their work on the design and production, Kathleen Westray, Ed Sturmer, and Pete Peters.

Finally, to Sarah Lazin, a closet metalhead if there ever was one.

And a very special thank you to Patty (the Iron Maiden) Romanowski, the world's best rock & roll book editor.

Contents

FOREWORD
viii

Foreword

I HAVE been invited to try my hand at explaining heavy-metal music. First, heavy metal is power. It's controlled aggression; it's a unification of the artist and the audience into one. Without making it sound too much like Zen, you might say that heavy metal is all of those things, though probably its most important element is the bond that exists between the musician and the fan. At a heavy-metal concert, the entire arena becomes a stage, and though the band is the focal point, no barrier separates what's happening on the stage from what's happening in the audience. It's total involvement for everyone.

Though I've always said that you shouldn't analyze heavy metal but simply enjoy it, I do know that its power and appeal go far beyond that. One only has to listen to the fans to understand that there's more to loving heavy metal than banging your head at a concert. Heavy metal speaks to its fans. When you're fifteen or sixteen years old, it seems as though everybody's against you, your parents don't know anything about you, and you're constantly slamming the door and stalking out of the house, feeling frustrated and confused. But at a heavy-metal concert, where everyone else is about your age and probably has the same sort of feelings, you're all there together, relating to the music, understanding it, singing about it, sharing it.

Heavy metal has been around for a long time and with good reason. For one thing, metal is as true to its roots today as when it first began back in the late Sixties and early Seventies. In all this time, while other styles of music go through a one- or two-year period of being fashionable before the public goes off looking for something new, heavy metal has the remarkable distinction of still being a strong and positive force.

When I'm in a particular mood, I'll listen to a particular style of music; that's exactly what heavy-metal fans do. If they're feeling frustrated or angry, they throw on a Judas Priest record, crank up the volume as loud as possible, and get it out of their systems. It's very therapeutic. Of course, there is always a certain amount of rebelliousness that goes with heavy metal, just as there was with Elvis Presley, Little Richard, and rock & roll in general. For that, and other things, heavy metal gets a lot of negative response and criticism from certain factions, including the Moral Majority, who claim that this music sets out to somehow bend young people's minds and to inspire violence, disruption, even Satanism. In fact, heavy metal's effect is quite the opposite, for it provides a catharsis for its audience. When a show ends, fans are as physically and mentally drained as we are; they're not going to start smashing windows or people. Ironically, the fact that the music is so often under attack only serves to make its fans even more loyal and protective.

"No," they'll say firmly to the critics, be they parents, teachers, or peers, "you're completely wrong; that's not what this music is about. This music is my music. It gives me a great deal of pleasure, of understanding, of release. And I don't want you messing with it." And that is how it should be.

On a more superficial level, what most critics find most frightening—and fans, most appealing—is heavy metal's look, which always has been and always will be very important. In concert, heavy metal is larger than life, so we performers try to look larger than life ourselves, as a sort of visual representation of the music. How else can I look other than the way I do? In what other costume could I perform heavy-metal music? That's pretty clear. But when a teenager comes down from his or her bedroom dressed in leather and studs, the parents stand there, no doubt gaping in disbelief, unable to understand how this could have happened to their child. The leather and studs is merely the audience's uniform, their gang colors, if you will. Again, the controversy over appearance is one of many scenarios that have been played countless times since rock began, and I don't think that will change.

But on a deeper level, I believe that heavy metal has more meaning now than ever before. Considering the current state of the world, being young is a very intimidating experience. I just find it remarkable to look down from the stage and see more and younger people in our audience every year. It makes me think that heavy metal will always be there, because, you see, it isn't just for that one period of your life. The proof is that I am in my mid-thirties and I still get the same tremendous joy from heavy metal that I did when I first started playing it all those years ago. Heavy metal is, I believe, forever.

—ROB HALFORD

Heavy Metal Thunder

Preface

⊂⊨ ⊂⊨ ⊂⊨

SUPERFICIALLY, much of heavy metal would appear to have little redeeming value—it can be musically primitive and lyrically inscrutable and seems to encourage behavior that could land you five to ten in some of the more conservative sections of this country. That it is so immensely popular with such a large segment of the international rock & roll audience is what makes heavy metal one of the cultural, let alone musical, phenomena of our time—as much for the sway it holds over its millions of fans as for the revulsion it inspires among critics, the media, and, needless to say, older listeners.

Because of its pariah status in rock-critical circles, heavy metal, both as a music and as a scene, has been woefully neglected by the media. And the press that it does receive, by way of the rock fan-mag glossies, is usually mawkishly adoring, as if showing any trace of objectivity or expressing criticism of the music or its idols would be blasphemy.

Hence I believe the need for such a book as *Heavy Metal Thunder*. While certainly this is a book for heavy-metal fans, it is also for those on the perimeter of the movement who are trying to comprehend just what it is about metal's mixture of honest musicianship and outlandish image that attracts its fans. It is as much for those who cheer wildly while being assaulted by a numbing mélange of volume, voltage, and visuals as it is for those who clap their hands over their ears but remain curious about what they are missing.

Heavy Metal Thunder looks at heavy metal as music, tracing its roots back to rock & roll's own adolescence, and as an intriguing part of rock culture, the one rock & roll genre to appeal almost exclusively to those in the throes (or agony) of adolescence. It is about the audience and the musicians, for as you will see, the two are intertwined as in no other music—perhaps the ultimate reasons for hard rock's longevity and commercial success. You will find that, contrary to popular belief, the majority of heavy-metal musicians are as passionate about their music—and can articulate their feelings and thoughts as convincingly as the staunchest jazz musician or the most ardent proponent of folk.

The ten acts featured in the second section of this book do not necessarily represent the best of heavy metal but those who best embody what the music stands for and who raise certain relevant issues regarding the music and its culture. There is here a certain detachment from the music, and that is quite intentional. Both metal's positive and destructive aspects are explored, because, after all, part of what makes heavy metal so good is its capacity to be so bad.

In the end, *Heavy Metal Thunder* attempts to provide historical and cultural analysis, but also to make the music and its musicians come alive. By the time you put this book down, your ears will be ringing.

—PHILIP BASHE

I N T R O D U C T I O N

BEFORE there was heavy metal, there was heavy metal. Long before it took on its metaphorical name, heavy-metal music was part of rock & roll's fabric and attendant culture, just as rock & roll, in the form of rhythm & blues, had been part of popular culture before it was so named.

Best indications are that the term *heavy metal* comes from Beat generation author William Burroughs's novel *Naked Lunch* (published in Paris in 1959, in the United States in 1962). In song the group Steppenwolf—whose music was a hybrid of hard rock and psychedelia—sang of "heavy-metal thunder" in their 1968 highway anthem, "Born to Be Wild," although in the context of taming a motorcycle. The rock press began using *heavy metal* as a descriptive adjective in the late Sixties, and by the early Seventies it was being used as a noun. Heavy metal had its own identity as a rock & roll genre.

While part of heavy metal's popularity is due to its musical simplicity, it is ultimately a combination of factors that is responsible for metal's commercial success. In addition to the music's relentless volume and the frequent repetition of progressions, there are the equally single-minded lyrics, which touch on a handful of themes that the groups' audiences never tire of. And this aural assault on the senses is delivered by cartoon characters dressed in costumes out of a teenager's wildest fantasies, most of which are based on power, be it physical, musical, or sexual. Other rock-music genres may include one or two of these elements. Heavy metal encompasses them all.

Today heavy metal is used to describe not only a particular type of music, but that music's philosophy and values. Its appeal to fans derives from its musical values and its milieu, particu-

Of all rock's tribes, the heavy-metal audience is the one most feared by rock-concert promoters, city fathers, and occasionally the acts themselves.

larly the concert arena, where the music itself often becomes a live soundtrack to an audience's celebration of uninhibited fun and freedom from the restrictions of home and school.

In that sense, even though it is often derided as an aberrant rock form, heavy metal is in many ways rock & roll's quintessential genre. If rock & roll is loud, heavy metal is louder, volume being an integral element in both its construction and its appeal. If rock & roll is about rebelliousness, heavy metal is positively anarchic, defying even rock's own conventions. If rock & roll is about breaking down the barriers between performer and audience, heavy metal completely erases the line separating the two, for its musicians are as much fans as the audience itself. In fact, in their vociferous support of that music, heavy-metal stars become the ultimate fans. If rock & roll is about extremes, amplify that for heavy metal, whose performers adopt the most outrageous personas, detonate their music from skyscrapers of amplifiers while parading in front of some of the most costly, elaborate stage sets outside of a Dino De Laurentiis production, and are received by their fans with a fervor that is unequaled.

Rock & roll has always been youth-oriented music, but heavy-metal fandom is almost exclusively restricted to the teenage years. For many kids, their first musical love—their first concert, record, or video—is heavy metal. One of the original though unspoken tenets of rock & roll was that it not be absorbed by mainstream culture. But as its first and second generations grew into adulthood, rock & roll accompanied them, though it probably no longer held either the importance or the mysticism it seemed to have had during their youth.

Heavy metal, on the other hand, invariably gets left behind with memories of high-school dances, first cars, and first sex, a vestige of youth, part of a phase one is expected to outgrow. Perhaps for that reason, though it has been one of the dominant and most commercially successful musical trends of the last five years, heavy metal has never been recognized and accepted by the media in the same way that such superficially threaten-

ing figures as, say, Culture Club's Boy George have been taken to heart. Especially among rock journalists, those arbiters of what's in and what's out, heavy metal has been handled only at arm's length. It has been scorned for its alleged musical primitivism (the same quality inherent in the mid-Seventies punk rock so hailed by critics), and its participants, both musicians and fans, have been ridiculed as living contradictions to the theory of evolution.

That it has never been embraced even within rock circles, however, has helped to fuel heavy metalers' protectiveness about their music and the musicians' collective image as outlaws stalking rock & roll's periphery. Without that shared feeling of ostracism, metal might lose its edge, its burning ambition to prove its worth, and hence its notoriety as the ultimate populist music.

Rock & roll itself began as a populist music form. Such Fifties rockers as Elvis Presley, Jerry Lee Lewis, and Little Richard—all Southerners raised on orthodox Christianity and gospel and blues—recorded music that provided American teenagers with a physical outlet for their unnamed frustrations, largely sexual. And the electric guitar was the perfect instrument with which to express that frustration, offering itself for steady punishment—the harder you smash it, the louder its wail, and you will see a wicked smile spread across its master's face. The guitar can be a lance that its owner can wield heroically, like a knight about to go into battle; it can be a phallic symbol, played from the loins; or it can be the ultimate weapon, aimed menacingly at the audience. Its portability made it the obvious rock & roll instrument; it is much simpler to be flamboyant with a guitar around your neck than it is from behind an arsenal of keyboards or a forest of drums and cymbals. At its most basic, rock & roll dances were sexual rites performed while standing up; they proffered a release that bingo tournaments and the chess club could not match. Sixties psychedelia, or acid rock—a forerunner to heavy metal but with a different uniform and code—sought to re-create the psychedelic experience, either as a replacement for or as a soundtrack to drug use. It, too, offered release and some sense of community among its fans and between them and their stars. It also offered a specific philosophy, a way of looking at life and its audience's shared experiences—a group *raison d'être* that transcended the simple teen rebellion that inspired the earliest rockers.

To say that the music of these decades changed the world would not be entirely correct. Had it really done so, we would not need rock & roll today. At its most basic, rock & roll gives expression to the frustrations, fears, and anxieties of what we call adolescence, that period of transition into adulthood our culture often romanticizes but to which few of us would return voluntarily. Though we may certainly continue to love that music for years, even decades, after the first dance or hangover, we can still recall the exhilaration of the communal feeling, the battle cry, the call to join together, whether we came as hep cats and chicks, Beatlemaniacs, Deadheads, or troops in the Kiss Army.

Heavy metal, though its origins stretch back further, is a music of the Seventies and Eighties, and it offers its fans both physical and mental release. Besides melody (not always, but it tries) and lyrical message (ditto), there is heavy metal's glorious white noise: Sit in the fifth row and be purged as the bass guitar resonates your chest cavity; gnash your teeth at the sting of the electric guitars. You want physical entertainment? Heavy-metal fans are called headbangers, jarring their gray matter loose with the constant shaking up and down of their heads in time to the thunderous beat. Heavy metal. Painfully loud, fiercely aggressive, and often in danger of dissolving into complete anarchy.

The fans—many of whom probably see their lives as most teenagers have, namely, dreary and hopeless at its worst; just plain boring, at its best—thrive on the electricity, getting swept up by the sonic tornado cutting a path to the back walls of the stadiums where they have come by the tens of thousands. Heavy metal gives meaning to its fans' lives. It makes more bearable those lives that seem to have little purpose (i.e., excitement) at the time, in the thick of pubescence, entrapped by school, parents, teachers, peer pressure, etc. Its stars offer themselves as examples of everyday people who have escaped the commonness of their own lives by believing in something.

Then there is heavy metal's darker side. While heavy metal often stresses individuality and the idea of persevering in a cruel, uncaring world ("Never Surrender" by the Canadian group Triumph is a typical sentiment), some audiences pervert heavy metal's antifascist ideology into something quite different and disturbing. The fans, so dedicated to what they consider *their* music, are often vehemently opposed to other forms of music and to acts that display the slightest hint of ambisexuality. Headbangers are notoriously homophobic—just read the letters column in any heavy-metal magazine—and generally regard any act that does not go in for metal's mucho-macho posturing as beneath contempt. As with the membership of any gang, individuality may be encouraged, but only as it is defined by the gang itself.

Of all rock's tribes—each with its own dress and protocol—the heavy-metal audience is the one most feared by rock-concert promoters, city fathers, and occasionally the acts themselves. Heavy-metal fans express their enthusiasm fervently, sometimes violently. The artists usually defend their fans' behavior by stating that the crowd is merely acting out its aggressions, and better it be done within the confines of a concert hall than at home or at school. The heavy-metal experience is often described as cathartic. It can also be violent. At a Judas Priest concert at Madison Square Garden in 1984, fans ripped out seats before security guards could move in to make arrests. The tossing of fireworks and other projectiles is a typical method of expressing one's appreciation for a great show. Aerosmith singer Steve Tyler suffered a serious eye injury after a firecracker exploded onstage during one show, and guitartist Joe Perry had an M-80 explosive blow up on his hand at a 1978 Philadelphia concert. Black Sabbath bassist Geezer Butler was once congratulated for a job well done by being conked on the head by a flying bottle, rendering him unconscious. There is, however, often more audience violence at many sports events. As Blue Oyster Cult's Eric Bloom says, "It can happen anywhere."

The heavy-metal audience's penchant for acting out is abetted by their use of alcohol with drugs. It's not untypical to see kids sleeping, vomiting, or being escorted out by harried security personnel. Since the late Sixties, a percentage of any rock-music audience has openly taken drugs in concert situations. It is nothing new. But what makes the heavy-metal crowd different is their seeming preference for alcohol (which is easy to obtain) and barbiturates. Those who indulge can be observed staring intently at their laps, jaws slack, heads rotating 360 degrees. Then again, the greater number seem content to play air guitar, scream and dance, punch at the hot smoky air with their fists in time to the music, and have a good time. The next morning, they go to school.

The bands may change and the vices may change, but the heavy-metal code of ethics and uniform have remained consistent even as the bands themselves have become more stylized and less apt to dress like their fans. Blue jeans, sneakers, T-shirts, and denim jackets held together with patches that proclaim its wearer's loyalty to one or several bands comprise appropriate concert-going apparel. The video age, however, has brought with it a more elaborate dress code: tight Spandex pants, studded leather wrist and arm bands, and colorful bandanas tied to every conceivable appendage. The color of choice is black, the favored material is leather. Fans' hairstyles have gone from wild (long and apparently unkempt) to wilder, with elaborate shag cuts and streaks of color (usually temporary). Braver young men may also wear a dollop of mascara to the right show. More noticeable than ever—though still vastly outnumbered by boys— are girl headbangers. They are evenly divided between those who dress like the boys and those who try to emulate the bitch goddesses they see in their heroes' videos. For the latter group miniskirts, fishnet stockings, lots of cleavage, spiked heels, and anatomy-defining pants make up the costume. Before a show, the fans are out en masse strutting their finery.

Heavy-metal fans behave the way you'd expect them to, and in a manner that reflects the music: hard and unrelenting. They relate to the music on a surprisingly sophisticated level (the above descriptions of concert behavior notwithstanding). For heavy-metal fans, unlike, say, the modern-day bobbysoxers who salivate over such pinup pop groups as Duran Duran, the music comes first. Heavy metal's ultimate appeal remains in the musicians' musical ability, and this emphasis (another rock tradition) makes heavy metal a live form. On the stage, you can't fake it. Unlike performers working in almost every other rock genre, heavy-metal acts rarely use backup musicians, prerecorded tapes, background singers, or anything else surreptitious. What they offer is live rock & roll played very loud. This ultimately brings us to the most significant aspect of heavy metal as a music and a culture: the bond of trust that exists between the heavy-metal artists and their audience. Rock & roll has always inspired fans, but few objects of that adoration are as forthcoming and involved in communicating with their audience as the heavy-metal stars.

The one place this mutual appreciation becomes most apparent is at a live concert. Exhortations to party, boogie, and have a good time are, of course, clichés. But after attending numerous concerts by a wide range of acts, it is hard to overlook the fact that heavy-metal performers generally seem concerned about their fans. Cynics will say this is just show biz, but even some kinds of show biz are better than others. On his much-acclaimed 1984 tour, Michael Jackson could not offer his fans any more than about five dozen well-rehearsed words. Heavy metal, on the other hand, demands some kind of exchange. The bands feed off the audience's excitement nearly as much as they inspire that excitement in the first place, resulting in a upward spiral that can either end in one of those truly magical concerts, provoke violence, or collapse under its own weight.

Heavy metal offers an invitation to conspiracy. Not surprisingly, the majority of hit heavy-metal videos involve comic depictions of the age-old struggle between us (teenage metalheads) and them (usually teachers, parents, and other authority figures; occasionally nonmetal peers). Tactics for dealing with the enemy range from slapstick violence (Twisted Sister's "We're Not Gonna Take It" and "I Wanna Rock") to transforming party-pooping peers or authorities into headbangers (Twisted Sister's "You Can't Stop Rock 'n' Roll"; Quiet Riot's "Party All Night"). In the best of all possible heavy-metal fantasy worlds, everyone is just like you; authority figures become willing participants in heavy-metal revelry (Van Halen's "Hot for Teacher").

There is one heavy-metal cliché that those not moved by heavy metal's charm will find ridiculously funny. It reveals a great deal about how heavy metal works and why. Kiss's Paul Stanley may ask tens of thousands of fans, "You know what it's like when you really *need* alcohol?" and they roar back "Yeah!" Another star may confess his problems: "You know what it's like when you've got fifty hot beautiful women, all dying to get at you?" And hordes of prepubescent virgins will scream back "Yeah!" Twisted Sister's Dee Snider will recount his fictional experience as a contender in the "cocaine Olympics," and the crowd nods its collective understanding. Chances are, only a small percentage of the audience can even begin to imagine what this fantasy, debauched, adult (i.e., unrestrained) lifestyle is all about. What is at work here is an exaggerated form of the locker-room (or drinking or fishing) story, but with an important twist. Here, and in countless other words and gestures, heavy-metal stars are essentially saying to their fans that no one is excluded from this party, that you can have a fantasy (albeit one you will surely outgrow before your SAT scores come in), and, that even though we all know that's all it is, I won't tell. Most important, I will share all of this with you. For that matter, many of the artists themselves are living out a fantasy—that of eternal youth—through heavy metal. Though it is such a youth-oriented phenomenon, the fact that a large percentage of hard-rock heroes are in their thirties does not seem to perturb their fans—many of whom are literally young enough to be their sons and daughters. If anything, it has the opposite effect: Because the musicians have not succumbed to the conventional trappings of middle age, their age heightens their rebel status.

Interestingly, unlike most rock fans, heavy-metal fans are probably the least compelled to meet their heroes outside the confines of the stage show. They feel their trust has been rewarded; that this is all there is to know; that they are part of it. In exchange for that trust, millions of fans all over the world have said repeatedly and loudly that heavy metal rules. For them, it does.

HISTORY

ꗧꗧꗧ

IN THE BEGINNING

THE sounds that make up heavy metal's lexicon of noise were abhorred in the past, providing at least one clear-cut definition of heavy metal: a music that seeks not to turn ugly into beautiful, but to make ugly acceptable. Not to turn noise into music, but to redefine that noise and use it as music. Recording engineers in the past would instantly halt a session at the first hint of guitar feedback—the squealing, metallic cacophony created when the sound from the amplifier speaker is picked up by the guitar microphone and re-fed to the speaker. In the hands of such Sixties rock guitarists as George Harrison (the Beatles' "I Feel Fine," 1964), Pete Townshend (the Who's "My Generation," 1965), and Jeff Beck (the Yardbirds' "Shapes of Things," 1965), feedback became a new musical tool.

Heavy metal is derided as primitive, but in

The uniform of heavy-metal fans has remained consistent even as the bands themselves have become more stylized and less apt to dress like their audience.

rock & roll primitive is considered a virtue. Like early rock & roll, heavy-metal music is based on a simple combination of drums, bass, and guitar. That does not mean that what those instrumentalists do on those instruments is primitive, especially on the latter. The greatest advancements in electric-guitar playing have come from heavy metal.

Ultimately, heavy metal is as much a progeny of advanced musical technology as any other form of rock & roll. You can trace its origins back to the development of the electric guitar in the Forties, in particular the introduction of the Fender Broadcaster in 1948, followed in 1951 by the Fender Precision bass guitar. Though electric guitars were employed by jazz, rock & roll, and country & western artists throughout the Fifties, electric-guitar consciousness had yet to be raised. Most musicians played these guitars and basses as if they were merely electrified versions of acoustic instruments rather than virtually new instruments possessing a revolutionary and expansive new musical vocabulary. Electric guitars were used primarily to amplify their acoustic counterparts' clean tone and to provide sustain of the notes; and the electric bass was a convenient alternative to the bulky, difficult-to-transport stand-up bass.

Electric-guitar style can be traced through such seminal rock singles as Bill Haley and His Comets' "Rock around the Clock," the first rock & roll song to assault the *Billboard* Top Ten, reaching Number One in June 1955. Comets guitarist Francis "Frannie" Beecher played with the amp cranked just under the point of distortion, giving his blistering twelve-bar solo a fiery, almost frenzied attack. The King of Rock & Roll, Elvis Presley, rarely did more with his guitar than wear it. But his backup band featured Scotty Moore, whose wailing, defiant leads on "Hound Dog" (1956) and "Jailhouse Rock" (1957) set these apart from other rock records of the time. Moore's influence was also felt in a more indirect way, since many Fifties kids first picked up the guitar after hearing Elvis Presley, and though he was their inspiration, it is most likely that it was Moore's licks they were trying to pick up off the records.

Gradually, the instrumental focus on rock recordings shifted from the rhythm section (piano, bass, drums), and the saxophone and piano as the soloing instruments, to the guitar. Guitar solos became such an integral part of rock recordings that players with the ability to transfix the listener's attention with a four- or eight-bar fill were designated as specialists: lead guitarists. By the late Fifties, pickers were just beginning to explore the electric guitar's possibilities, and the advancement of electric-guitar technique was singularly responsible for the evolution of rock & roll.

One of the first recordings to define a heavy-metal sensibility in terms of glorifying the guitar was Link Wray's 1958 million-selling instrumental "Rumble" (recorded in 1954). Wray, a country and bottleneck player from North Carolina, altered his guitar's voice by poking a pencil through one of his Premier amp's three speakers. The result was a fuzzy, highly distorted tone. A decade later, this sound, dubbed "fuzz tone," would become integral to hard-rock and heavy-metal bands and would inspire the invention of the fuzz box, a foot-controlled distortion device that allows the guitarist to switch between the dirty fuzz sound and the electric guitar's naturally clean tone.

Of his pioneering effort, Wray says, "I was just looking for sounds. I wanted a sound that nobody else had. And I found that. Today, even with all the sophisticated electronic gadgetry, hard-rock bands like the Scorpions are still doing the same thing—looking for that new, original sound." Trailing Wray's hit up the charts was Duane Eddy's "Rebel-'Rouser." Eddy achieved his trademark elastic, twangy sound by playing melody lines on his bass strings and integrating that with the echo setting on his amplifier and the tremolo bar on his Gretsch Chet Atkins model electric. This sound was immensely popular through the mid-Sixties, particularly on early-Sixties surf records, and still can be heard in country & western and neorockabilly. Eddy's shortlived but enormous popularity (in 1959, England's venerable music paper *The New Musical Express* voted him the number-two music personality behind Elvis) further helped to establish the guitar's dominance in rock & roll, and by the early Eighties, Eddy's worldwide record sales had exceeded 60 million.

The electric guitar's position in rock crystallized with the British Invasion of 1964. Most of the groups streaming out of England were combos with a bass-and-drums rhythm section and two guitars, occasionally augmented by a keyboardist (the Animals and Manfred Mann) or, a token of rock's past, a saxophone (the Dave Clark Five). With nearly every song featuring a four- or eight-bar break, the functions of the lead and rhythm guitars became further refined. In the Beatles, rhythm guitarist John Lennon always deferred to George Harrison when it came time for the middle eight. Keith Richards relinquished his role as a soloist only when the Rolling Stones essayed a blues tune like Muddy Waters's "I Can't Be Satisfied," for which Brian Jones would add his liquid, Elmore James–inspired bottleneck playing.

Out of the British Invasion came the first true heavy-metal single, the Kinks' "You Really Got Me," which readily distinguished itself from more buoyant, poppier English releases by its brittle guitars and the cement-hard snare-drum cracks. No doubt inspired by Link Wray, seventeen-year-old lead guitarist Dave Davies sliced his guitar-amp speaker with a razor blade and fed the distorted signal through a larger amp. With its thick barre chords, pre–heavy-metal sound, and pre-punk spirit, "You Really Got Me" was the era's most ferocious song. Fittingly, it would also be the hit single debut from a second-generation metal band, Van Halen, some fourteen years later.

Heavy metal's forebears also include drummers, and equally important to the Kinks' sound was drummer Mick Avory, who along with the Beatles' Ringo Starr attacked the drum kit with unprecedented aggression. While most British drummers of the day politely tapped their ride cymbal for a *ping-ping-ping* sound that merely embroidered the rhythm set up by the other instruments, Avory would hit the shank of his stick on his half-closed hi-hat cymbals, or ride his cymbals so hard that they generated a steady, frantic *shhhhh*.

The Kinks would temporarily eschew their hard-rock direction to concentrate on leader Ray Davies's tragicomic vignettes about the English working class. The unwitting originators of heavy metal would enjoy their greatest commercial success beginning in June 1979, when they returned to their hard-rock roots.

The June 1967 Monterey Pop Festival heralded a new era of pop music. Rock & roll suddenly had become a less frivolous art form, changed forever that same month by the release of the Beatles' landmark album, *Sgt. Pepper's Lonely Hearts Club Band*. As pop became "rock"—less innocent, more cerebral, more adventurous—its audience became more sophisticated and more demanding of its artists. Rather than screaming hysterically from their seats or dancing while the band played on, these new rock fans now sat and listened intently, even analyzing the music, the lyrics, and the musicians' playing ability. Displays of instrumental expertise became vital to the performance, and watching a talented guitarist execute a technically demanding solo—or one that looked that way—became the highlight of any concert. Keeping pace with the pioneering spirit that overtook rock & roll during 1965 and 1966, music technology was also charting new frontiers. New tools were introduced: the fuzz box, and the wah-wah pedal, a floor-pedal device which altered a guitar's tonal characteristics from muted to bright and which sounded much like its onomatopoeic name. Larger and more powerful amps, capable of producing their own natural distortions, were being built; and drum kits—traditionally just a bass drum, a snare drum, one or two tom-toms, a hi-hat, and one or two cymbals—were now expanded to include two bass drums and multiple tom-toms and cymbals.

Monterey Pop ushered in and celebrated this new era. Not only did it showcase many soon-to-be-influential acts—among them the Who, Jimi Hendrix, the Jefferson Airplane, and Janis Joplin—but it offered a challenge to established acts like the Beatles and the Rolling Stones that was immediately accepted, resulting in a second golden age for rock & roll.

The Who ranked right behind the Kinks as a prototypical heavy-metal band, not only in musical content but in showmanship and attitude, which in metal vie for equal importance. In their two-decade career, the Who presented some of rock & roll's most inveterate images: singer Roger Daltrey twirling his microphone cord like a lasso; guitarist Pete Townshend descending upon his guitar strings with an exaggerated windmill motion or offering up his instrument to his banks of amps to extract feedback; drummer Keith Moon hammering madly at his massive kit; and bassist John Entwistle standing in the shadows, stolidly plucking away with what seemed to be little interest in the surrounding mayhem. At the end of Townshend's anthemic "My Generation," which contained the prophetic—and for Townshend, troubling—line "Hope I die before I get old," the quartet would ritualistically demolish its gear in a display that was part show biz and part honest anger.

The Who's sound had much in common with Seventies and Eighties heavy metal because of its instrumentation: just guitar, bass, and drums. With no rhythm guitar, the burden was placed upon Entwistle and Moon to fill the hole in the sound. One way the entire band compensated was by performing at an ear-blastingly loud volume, Townshend playing what would later be called power chords—loud, ringing chords strummed savagely, in his case with a full arm motion. Entwistle and Moon elevated the rhythm section's status by abdicating their traditional supporting roles and challenging Townshend for the spotlight. Entwistle would often play lead bass lines while Townshend supported the band with his chord work.

That the Who was essentially a metal power trio fronted by a vocalist was best evidenced in its live shows, where the sound was stripped bare of the multiple guitars and keyboard parts Townshend would overdub in the studio. The sheer density of the Who's live sound made it difficult to record, and several early attempts at taping a live LP were scrapped because, Townshend admitted bluntly, "it was crap." Eventually the group would record two official in-concert albums, 1970's *Live at Leeds*, on which it sounds remarkably like Led Zeppelin (who by that time had already surpassed the Who in terms of record sales), and 1984's *Who's Last*, the recorded account of their swan song American tour of 1982.

At Monterey, the Who galvanized the crowd and elicited the most enthusiastic response with their equipment-wrecking display at the set's end. But waiting in the wings, clutching his Fender Stratocaster, was a performer about to make musical—and indirectly, heavy-metal—history.

In Jimi Hendrix's hands, the electric guitar truly became electric. He utilized every conceiv-able sound—like the cry of his Stratocaster being sawed against the microphone stand—and invented some along the way: the bleats and roars achieved through feedback on "Third Stone from the Sun" and the Woody Woodpecker cackle on "Bold as Love." An ardent student of bluesmen like B. B. King, the Seattle-born Hendrix had drifted through several backup stints during the early Sixties, at various points playing under the name of Jimmy James behind Little Richard, the Isley Brothers, and Curtis Knight. In 1966, Animals bassist Chas Chandler whisked Hendrix off to London, where he was teamed with two white musicians, bassist Noel Redding and drummer Mitch Mitchell. The racially mixed trio dressed like Edwardian dandies, and with Hendrix's visceral, sexually charged presence, quickly became the rage of London. Their first LP, 1967's *Are You Experienced?*, made most of the era's flower-power puff and hesitant experimentation seem trivial. At Monterey, a nervous Hendrix had the audience gaping in awe as he tongued and caressed his guitar, and climaxed his set by setting the instrument on fire with lighter fluid—a spontaneous sacrifice.

The following year Hendrix released his second and third LPs, *Axis: Bold as Love* and *Electric Ladyland*, the latter going to Number One in November 1968. *Ladyland*, on which Hendrix began breaking out of the pop-song format, included several lengthy, winding jams ("Voodoo Chile," "Moon, Turn the Tides"), evidence that rock & roll could no longer accommodate his ideas. Intrigued by the avant-garde, Hendrix was also becoming continually frustrated by his fans, who still yelled out for his older songs. "Why don't they take me seriously?" he would often lament.

Hendrix never got the chance to fully explore all of his ideas. After disbanding the Experience in 1969, he drifted through several interim lineups. Work began on his fifth studio album, *The Cry of Love*, but on September 18, 1970, Hendrix

The Jimi Hendrix Experience: Mitch Mitchell, Hendrix, and Noel Redding. In Hendrix's hands, the electric guitar became truly electric.

died in a London apartment after ingesting barbiturates and choking on his own vomit. He was twenty-seven.

In the years since his death, Hendrix's legacy has been somewhat tainted by posthumous LPs consisting of outtakes and material never intended for public consumption. His guitar style remains perhaps the most influential of any of his contemporaries'. That he created a lifetime's worth of important music in just four years makes his death one of rock's greatest tragedies.

With technical expertise becoming the prerequisite for late-Sixties rock artists, the music began to take on the often self-serious characteristics of jazz, as well as its emphasis on improvisation. No group better embodied that approach than Cream, one of the most important musical entities of the decade. On record the three players focused their talents within three- to four-minute song structures, and enjoyed several hit singles ("Sunshine of Your Love," "White Room"), but live, they expanded the boundaries of the pop group into a powerful triumvirate where the bass and drums rivaled the guitar for the spotlight as solo instruments, even more so than in the Who.

Cream also introduced the supergroup to rock & roll, though when they formed, only guitarist Eric Clapton—formerly of the Yardbirds and John Mayall's Bluesbreakers—had a substantial reputation. Bassist Jack Bruce had played with Manfred Mann and the Graham Bond Organisation; drummer Ginger Baker had also been in the Bond aggregation.

Cream's music was a mating of heavily amplified blues rock—Bruce and Clapton originals mixed with blues standards like Willie Dixon's "Spoonful" and Muddy Waters's "Rollin' and Tumblin' "—with the headstrong freedom one associates with jazz. Sometimes the trio would flail madly for several bars, making you think it would

Jeff Beck in 1983. Beck began in the premetal group the Yardbirds but by 1975 was playing jazz-rock fusion. His impetuous, volatile nature fuels his guitaring, which is truly heavy metal in spirit, regardless of genre.

never get out alive. Then one of the three would kick into a remarkable passage, the other two would rush back to greet him, and off they would go.

Their instrumental autonomy also resulted in problems and eventually insurmountable ego conflicts. Onstage, where the songs were merely launching pads for instrumental jams that could last up to fifteen minutes, each of the three musicians would wander off into his own universe. For Clapton the freedom of soloing lost its appeal when what had once been spontaneous became an obligation. Amid growing tensions, the trio announced its disbandment in the summer of 1968, just as its third album, *Wheels of Fire*, hit Number One. On November 26, 1968, at London's Royal Albert Hall, they gave their final performance, as fans shouted, "God save the Cream!"

Cream's influence far outlasted its own career; the supergroup concept continued into the Seventies, and with Cream's breakup, rock fans and critics searched frantically for its successors. While awaiting Clapton's next career move, rock came up with its latest guitar hero: Jeff Beck.

Ironically, Beck was the guitarist who had replaced Clapton in the Yardbirds in late 1964. Originally conceived as a white blues quintet, with Beck in the lineup the group's sound changed dramatically. Clapton was a relatively rigid blues purist, but the temperamental Beck had little reverence for either blues or rock & roll, and his originality as a player is rivaled only by Jimi Hendrix; Beck's successor in the Yardbirds, Jimmy Page; and late-Seventies and Eighties guitar superstar Eddie Van Halen.

Beck was capable of creating a wide range of sounds, which he would spontaneously apply where needed. For a 1965 single, "Heart Full of Soul," producer Giorgio Gomelsky imported a sitarist and a tabla player, but after hours of watching them fail to grasp the rock feel, Beck approximated the Eastern melody on his Fender Esquire guitar plugged into a fuzz box. Feedback was another of his weapons, but Beck's style is most notably characterized by his acute wit and emotion.

Beck's first post-Yardbirds band, the Jeff Beck Group, not only was a superb, fiery blues-rock unit, it was also the training ground for two Seventies and Eighties stars, singer Rod Stewart and bassist Ron Wood, later to join the Rolling Stones as guitarist—the same position Beck had rejected in 1975. The band could not remain together beyond two years and two celebrated albums, 1968's *Truth* and the next year's *Beck-Ola*.

By the mid-Seventies, the mercurial Beck would confound his audience, typically, by changing gears and opting for a jazz-rock direction that brought him the greatest commercial success and public recognition of his career. Even in that usually cool style, Beck still played the guitar with the intense emotional fervor that is truly heavy metal in spirit.

Beck's impetuosity ensured that his career would never reach superstar status—at least not in commercial terms—and upon leaving Cream, Clapton thoroughly rejected his position as a guitar deity. In 1974, following a three-year period of self-imposed exile, he began a highly successful career as a pop songwriter/blues singer and guitarist, but never again would he play as he had in Cream. Of the trio of ex-Yardbirds guitarists, Jimmy Page would go on to achieve the greatest amount of fame, as both a guitar player and as leader of the quintessential heavy-metal band, Led Zeppelin.

Page, born on January 9, 1944, in Heston, England, was a premier British session guitarist between 1963 and 1965, appearing on records by the Who, Tom Jones, Cliff Richard, the Kinks, and many others. (A long-standing rumor was that it was Page, and not Dave Davies, who played lead guitar on the Kinks' "You Really Got Me," a story angrily refuted by Ray Davies.) In 1964 Page turned down the chance to take Clapton's spot in the Yardbirds, but a year and a half later, he replaced original bassist Paul Samwell-Smith. And for an all-too-brief time, he and Beck shared lead guitar, their only recorded legacy being two 1966 tracks, "Happenings Ten Years Time Ago" and "Psycho Daisies," with Page on bass. Beck left the group, rhythm guitarist Chris Dreja switched to bass, and Page became the sole lead guitarist.

The Yardbirds enjoyed several U.S. hit singles in 1965 and 1966, but by the time Page joined, record sales had taken a downturn, and Page and the band recorded just one LP, *Little Games*, before disbanding in 1968. Page had managed to shift artistic control of the group by that time away from lead vocalist Keith Relf, and a live LP recorded at one of their last performances, at New York City's Anderson Theater on March 30, 1968, testifies to Page's sway over the band. Throughout the set, Relf refers to Page as "the grand sorcerer of the electric guitar," and at one point leaves the stage to Page for an acoustic guitar workout, the haunting "White Summer." Included was "I'm Confused," which would appear on the first Led Zeppelin album as "Dazed and Confused," a hard-rock classic. Though today listeners can appreciate this album for its historical value, at the time, the group was so displeased by its performance and by the LP's recording (which included ludicrous bullfight cheers overdubbed) that it forced Epic Records to shelve it shortly after its 1971 release (which had been prompted by the success of Led Zeppelin). The LP does, however, illustrate the similarities between the Yardbirds and the early Zeppelin, prompting one to speculate that the former group might have enjoyed similar success had it remained together long enough to take advantage of rock's new emphasis on albums instead of hit singles.

Relf, Dreja, and drummer Jim McCarty left the Yardbirds to Page, who initially intended to carry on under the moniker the New Yardbirds, with three replacements: singer Robert Plant, a twenty-year-old from Bromwich; respected session bassist John Paul Jones, who hired Page to play lead guitar on Donovan's acidy 1968 single "Hurdy Gurdy Man," and who arranged the cello part on Page and the Yardbirds' "Little Games"; and drummer John Bonham, a two-fisted player from Redditch who had played previously with

Led Zeppelin's Robert Plant and Jimmy Page (with bassist John Paul Jones, background). From 1969 to 1980, Zeppelin reigned as the preeminent hard-rock act.

Plant in a Birmingham outfit called the Band of Joy.

After touring Scandinavia in October 1968 as the New Yardbirds, the quartet returned to England, where it recorded its first album in just thirty hours and adopted the name Led Zeppelin, allegedly coined by Who drummer Keith Moon. Until their 1980 dissolution following the death of Bonham on September 25, 1980, Zeppelin was the most popular heavy-metal act in rock & roll, if not its most popular band, period, outselling such stalwarts as the Stones and the Who. And although critically snubbed, Zeppelin was the most independent and experimental of the Seventies metal bands. Its music often incorporated elements of reggae ("D'yer Mak'er," from 1973's *Houses of the Holy*), raga ("Black Mountain Side," *Led Zeppelin*, 1969), Eastern melodies ("Kashmir," *Physical Graffiti*, 1975), and folk (the classic "Stairway to Heaven," *Led Zeppelin IV*, 1971), but it was always based in the blues. Their weighty debut contained two Willie Dixon tunes, "I Can't Quit You Baby" and "You Shook Me," the latter of which Jeff Beck had recorded on *Truth*. Zeppelin's vast wealth and intense audience loyalty afforded the group the freedom to experiment on a scale rare in popular music. Also, Zeppelin set the thematic tone for other heavy-metal acts. An interest in the occult (Page lives in the former home of Satanist Aleister Crowley), alleged use of backmasking to disguise what were supposedly Satanic messages ("My sweet Satan" on "Stairway to Heaven," it is claimed), monolithic, dramatic music with cryptic or myth-inspired lyrics (all open to and subject to intense scrutiny by fans and critics) were all factors in Led Zeppelin's success and mystique.

In addition, Zeppelin's lead vocalist Robert Plant set something of a standard that most heavy-metal vocalists—male and female—seek to match today. Besides his inspired phrasing and his extemporaneous howls and asides, Plant could convincingly convey slow blues ("You Shook Me"), gutbucket rock & roll ("Rock and Roll"), and even folk ballads ("Going to California"), in a strong, cutting voice that remains one of the most distinctive in rock. In 1982 he commenced a highly successful solo career that demonstrated his versatility, particularly on 1984's Top Five *The Honeydrippers*, an EP of Fifties and Sixties classics, recorded with Page and Beck, among others. After a lengthy sabbatical, Page formed a hard-rock quartet called the Firm with singer Paul Rodgers in 1984.

While Jimmy Page's greatest acclaim in Zeppelin was as a guitarist, his production played an equally important part in the unit's overall sound: sonorous and elephantine. The drums in particular were brought up in the mix like never before, as on *Led Zeppelin IV*'s "When the Levee Breaks," all cannoning bass drum and snare.

Of Led Zeppelin's nine albums prior to Bonham's death, six went to Number One, two to #2, and one to #10. Zeppelin remains heavy metal's most enduring act.

But were they the first? Clearly heavy metal is as much an attitude, a way of seeing oneself in the world, as it is a music. Indeed, were there no heavy-metal attitude, much of what we call heavy metal might just be called hard pop. In terms of being the first to fully personify heavy metal's embrace of rebellion and love of excess, that distinction might belong to Blue Cheer, a hard-rock trio from California that enjoyed fleeting fame with its bombastic version of rockabilly Eddie Cochran's 1958 hit "Summertime Blues" (a staple of the Who's repertoire and a moderate hit for them in 1970). Blue Cheer—guitarist Leigh Stephens, bassist Dickie Peterson, and drummer Paul Whaley—expressed an aggressive attitude that, when mixed with what appeared to be a woeful lack of musicianship and finesse, bucked sharply against that of such virtuosos of the day as Cream or Ten Years After (a British blues quartet fronted by guitarist Alvin Lee, who, if nothing else, was one of the speedier riffers of the Sixties). The trio was managed by an ex–Hell's Angel named Gut, who boasted that Blue Cheer were so heavy they could churn the air into cottage cheese. Their *Vincebus Eruptum* (even its title

conjures up the pompous, weighty, pseudo-Gothic aura that later became a cornerstone of heavy-metal imagery) may be the earliest pure-metal artifact.

Another early proponent of metal, though rarely thought of as such and most often cited as godfathers of punk, was the MC5, a self-described guerrilla-rock group from Detroit. Heavy metal has rarely demonstrated a political consciousness, much less the militant stance of the White Panther Party members MC5, whose incendiary "politics," though well intentioned, were, to be generous, naive. Its music, however, was powerfully loud and primitive hard rock, as captured on its debut, *Kick Out the Jams*, recorded live in October 1968 at Detroit's Grande Ballroom. The group's music was adventurous even though its members' musicianship was lim-

ited. Like Blue Cheer, the MC5's direction softened with subsequent albums. Both groups broke up in the early Seventies.

By the dawning of the Seventies, rock & roll had become as fragmented as its primary medium, radio, which had been irrevocably split into pop-chart, single-happy AM, and album-oriented, progressive FM. The music followed suit, developing its own subgenres. There was the burgeoning Southern rock movement, led by the Allman Brothers Band; singer/songwriters like James Taylor and Carole King; pop, jazz-rock, progressive rock, symphonic rock, folk-rock, country-

Was Blue Cheer the first true heavy-metal band? Maybe. The band's manager boasted they were so heavy, they turned the air into cottage cheese.

rock, etc. As the music itself was split into sub-groups, so was the rock & roll audience, and the tribal rites of each became more defined. By 1970, heavy metal was becoming recognized as a genre all its own, and one that was largely disparaged by the burgeoning rock press.

Under the banner of heavy metal came hordes of Cream/Zeppelin imitators. One of the most popular of these was Mountain, essentially a metal trio augmented by keyboards for color and texture, with a sound as weighty as its lead guitarist, 250-pound Leslie West. Between 1970 and 1973, West (Leslie Weinstein of Queens, New York) vaulted to star status as one of the most highly acclaimed white blues players of the early Seventies and was hailed by such peers as Jimmy Page. West's style was characterized by a series of

Mountain, whose career prospered between 1970 and 1973, had a sound as weighty as its lead guitarist, 250-pound Leslie West (far right).

teasing staccato phrases that would climax in a long, loud wail. Like another guitarist of the period, Free's Paul Kossoff, Leslie resisted the temptation to be the fastest gun in the West, playing instead with dynamics and bluesy emotion. On much of Mountain's heavier material, such as its hit "Mississippi Queen," the hulking West also fronted the band with his gruff, furnace-blast voice.

Musically, Mountain owed a considerable debt to Cream, not surprising since bassist Felix Pappalardi had produced and written for all of Cream's albums. In concert, Mountain would often use a single riff as a springboard for a lengthy jam, with West's guitar always the centerpiece; in that respect, Mountain was more of a traditional band than was Cream. Another of Mountain's most memorable songs was a version of Cream bassist Jack Bruce's "Theme for an Imaginary Western," one of the early FM radio "hits," though it never actually charted. Mountain was often criticized for a one-dimensional approach, but Pappalardi's satiny voice did afford them some variety.

Though Mountain's popularity was brief (sales began plunging with the fourth of nine albums, 1971's *Flowers of Evil*), it did leave something of a modest musical legacy: Many of the metal bands to follow would pattern their style after the group's frequent use of the guitar and the bass playing concurrent lines, instead of bass notes supporting guitar chords. Another commonly used metal technique was call and response, long a staple of vocal groups, which originally had come from gospel singing. In call and response, the lead vocalist trades off phrases with the backup singers, who either repeat them or answer them in some way. Early black rock & rollers—the Isley Brothers (on "Shout," 1959), Sam Cooke, James Brown, and Otis Redding, to name a few—used call and response effectively. In metal the call and response could be between voice and guitar (Zeppelin's Plant and Page on "You Shook Me," or Jeff Beck and Rod Stewart on "Let Me Love You"); between guitar and harmonica (Beck and Keith Relf on the Yardbirds' "Lost Woman"); or

between guitar and organ (Ritchie Blackmore and Jon Lord on Deep Purple's in-concert version of "Smoke on the Water").

Metal groups such as Mountain, Deep Purple, and Black Sabbath attained their popularity at the same time that the rock & roll press assumed the mantle of tastemakers of the counterculture. Their reviews appeared in such youth-oriented magazines as *Rolling Stone*, *Creem*, *Crawdaddy*, and *Circus*. Each publication clearly had its own tone and philosophy. This was an era in which anything that seemed even vaguely successful was suspect, regardless of its quality. Many regard this time as the golden age of rock journalism. While there is certainly a case to be made for that view, it was also a time when rock journalism was in many ways an older, more sophisticated form of fandom. Regardless, some artists did take the reviews seriously: Eric Clapton laid part of the blame for his decision to break up Cream on Jann Wenner's published putdown of *Wheels of Fire* in *Rolling Stone*.

During this era, some critics literally did make their heroes stars. For many fans, critics did indeed have the last word. It was through critics that many people discovered and learned to appreciate and support the work of urban blues musicians. It was also the work of critics that helped create a body of information on the subject and led in the battle to legitimize rock & roll as a valid and important aspect of the culture.

The other side of the coin is that most writers understand lyrics much better than they actually understand the music. As best proven in the punk era, image is as important to them as to their "uneducated" readers. Hard rock and heavy metal immediately became the critics' targets.

Never had critical and popular opinion been so divided as in the case of Grand Funk Railroad, truly one of the earliest "people's" rock bands. Despite suffering unequaled critical contempt, the trio (which added a keyboardist in 1972) from Flint, Michigan, was one of the most consistently charting American bands from 1969 to 1976, and was one of the few metal acts to garner hit singles in an era in which LPs were the top priority.

Grand Funk, also known as GFR, built their populist reputation early in their career, at the 1969 Atlanta Pop Festival. Unknown and unsigned, they inspired such a feverish response from the 250,000 assembled that after their third encore, they were carried off the stage on the crowd's shoulders. Capitol Records signed them on the spot. Ten of the group's fifteen albums went Top Twenty, eight reached the Top Ten, and in 1973 and 1974 Grand Funk had two Number One singles, "We're an American Band" and a hard-rock version of the oldies dance hit "The Locomotion."

Of the critics' slagging of the group (a full decade after the group's debut, critic Dave Marsh wrote in *The Rolling Stone Record Guide*, "Wretched is the word to describe Grand Funk's music") lead guitarist/singer Mark Farner says, "It was actually easy for us to deal with because we had the people. But it was hard to understand how writers could come and observe such a positive audience response and then slam it; it was like telling those people who were clapping and going crazy that they were out of their minds. Luckily," he adds, "it didn't make a difference."

As time went on, it would appear that what critics had to say made less and less difference. Just as they could not help boost a band with good reviews (the punk/new-wave movement is a classic example of the critics' split with popular taste), their power to "ruin" a band was essentially nil.

Virtually all heavy-metal acts since Grand Funk—including Led Zeppelin—have received similar treatment from the rock press, leading one to speculate that the scribes' influence is greatly overplayed. Just how seriously readers regard rock-album reviews is unclear, but an artist whose latest vinyl offering is disparaged in print can easily take umbrage. Like any of their colleagues in other fields, rock critics' judgments range from fair and even constructive to clearly prejudiced and uninformed. Some choice diatribes directed at metal acts include:

Led Zeppelin: "Unfortunately, Jimmy Page is also a very limited producer and a writer of weak, unimaginative songs." John Mendelsohn, *Rolling Stone*, 1969.

AC/DC: "AC/DC have nothing to say musically. [Their] calculated stupidity offends me." Billy Altman, *Rolling Stone*, 1976.

Black Sabbath: "The group performs with all the restraint and sophistication of four Cro-Magnon hunters who've stumbled upon a rock band's equipment after a bad day chasing meat." Paul Battiste, *Creem*, 1972.

As David Fricke wrote in the 1983 edition of the *Record Guide*, "What the critics don't know, the heavy-metal kids understand."

Rock writers may have been intolerant of heavy metal because it is often not as "literate" as other music styles, such as progressive rock, which often was based on literature or ancient myths (but was roundly criticized for being *over*ambitious, and musically and lyrically pretentious). Nor is it as concerned with a lyrical message outside of the usual exhortations to party or to retain one's individuality or to hail, hail rock & roll.

Much of heavy metal *is* lyrically vacuous and at times offensive—sexist, misogynistic, violent. But sexism is certainly part of the blues and reggae, and as for being offensive, there were scores of punks, praised by the critics, who wore swastikas in a simple-minded attempt at public offense.

A final factor that applies particularly to heavy metal in this decade—and to which virtually none of the critics will admit—is that the majority of writers are now in their thirties and beyond. They no longer have an interest in a music that is directed at a younger, adolescent audience. That the tenor of the critics' in-print revulsion echoes the long-standing intolerance all adults and authority figures have expressed for rock & roll in general is an irony not missed by many bands. "The real truth," theorizes David Lee Roth, the outspoken lead singer of Van Halen, "is that many of the critics have kids of their own. It scares the hell out of them to think that their kids could be anything remotely like David Lee Roth."

This battle will no doubt rage indefinitely.

Hard-rock fans, however, will never pass up the next Judas Priest album because of a negative review. The press's abhorrence of heavy metal only seems to unify the fans and make their protectiveness and defensiveness of the music an even more important aspect to their enjoyment of it. Heavy-metal fandom is a large and, by requirement only, exclusive club.

As hard rock prospered in the early Seventies, it became increasingly diverse. Bands categorized as heavy metal often seemed at odds with one another in terms of approach: The ominous downer rock of Black Sabbath, Black Widow, and Coven was countered by the uproarious boogie of Humble Pie, Nazareth, and Foghat. Each faction of course had its share of classics and clinkers,

the latter surely still more entertaining to lovers of junk culture. There was Bloodrock's unforgettable 1971 Top Forty hit "D.O.A.," a horrifyingly graphic first-person account of perishing in an airplane crash; conversely, there was histrionic amphetamine rock that was as dizzying as a roller-coaster ride, by such groups as Sir Lord Baltimore, the Frost, Cactus, Dust, and others quickly banished to the annals of rock history.

Hard rock's lack of rules afforded musicians a whole new freedom of expression, and its audience was more than willing to encourage the artists' indulgence. This era of experimentation and acceptance attracted musicians whose training encompassed other, more formal musics.

The classic Deep Purple lineup: Jon Lord, Roger Glover, Ian Gillan, Ritchie Blackmore, and Ian Paice. They regrouped in 1984 after eleven years apart.

In the case of the British band Deep Purple, who rivaled Led Zeppelin from 1973 to 1976, the intraband disparities resulted in some of the most memorable metal of the period. Anchored by a conventional rock rhythm section (bassist Roger Glover and drummer Ian Paice) and fronted by a series of rock & roll shouters (Rod Evans, then Ian Gillan, who was succeeded by David Coverdale), Deep Purple created riffy hard rock imbued with dramatic, symphonic chord changes and orchestral dynamics, the influence of keyboardist Jon Lord and guitarist Ritchie Blackmore.

After its debut in Tastrup, Denmark, in 1968, it took the group several years to sort out its many influences, and there were some embarrassing gaffes made along the way. They cracked America with keyboard-heavy versions of the Joe South tune "Hush" (#4) and Neil Diamond's "Kentucky Woman" (#38). The classically trained Lord then convinced the group to essay his *Concerto for Group and Orchestra*, which they recorded on November 15, 1969, with the Royal Philharmonic Orchestra at London's Royal Albert Hall. The album failed miserably, both musically and commercially, and only succeeded in obscuring the group's musical identity.

For *Deep Purple in Rock*, guitarist Blackmore exerted his hold over the group, and though it fared poorly commercially, *In Rock* is now deemed an important hard-rock LP. Blackmore is a lover of classical music who claims to disdain most rock & roll, his playing combining the simplicity of blues guitar with classical motifs.

Purple rebounded in 1971 with *Fireball*, a Top Forty LP, and went to #7 the following year with *Machine Head*. The latter contained "Smoke on the Water," a song chronicling the December 3, 1971, concert the band opened for Frank Zappa during which the Montreux Casino burned to the ground. "I didn't think that song was anything special," claims Roger Glover. "In fact, I didn't like it very much at all." A full year later, following the successful *Who Do We Think We Are!* (#15) and *Made in Japan* (#6) albums, "Smoke on the Water" became Purple's biggest hit of its career, but by that time, the band was in sham-

bles. Gillan and Glover left, to be replaced by David Coverdale and Glenn Hughes, and though subsequent releases *Burn* and *Stormbringer* went Top Ten and Top Twenty respectively, Blackmore was dissatisfied with the band's meandering direction, and quit. In 1975, he started Blackmore's Rainbow with singer Ronnie James Dio of Elf. Purple persevered for one more album, *Come Taste the Band*, with guitarist Tommy Bolin, before disbanding in 1976. In 1984, Rainbow (who had endured constant personnel changes and middling success) disbanded and Deep Purple's most successful lineup re-formed, after years of rumors about such a reunion. An LP, *Perfect Strangers*, was released in October.

The mid-Seventies were dire years for heavy metal. Not only were album sales slipping for most of its groups (with the exception of the perennially popular Led Zeppelin) as rock radio veered toward soft-rock acts like Fleetwood Mac and the Eagles, but the bands' collective creativity seemed to have sunk to its nadir. There were a few bright spots, however. Bad Company, a quartet in the style of Zeppelin but with more traditional, simplified rock values, hit Number One with its eponymous debut album in 1974. Its sound was heavy yet economical, and instead of guitarist Mick Ralphs being pushed out front as in most hard-rock outfits, Bad Company's primary soloist was singer Paul Rodgers, blessed with a throaty, commanding voice and remarkable phrasing. Bad Company's infrequent recorded output extended their career into the Eighties despite a paucity of ideas. They heralded a new, more melodic and song-oriented approach for hard rock, which had fallen to the mercy of FM rock radio stations. Those bands that acquiesced received airplay; those that didn't received little or none.

Many heavy-metal bands took to the road in lieu of radio support, cultivating their audiences that way. Aerosmith, Blue Oyster Cult, and Ted Nugent stayed on the road more than forty weeks out of the year. Stage shows became more theatri-

cal and elaborate, thanks to the likes of Alice Cooper, who had enjoyed tremendous success beginning in 1971 with a shock-rock theater-of-the-absurd presentation: a boa constrictor curled around a ghoulishly made-up Cooper as he sang. Guillotines and other props were as necessary to the stage show as amps and guitars. Two of the few hard-rock groups to prosper during this period were Kiss and Queen. The former wore makeup that took over an hour to apply, each member assuming a different cartoon-character persona; its bass player, Gene Simmons, a onetime school-teacher, wore Kabuki-style hair and giant plat-form boots, breathed fire, and wiggled his ser-pentlike tongue (not a stage prop). Kiss's music was pedestrian heavy metal, but they had a flair for penning teenage anthems about the joys of overamplification ("Rock and Roll All Nite") and overamped sex drives ("Love Gun"). It was calcu-lated and ludicrous, scoffed critics, and after their first three LPs stiffed, the band was ready to cash in the chips.

In late 1975, the masterstroke of *Alive!* cap-

The original Kiss: Paul Stanley, Ace Frehley, Peter Criss, and Gene Simmons. At the band's peak, its fan club was 100,000 strong.

italized on the quartet's live appeal. From that point until 1979, each of Kiss's five subsequent new LPs went Top Thirty. But the records were always secondary to the live show. The band performed amid smoke and explosions, while drummer Peter Criss would be elevated into the air on a hydraulic lift. Little more than circus tricks, perhaps, but fully entertaining. Their cartoon-character images became so ingrained that the group was the subject of a TV cartoon show, as well as two Marvel comic books. By 1978, its popularity was at its pinnacle: the band's official fan club, the Kiss Army, was some 100,000 strong, and each band member—Simmons, Stanley, Criss, and guitarist Ace Frehley—simultaneously released his own solo album, each of which went platinum.

By 1983 Kiss had sold 50 million records and racked up eleven platinum and fifteen gold LPs, though sales began dropping with 1980's *Unmasked*. To rejuvenate their imperiled career, Kiss finally removed their makeup, rekindling fan enthusiasm enough for 1984's *Animalize* to sell one million copies.

Queen represented the less primal, more sophisticated side of heavy metal, and was one of the few hard-rock groups besides Led Zeppelin to adapt comfortably to—and further the art of—making records. Its 1976 hit "Bohemian Rhapsody" was a mini-opera in three movements that featured multiple layering of voices so that it sounded like dozens of choral singers—recorded on just a sixteen-track machine.

Queen became one of the most successful hard-rock bands of the decade, peaking in 1980 with *The Game*, Number One for five weeks. Lead singer Freddie Mercury's persona was unusually fey, but there was always a bit of tongue-in-cheek to the group's made-up appearance, which they modified by the late Seventies. "I look at old pictures of the group and cringe," says drummer/vocalist Roger Taylor.

Queen's and Kiss's careers both illustrate, however, the hard-rock audience's intolerance for experimentation on the part of their idols. The former tried its hand at heavily synthesized dance music on 1982's *Hot Space*, and it became Queen's poorest-charting album since 1974's *Queen II*. The group returned to a hard-rock direction on 1984's *The Works*. And Kiss's ambitious but ill-conceived concept LP, *(Music from) The Elder* (with songs cowritten with Lou Reed), was received with cries of horror from the group's fans, prompting them to reverse gears and return to heavy metal on the following LP.

Aerosmith, by contrast, held steadfastly to its hard-rock direction. Right from the start, the group—formed in New Hampshire in 1970—wore its Stones/Yardbirds influences proudly, and even played the latter's "Train Kept a-Rollin'" years after allusions to rock's past were fashionable. Like first-generation metal groups such as Grand Funk Railroad, part of Aerosmith's appeal was its kinship with its audience. Once, after a show in Fort Wayne, Indiana, the band posted $3,650 bail for fifty-two fans who had been arrested for possession of marijuana.

Vocalist Steve Tyler and guitarist Joe Perry aped the onstage chemistry of the Stones' Mick Jagger and Keith Richards rather than Zeppelin's Plant and Page, the usual heavy-metal prototypes. When Perry left to pursue a solo career, that chemistry was lost, and with it the level of success they'd enjoyed since 1975, when their third album, *Toys in the Attic*, went to #11. Five years after Perry's departure, the group had recorded but one LP, the moderately successful *Rock in a Hard Place*, and in 1984 Perry—whose solo career had floundered—and rhythm guitarist Brad Whitford rejoined Tyler, bassist Tom Hamilton, and drummer Joey Kramer. Tyler contended that "the time is right" for a comeback, though he admitted that "there are a couple of bands who kind of took over where we left off."

While the second generation of metal bands was struggling to maintain its audiences, a third generation of groups was exploring two new directions for heavy metal, each a response to the sorry state of mid-Seventies rock & roll. By 1976, rock was monopolized by so-called corporate rock artists whose output was aired repeatedly by rock radio regardless of its quality. Radio's influence (stranglehold) over the record-purchasing public became alarming; with the key to advertising being repetition, these tightly formatted stations did little more than advertise certain songs. Most rock historians agree that 1974 and 1975 were low points for rock & roll.

In England was festering a movement determined to wipe out what it saw as fat-cat rock & roll stars who had lost touch with their audience: punk. Groups such as the Clash and the more notorious Sex Pistols possessed little in the way of instrumental technique, but this only heightened the music's aggression. The punk movement was instantly embraced by rock critics for its musical primitivism, angry, alienated lyrics, and flamboyant sense of style, many of the bands and their fans dressing up in leather, studs, and chains.

The arbitrary nature of rock-critic categorization is best illustrated by the schism that quickly developed between "punk" and late-Seventies "heavy metal," for there was relatively little difference between the two. What made the Sex Pistols punk and Judas Priest heavy metal? Both played thickly chorded, high-decibel music, but while punk relied on inspired amateurism, metalers still abided by their fans' demand for technical expertise. The Pistols' anarchic anthem "God Save the Queen" is as much a heavy-metal song as Priest's "Breaking the Law" is punk.

Motorhead, a ponderously loud trio whose popularity in Britain never crossed the Atlantic, is a perfect example of the murky differences between the two musics. They broke around the same time as the Clash and the Sex Pistols, "and if you didn't see a picture of us," observes Motorhead's hirsute bassist/leader, Lemmy Kilminster, "you'd probably think we were punks." Indeed, the group's songs shared the punks' spirit, and on such tracks as "Back at the Funny Farm," Kilminster demonstrates a Ramones-like, absurdist sense of humor. "We always crossed over," says Lemmy. "I think we'll best be remembered as the ones who upset all your theories about categorization. Also the ones who sent you home deaf."

The Sex Pistols and the majority of the punk movement (with the exception of the Clash and the Jam) would self-destruct by 1978, evolving/devolving into the safer "power pop" or "new wave." Several of its principles, such as an emphasis placed on concise songs and fewer guitar solos, would be adopted by the new generation of hard-rock groups.

Just as 1970 heralded a fruitful period for heavy metal, so did 1980 auger well for the music, though the so-called heavy-metal renaissance that would occur that year would last far longer and have a more profound influence than the earlier hard-rock movement.

We say "so-called" heavy-metal renaissance/revival, because that implies hard-rock acts had ceased to exist during the late Seventies. Hardly. While rock & roll was dominated by punk/new wave in 1979, and disco from 1977 to 1980, metal bands continued to ply their trade. In basements all over the heartland of America, copies of *Led Zeppelin II* and Black Sabbath's *Paranoid* still were being ground down on turntables.

What expedited the metal revival of 1980 was the fact that the majority of metal bands hailed from England, just as had the groups that comprised the British Invasion of 1964, or those that would lead the New Romantics in 1981. Americans have always harbored a preference for the U.K. artists' distillation of their very own rock & roll, and the 1980 invasion was headed by such English acts as Judas Priest, Def Leppard, Iron Maiden, and Ozzy Osbourne, the former Black Sabbath singer gone solo. To a lesser extent, there was Whitesnake, Saxon, Tygers of Pan Tang, Angelwitch, Samson, and Girl. By this time, heavy metal had gone international. AC/DC, whose 1980 LP *Back in Black* went to #4, was based out of Australia; Van Halen, who had already seen each of its first three albums go multiplatinum, was a former bar band from Pasadena, California; Krokus was from Switzerland, never exactly a hotbed of musical activity; Scorpions and Accept came out of Germany; Triumph, Max Webster, and Helix all hailed from Canada.

The plethora of heavy-metal bands for the first time included women, who had generally been excluded from hard rock for many reasons, among them a lack of role models. Until the mid-Sixties, the impact of women on rock & roll had been minimal. The blues boasted legends like Bessie Smith and Billie Holiday, but in rock, women usually had supporting roles. They were either songwriters (Carole King, Ellie Greenwich), teary-eyed victims of romance (Lesley Gore), or members of girl groups who manufactured hits under the dictims of such male producers as Berry Gordy at Motown and Phil Spector.

Sixties soul had its share of female stars, Aretha Franklin, Lady Soul, being the best known. In rock there was Grace Slick of the Jefferson Airplane, the closest thing to a female hard-rock singer at the time. Rather than shrill the lyrics, however, Slick's delivery was more incantory. Janis Joplin was more of a heavy-metal belter. When her original band, Big Brother and the Holding Company, performed its distillation of blues and rock & roll, they were so loud that they intensified Joplin's impassioned singing, simply so that she could be heard over the din. Other women picked up on the leads of Slick and Joplin, such as Fanny, an all-female hard-rock quartet that formed in California in 1970 and recorded five marginally successful albums before disbanding in the mid-Seventies.

With the next wave of female groups, two surprising role models became apparent: for guitarists, Keith Richards; for singers, Robert Plant. Heart was a two-woman, four-man group from Seattle who had begun its career by playing Led Zeppelin cover tunes in local bars, and lead singer Ann Wilson at times sounded identical to Zeppelin's Plant. Even through Heart's multiplatinum heyday in the late Seventies, a highlight of its set was the Zep's "Rock and Roll." Heart variated between heavy metal ("Barracuda," #11, 1977) and softer, poppier fare such as "Straight On" (#15, 1978), and following some personnel changes, Ann's sister Nancy moved

from rhythm to lead guitar for 1980's *Bébé le Strange*, providing the next generation with a bona fide woman guitar star.

Part of the British new wave of heavy metal was Girlschool, a quartet that in its original formation included American guitarist Kathy Valentine, later to join the successful U.S. all-girl pop band the Go-Go's. Taken under the wing of Motorhead's management, Girlschool had several British hits, beginning with 1980's "Race with the Devil." Metal fans tend to be a chauvinist lot, but the group gained credibility with them, getting voted the second-best new band of the year in a *Sounds* magazine 1981 readers' poll.

Girlschool and the female metalers to follow—Lita Ford, former member of the late-Seventies female punk-metal act the Runaways, and Rock Goddess—did not vary the metal formula much, including the sexually charged aggression, with the genders simply reversed. Men and women sometimes found it unnerving, as when Joan Jett—also a former Runaway and a pop-metal classicist who weds grinding guitars to Sixties-inspired tunes—sings "Handy Man" (a tribute to a sexually adept boyfriend) with the leer of a Times Square sidewalk barker. Of Girlschool, Ford, Rock Goddess, and the many mixed-gender metal acts flourishing by 1984 (such as L.A.'s Madame X), only Jett has been able to achieve far-reaching commercial success. No one ever denied that heavy-metal fans were in need of a little consciousness-raising.

Heavy-metal groups began ascending the charts higher than they had during the music's early-Seventies heyday, a phenomenon partially attributable to the music's more melodic quality and, of course, to music video. Another factor that added to heavy metal's resurgence in mass appeal was the fact that the so-called new music

Women hard-rockers such as former Runaway Lita Ford have kept to the metal formula, including the genre's sexually charged aggression. For the first time, young female metal enthusiasts have role models of their own gender.

that was being heralded by the industry at large as the next big thing for the youth market held little appeal for many younger would-be fans. While new wave supposedly expressed a rebellious attitude, its allusions to mid-Sixties pop, its moody, introspective but obtuse lyrics, and its obsession with fashion were largely lost on the younger audience. Hard-rock bands began to have hit singles: AC/DC with "You Shook Me All Night Long" (#35, 1980); REO Speedwagon with the hard-pop ballads "Keep On Loving You" (#1, 1980) and "Take It on the Run" (#5, 1981); Journey with "Who's Crying Now" (#4) and "Don't Stop Believin'" (#9), both 1981; and Billy Squier with "The Stroke" (#17, 1981). Van Halen, Def Leppard, and Squier all played what could be termed "pop metal." The latter, in fact, had been a member of two pure pop groups, the Sidewinders and Piper, in the Seventies. The imagery and the decibel level were heavy metal, but the melodies were far more tuneful than most of the metal music of the Seventies.

By 1983, heavy metal had truly come of age, aided by the advent of MTV—the TV channel that broadcast rock videos twenty-four hours a day beginning on August 1, 1981, and singlehandedly revolutionized the record industry. Always a highly visual medium, hard rock thrived on MTV, its groups able to come across effectively whether "starring" in elaborate concept videos or in simple set-up-and-shoot in-concert videos. MTV's acceptance eventually provided acceptance from rock radio. But, interestingly, the same metal acts who have benefited from their video exposure are skeptical of a medium that is still largely regarded as the promotional tool for Britain's sartorially dressed Analog Army.

Because they were seen by millions of fans daily, videos stimulated record sales. Their most important contribution to heavy metal as a genre was that they allowed fans to visualize the music's colorful, sometimes violent, sexy, and fantastic

Twisted Sister: For years this veteran bar band was considered an anachronism, but by 1984 fans began regarding it as the originator of a new metal style.

imagery. In a general crop of rock videos, heavy-metal clips almost always stand out. Whether the influence of video on rock—and heavy metal—is good or bad is too complex a question to answer. But it is impossible to dismiss rock video, especially since heavy-metal videos usually accomplish what they set out to do, and usually do it quite well. Story lines that deal with rebellion, thwarting authority, joining in the battle between good and evil, the search for lost treasure, quasi-religious symbols of redemption, or just good-looking members of the opposite sex are staples of heavy-metal video. Some groups stick with performance video clips; others, like Van Halen, Twisted Sister, Judas Priest, Quiet Riot, Def Leppard, to name a few, successfully exploit the music's highly visual, stylized form. The results are sometimes arresting and often intentionally humorous. Heavy metal's songs and stars seem to have been made for the small screen. With video behind it, heavy metal took off.

Yet there were still plenty of nonbelievers who needed to be convinced of heavy metal's rising popularity, and the groups who appeared at the US '83 Festival's Heavy Metal Day were as much making a declaration to the heretics as they were hosting a celebration with their fans.

It came as little surprise—even to festival organizer Steve Wozniak, the thirty-two-year-old Apple Computer, Inc., founder—that Heavy Metal Day drew nearly more than the combined attendances of days number one and three, on which new-music and more mainstream rock acts were presented, including David Bowie in his first U.S. appearance since 1978.

US '83 was Wozniak's second attempt at such an event; the first, held on Labor Day Weekend in September 1982, lost a reported $5 million. Wozniak and his UNUSON corporation sought to gather an audience under an umbrella of togetherness—the Me Generation's Woodstock—but, ironically, the only evidence of community was found among those 250,000 (promoter's estimate) who attended Heavy Metal Day—although it was also on that day that more arrests were made by the festival's 700-strong police force

than during the entire three days of the first festival.

Sunday, May 29, was blisteringly hot, with temperatures in the high 90s. The first two acts were Los Angeles bands Motley Crue and Quiet Riot, both relative unknowns at the time; Crue did not even have a major label. By the end of the year, however, both acts would be top metal bands. US '83 was heavy metal's Monterey.

Besides being the largest crowd of the festival, it was also the most violent, causing headaches for San Bernardino County Sheriff Floyd Tidwell, who described the mob as "a younger crowd that's primarily interested in the four *s*'s: *smoking*, *snorting*, *shooting*, and *screwing*." Tidwell kept his attention focused anxiously on the audience while the fans roared their approval during Ozzy Osbourne's afternoon set, followed by Judas Priest. The leather-clad quintet was frying under its black leather stage gear, but, vocalist Rob Halford later exclaimed, "When we started the opening bars of 'The Electric Eye,' it was like when there's lightning and you feel the air crackling with energy. It was like walking into the middle of a storm. It was most enjoyable."

At approximately 6:00 P.M. Steve Wozniak himself introduced Triumph to the crowd. Stripped of its usual pyrotechnics display, Triumph had to work extra hard, and though they acquitted themselves well, by most accounts their set was not one of the day's highlights. In fact, Mike Levine, guitarist Rik Emmett, and drummer Gil Moore might have been more overwhelmed than the crowd as they looked out upon the audience. "It was awesome," says Levine. "It seemed to go on forever."

Germany's Scorpions were next, having warmed up for the festival with a small series of dates in the Southwest, and their fiery set whetted the crowd's anticipation for headliners Van Halen, who earned $1.5 million for one set.

As a gathering of the Me Generation, US proved little other than that the appellation was apt; it was a giant frat party—not much more. For heavy metal, however, it was a sign to the music industry and to the media that it could no longer be ignored. In the months following US '83, hordes of hard-rock bands began scaling the album and singles charts. A few were brand-new entities, but most were comprised of refugees from other, older bands or local-scene veterans: Dio, the outfit led by heavy-metal lead singer Ronnie James Dio, formerly of Elf, Rainbow, and Black Sabbath; Fastway, which included ex-Motorhood guitarist Fast Eddie Clarke and former Humble Pie drummer Jerry Shirley; Alcatrazz, formed by Graham Bonnet, onetime lead vocalist for Rainbow and the Michael Schenker Group; Ratt, a hard-rock quintet in the Aerosmith vein and yet another graduate of the L.A. club circuit; Zebra, a transplanted band from New Orleans who, only months before recording its debut LP, was still playing Led Zeppelin cover tunes in New York bars; and Twisted Sister, whose story emulates that of heavy metal.

Formed in 1973, this New York–based group wore ghoulish makeup and Spandex in the tradition of Alice Cooper and the New York Dolls. Eight years later, it was a staple on the New York, New Jersey, Connecticut tri-state bar circuit but considered a hopeless anachronism. The band took off for England, where it found enough fame to keep it afloat until it was signed by Atlantic Records. When its second album, the sardonically titled *Stay Hungry*, was released, Twisted Sister was so far behind the times that fans suddenly began regarding it as the originator of a new metal style, much in the vein of war-painted Motley Crue. *Stay Hungry* sold over one million copies, and heavy metal had its newest heroes.

The mid-Eighties may have been a fruitful period for heavy metal commercially, but it was not necessarily a creative renaissance. As has been the pattern for nearly every musical trend in rock history, with the eruption of hard-rock groups in 1980 and 1981 record labels began signing metal bands recklessly, and standards sagged, as groups were inked to contracts based on their style rather than their talent or vision.

The new crop of bands had discovered the formula and mined it gleefully, to the point where it seemed as if every successful hard-rock group had its own poor-cousin clone: Heaven and Rose Tattoo tried to cash in on AC/DC's raunch and roll; with the success of L.A.'s Quiet Riot and Motley Crue, acts from the City of Angels were snapped up quickly. Wasp, who merely replayed the Black Sabbath songbook at blistering volume while wearing the mandatory leather, studs, and leers, followed in the wake of Motley Crue, themselves a third-generation band with little new to offer—by their own admission.

A sign that imagination in metal was at a new low was the fact that suddenly acts that for years had languished in obscurity suddenly began selling records, as fans seemed to blindly embrace anything that was heavy metal (e.g., America's Y&T and Twisted Sister and Britain's Saxon). The most basic element of the formula, besides looking the part, was to write *the* anthem, the ultimate paean to heavy metal. After Def Leppard's 1983 success with "Rock of Ages," it seemed as if every heavy-metal newcomer and veteran marginal act was attempting to write its own, with the tribal chorus and heavy drums and guitars—and, quite noticeably, a sense of calculation and desperation, as in the case of T. Sister's "We're Not Gonna Take It," teen rebellion at its most banal. The future of metal is simple: the acts possessing originality and vision will endure and the great pretenders will fall by the wayside.

That it's taken heavy metal nearly two decades to be accepted as a significant rock genre is, in some ways, proof of its success. Fashions come and go, but the youngest stratum of the rock audience renews itself annually with a new crop of kids whose attitudes and problems are basically no different than those of young teens two years, or even two decades, earlier. Their trials may be as profound as the search for oneself, as banal as a bad case of zits. But no matter. The fans support heavy metal because heavy metal—however temporarily, and however mysterious its ways to those who do not partake—supports them.

OZZY OSBOURNE AND BLACK SABBATH

NEVER SAY DIE

OZZY Osbourne has often sung about graveyards, but much to the wonder of his critics, he has yet to end up in one. His notoriety for a series of egregious offstage stunts—such as biting off the head of a live dove just to shock a roomful of record-company executives—has caused many to scorn him as nothing more than a buffoon. While that stigma has made Ozzy Osbourne a personality whose celebrity extends beyond rock & roll circles, it has also prompted many to overlook his music.

Despite his tendencies toward self-destruction—drinking and drugging have threatened to end his career several times—Osbourne is the most successful heavy-metal performer of all time. As of 1985, he had recorded thirteen albums over seventeen years—five as a solo artist, eight as lead vocalist for the group Black Sabbath. Eleven of those have been certified either gold or platinum.

Osbourne's madman-of-metal image has not only made him a wealthy man; ultimately, it has helped him to endure. Thirty-two years old when he began his solo career, Osbourne evokes a sense of trust from his fans, many of whom really are young enough to be his children. At the same time, Osbourne possesses a childlike impetuosity, and his audience sees him through his various personal trials with the concern of doting parents. It is a testimony to just how much they trust Osbourne that his solo career has prospered on music that does little more than echo the seminal heavy metal he made with Sabbath, who, just as surprisingly as their former singer's success, have been able to survive into the mid-Eighties.

John Michael Osbourne was born December 3, 1948, in Birmingham, England, the son of a steel worker and a factory worker and one of six children. In a macabre example of art later imitating life, one of the first jobs he took after quitting

school was working in a slaughterhouse, which inspired recurring nightmares "of all those mad cows running after me." His dreams also turned to music, particularly Cream, Jimi Hendrix, and the Beatles. He played *Sgt. Pepper's Lonely Hearts Club Band* continuously. With schoolmate Terry "Geezer" Butler, born July 17, 1949, in Birmingham, and who was studying to be an accountant, he formed a blues-rock band called Rare Breed.

In another aspiring local outfit, Mythology, were guitarist Tony Iommi and drummer Bill Ward, both twenty, Birmingham born, and primary schoolmates of Osbourne's and Butler's. The former had a taste for jazz and the ability to execute speedy runs even though he had lost parts of two fingers on his strumming hand in a metal cutter years earlier. Iommi was working then as a typewriter repairman; Ward, as a truck driver.

In 1968, Osbourne and Butler and Iommi and Ward formed Earth, and except for a two-week

spell in 1969 when Iommi defected to join the band Jethro Tull, this lineup would remain intact under different names until 1979. Even that far back, Osbourne would go to any length to stir audience response. Before going onstage at Hamburg, Germany's Star Club, legendary for its blasé patrons, Osbourne painted his entire body purple.

Earth's sound gradually moved in a heavier direction inspired by Cream and Led Zeppelin, as opposed to their original pop-rock material modeled after another Birmingham group, the Move. A name change seemed in order; Butler suggested Black Sabbath, which was in keeping with the group's excessive volume and sinister presence, elements that were not always fully appreciated by its audience. Once, the group was pelted with red-hot pennies by irate locals in a

The original Black Sabbath: Ozzy Osbourne, Bill Ward, Terry "Geezer" Butler, and Tony Iommi. All seemed to see the shadows instead of the sun.

Scottish roadhouse. Osbourne and the band just turned up the amplifiers louder.

That strength of conviction infused Sabbath's music, and the band was soon signed by Vertigo Records in England and to Warner Bros. Records in the U.S., though one Warner executive was heard to call its music "so bad, it's painful." In a rock scene that had discovered the "new Cream" the year before in Led Zeppelin but was already searching for *their* successors, the February 1970 releases of a single, "Evil Woman, Don't You Play Your Games with Me," and *Black Sabbath* were well timed. Both were successful for reasons even the band's own label could not explain.

⊂⊂⊂⊂⊂⊂⊂⊂⊂⊂⊂⊂⊂⊂

"Before the press was slamming us, they were slamming Led Zeppelin. I used to get brought down by it, but I don't anymore." —Ozzy Osbourne

Recorded in just two days for £600 (roughly $1,200), *Black Sabbath* forged this band's image in no uncertain terms. Musically it was crude, with patchworks of song ideas threaded together by loose jams, such as "The Wizard," a wildly syncopated Yardbirds-derived rave-up punctuated by blasts of blues harmonica. The title song, however, remains the essential Black Sabbath track and contains one of Osbourne's most dramatic performances. The music is raging and foreboding, with drummer Ward adding death-knell bells to the tempest. In it, Osbourne is a soul beyond redemption being confronted by a "black shape with eyes of fire"—Satan. As the flames of hell shoot higher and higher, about to engulf him, Osbourne emits a blood-curdling "Oh, no, no, please, God, help me!" His keening, mournful voice sounds as if it belongs in a horror-movie murder scene rather than a rock & roll album. It is a remarkable performance.

Sabbath was almost instantly branded a Satan-ic band, an accusation that greatly disturbed Osbourne, himself a baptised Christian. On its maiden U.S. tour in 1970, Black Sabbath was frequently mistaken for a band called Black Widow. The latter's songs really did promote witch-craft; the band performed mock human sacrifices onstage. Adding to the confusion was the fact that one of Black Widow's songs was titled "Come to the Sabbath (Satan's There)." Black Sabbath, though they did profess a fascination with man's wickedness and the devil, were never didactic, and in their songs Satan was presented as something to be feared, not worshiped. One defense of the band came from, of all places, *The Christian Science Monitor*. In a review of Sabbath's *Master of Reality*, the publication stated that the group did not "condone or promote the less seemly aspects of . . . an interest in occult matters."

But in the long run, being condemned as Satanists proved a mixed blessing, for as much as it may have bothered the band members, it bestowed upon them a dark, alluring mystique that soon proved worth its weight in gold records. *Black Sabbath* bowed impressively at #23 and remained on the charts for over a year. Sabbath's records were played by "underground" FM radio stations, and Warner Bros., which had spent relatively little on promoting the group, was shocked to see it easily sell out the Whisky a-Go-Go in L.A.

In interviews, the members of Sabbath were usually asked about their views on devil worship and witchcraft. Though they seemed more than willing to go along with the angle that was giving them so much commercial mileage, they often contradicted one another's statements. "We're into God," Iommi once defended, while Ward countered, "But sometimes I feel Satan *is* God." And Ozzy Osbourne would later confess to having sat through no fewer than eight screenings of *The Exorcist*.

Ozzy Osbourne: shaman, sham, or showman? Mostly the latter. Never a hypocrite, he continues to express an honest commitment to rock & roll.

Sabbath expanded on the debut album's melancholy themes on its next album, *Paranoid*, recorded in just six days and released in January 1971. Its original title was *War Pigs*, but after the "Paranoid" single went to #4 in Britain, the album was retitled. To describe the music's turgid, soporific rhythms and generally gloomy outlook, one pundit coined the phrase "downer rock," and it was cynically suggested that Sabbath LPs come packaged with razor blades, presumably to assist listeners in taking their depression to the most extreme conclusion. Iommi responded at the time by saying, "If we come across doomy and evil, it's just the way we feel." And Butler, along with lyricist Osbourne, seemed quite pleased with the label. "The world's a right fucking shambles. Anyway, everybody has sung about all the good things already." And it was Bill Ward's view that most people were on what he called "a permanent down" and that Sabbath was simply expressing it for them.

The band looked the part: the otherwise angelic-looking Ozzy covered with tattoos, the knuckles of his left hand tattooed, one letter on each, to read Ozzy; drummer Ward with his dark, Rasputin-like beard; Butler almost always wearing a sly, somewhat unnerving grin; and Iommi, mysterious and distinguished looking, with dark, hirsute features. All wore the large inverted steel crosses Osbourne's father had forged and given to them to ward off evil spirits. All seemed to see the shadows instead of the sun.

Yet the band's singer claimed that his goal was to "make people happy," and that ultimately is what Sabbath accomplished. By playing music so dark and despairing, it succeeded in making you feel *good*. (Though not always: One English fan committed suicide by swallowing a bottle of pills as *Paranoid* blared in the background.) Perhaps being in the presence of the dead only served to make one feel more alive.

Although their general image was that of high-decibel doomsayers, a careful look at Sabbath's lyrics reveals an almost flower-power ideology. In concert, Osbourne, outfitted in pants and top festooned with fringe, leaped up and down excit-edly throughout the set, flashing peace signs in the air and shouting "We love you!" at the audience.

Sabbath spent much of 1970–72 touring the United States, where its music found an enthusiastic audience, *Paranoid* going to #12. In one eighteen-month stretch, the group played the United States eight times, and their lyrics reflected American youth's outrage over the Vietnam War. Sabbath's "War Pigs" is perhaps the most vicious antiwar diatribe outside of Bob Dylan's snarling "Masters of War" from 1962. Opening with foreboding, sweeping chords and air-raid sirens, it then steers into tightly syncopated interplay among the guitar, bass, and drums as Osbourne intones: "Politicians hide their tails away / They only started the war / Why should they go out to fight / They leave that to the poor." And just as Dylan had prayed for retribution in his earlier protest song, so did Osbourne, sure in the knowledge that come judgment day, justice would be served.

Many of Sabbath's songs were cries of alienation with an us-against-them stance that was readily embraced by those on the younger side of the generation gap, such as "Children of the Grave" from 1971's *Master of Reality*: "Revolution in their eyes, the children start to march," Osbourne begins. But the group's rebelliousness was always tempered by Osbourne's love-and-peace ideology, and at the song's end, he cautions them, "Tell the world that love is still the way, you must be brave / Or you children of the world are children of the grave."

Black Sabbath was overwhelmingly reviled by the critics, but except for one occasion in 1974, when Iommi punched a journalist from the British music paper *Melody Maker* for expressing disapproval of the guitarist's offstage lifestyle, the band took little heed. "Before they were slamming us, they were slamming Zeppelin," Osbourne remarked in 1971. "I used to get brought down by it, but I don't anymore." A review by Henry Edwards of 1971's *Master of Reality* was typical of the brickbats tossed their way: "Just ten seconds into the first cut on the new Black Sabbath album, my

bathtub drain miraculously unclogged itself for the first time in three months. . . ."

Regardless, Sabbath's popularity was soaring by late 1971, with *Master of Reality* becoming the group's first album to crack the Top Ten. They were even able to sell out their show in Salt Lake City, Utah, home of the Mormons. But the constant touring had worn down the band. Osbourne's nerves were so shattered from the 1970 campaign that upon his return home, he checked into a

hospital to rest. The following year, ten months on the road left him weakened with a throat infection and 106-degree fever. The subsequent 1972 tours were so grueling that Osbourne said afterward, "We were almost crashing out on the stage." Bill Ward had to be hospitalized for hepatitis, Geezer Butler developed kidney trouble, and Osbourne

Lead guitarist Tony Iommi defected briefly from Earth to join Jethro Tull in 1969. The following year, Earth changed its name to Black Sabbath.

spent much of his time combating laryngitis and homesickness. He longed to be back in Birmingham with his wife Thelma and their two children, and also to escape the groupies and the more eccentric fans who reveled in the band's supposed darker side. Osbourne once snarled, "It's a wonder half of them [fans] didn't bring coffins to the gigs." At one show, in Nashville, Osbourne, glancing out of his dressing room, saw several fans dressed in black robes, holding candles. With a shudder, he commanded a roadie standing nearby to "get rid of these people." On the whole, Osbourne was made so unhappy by touring that he took antidepressant drugs, which did not help his physical health.

Black Sabbath spent 1973 convalescing and living off the substantial royalties of *Black Sabbath— Volume 4*, which portended musical growth with a new producer, Patrick Meehan, in place of Roger Bain. One song, "Changes," was a wistful ballad with piano and Mellotron backing. "Laguna Sunrise" was a tranquil acoustic guitar interlude by Iommi. Were the Sabs going soft? The answer to that came in their next album, late 1973's *Sabbath, Bloody Sabbath*, described by Osbourne as "less aggressive and raw than in the old days." And Bill Ward explained, "We're not angry young men anymore. We're getting into happier things." Presumably he was not referring to material like the title track, a characteristically apprehensive song about a Big Brotherly world right out of George Orwell's *1984*.

Such changed perspectives have been known to capsize the careers of rock & roll bands, but not in Sabbath's case. *Sabbath* went to #11, and the group's 1974 tour with Black Oak Arkansas sold out countrywide. At Pittsburgh's Civic Auditorium, the band set a record for top-grossing show.

Sabbath's popularity began to erode the following year. Other music forms were eclipsing hard

Terry "Geezer" Butler and Osbourne first played together in a local band called Rare Breed. Despite sagging record sales and personnel problems, Butler and Iommi were still leading Sabbath fifteen years after its debut.

rock in terms of radio airplay and record sales. Nineteen seventy-five's *Sabotage* reached only #28, though Sabbath's U.S. tour was successful, with the band selling out shows in thirty cities. But when a best-of album and the next studio LP, *Technical Ecstasy*, fared dismally in 1976, the band's morale, especially Osbourne's, dipped dangerously low.

Just the year before, the singer had committed himself briefly to a British mental hospital; he was agonizing over his father's death from cancer and seeking solace in drugs and alcohol. He was also unhappy that the band seemed to be veering away from its original hard-rock direction. In 1976 he quit Black Sabbath and announced plans to form Ozzy Osbourne's Blizzard of Ozz, which did not materialize. So, in 1978 the four regrouped to record *Never Say Die!*, which, despite its confident title, was the work of a faded, lethargic band. On what would be their final U.S. tour, in fall 1978, Sabbath was upstaged night after night by the newcomers Van Halen. Osbourne knew then, he would later say, that Sabbath's career was over.

In early 1979, Osbourne left Black Sabbath again, this time for good. He retreated to Birmingham in hopes of finally solving the drinking and cocaine problems he had developed. Plus, at age thirty, with serious limitations as a composer, he needed to hook up with a songwriter or songwriters that would produce a relationship as fruitful as the one he had enjoyed with Iommi, Butler, and Ward.

The other members of Sabbath, meanwhile, were ready to break up. The band had long been derided by critics as a dinosaur, but in light of the new-wave movement, that putdown seemed more appropriate than ever.

After an unsuccessful try as Sabbath, with singer Dave Walker in Osbourne's place, Tony Iommi made up his mind to form a new band. For the lead vocalist he chose Ronnie James Dio, former singer for Ritchie Blackmore's Rainbow and, before that, an upstate New York band called Elf. The two met and hit it off, but they could not decide on a bass-and-drums team, so Iommi suggested Butler and Ward, and quickly, Black Sabbath was raised from the dead.

For Dio, it was a logical move, since in Rainbow he had cowritten material with a similarly mythological bent. "I've always been interested in science fiction and medieval art and literature," he pointed out. Not everyone shared his and Iommi's optimism about a resurrection, however, and management problems and Butler's needing to take time off due to some personal and family problems delayed their recording comeback until 1980. Dio, acknowledged as a technically superior singer to Osbourne, was in the unenviable position of having to match Osbourne's enormous popularity with the fans. "I've always been one for challenges," he said at the time of *Heaven and Hell*'s summer 1980 release, "and I'm damn well proud of these guys and myself. Black Sabbath are again a band to be reckoned with."

He was right, albeit temporarily. *Heaven and Hell* shot into the Top Thirty, selling in excess of 500,000 copies. But on the subsequent tour, the band was tormented by the kind of problems that would haunt it through the early Eighties. In mid-tour, Bill Ward dropped out, due to, Dio later explained, "family problems"; specifically, the deaths of his mother and father within six months of each other. Feeling that he needed some time to himself, Ward left, and the band willingly absorbed the financial losses that resulted from the cancellation of several concerts. But when Ward decided to leave a second time in 1981, says Dio, "We just couldn't take that time off, and it was a case of never looking back." Vinny Appice, younger brother of veteran rock drummer Carmine Appice (who in 1983 would drum briefly for Ozzy Osbourne), joined the band on three days' notice and completed the tour.

By the time Ozzy Osbourne was ready to form his own band, it appeared that his old Sabbath mates had already reclaimed their former audience.

And with such new acts as Judas Priest, Def Leppard, Van Halen, and Scorpions monopolizing the affections of heavy-metal fans, it was questionable whether Osbourne would find any place in which to stake his claim.

The single most important turn in Osbourne's career came when he spirited twenty-three-year-old guitarist Randy Rhoads away from Quiet Riot, then a struggling California quartet with two Japanese LPs to its credit and scant hopes of a U.S. record deal. In Rhoads, Osbourne found a songwriting partner; together, they and bassist Bob Daisley, formerly of Rainbow, and drummer Lee Kerslake, of the band Uriah Heep, composed and recorded two albums' worth of songs. In case anyone had forgotten his demonic presence with Black Sabbath—it had been over two years since he was last heard from—Osbourne posed on the cover of *Blizzard of Ozz*, clutching a cross and wearing a suitably crazed expression.

"Black Sabbath are again a band to be reckoned with."
—Ronnie James Dio

"Black Sabbath today is Black Sabbath in name only."
—Ozzy Osbourne

That Osbourne's solo debut streaked into the Top Thirty was even more surprising than Sabbath's comeback of the previous year, and Osbourne's lengthy 1981 American tour (with ex–Quiet Riot bassist Rudy Sarzo in place of Daisley, and former Black Oak Arkansas/Pat Travers Band drummer Tommy Aldridge taking over for Kerslake) was a success. With the second LP, *Diary of a Madman*, already in the can, Osbourne capitalized on his momentum by releasing it late in the same year, at about the same time as Sabbath's second with Dio, *Mob Rules*.

Ronnie James Dio found his tenure in Sabbath as Osbourne's replacement less than satisfying. By late 1984, his first two solo albums had gone gold.

The break between Osbourne and his longtime partners had been friendly at first, with Osbourne praising their choice of Dio, and Dio saying respectfully that he realized the enormity of the role Osbourne had left for him to fill. But by late 1981, a bitter rivalry had arisen between the two. Osbourne was prone to making such statements as "Black Sabbath today is Black Sabbath in name only." A midget who later appeared in Ozzy's stage show was nicknamed Ronnie, a swipe at Dio's five-foot-four height. There were also some personal attacks on the normally mild-mannered Iommi, which hurt him deeply.

"Yes, it's upsetting," Iommi admitted with a combination of bemusement and bewilderment in his voice. "He's been slagging the band—particularly me—and I don't know why. He's doing his thing and doing well, and we're doing our thing and doing well, so I don't understand why he doesn't leave the whole thing alone."

Iommi was especially rankled by Osbourne's claim that he was the image of the band, since one of the last statements Osbourne made before leaving Black Sabbath was that no one member defined that image. "Well, that's Ozzy," Iommi shrugged. "He says one thing one day, then says something entirely different the next."

Admirably, Sabbath's members refrained from returning Osbourne's fusillade of name-calling, but as far as the public was concerned, Osbourne apparently did embody the image of the band: *Diary of a Madman* went into the Top Fifteen and sold over one million copies, whereas *Mob Rules*, by Dio's own admission an unfocused record, stalled at #29.

While Sabbath toiled dutifully, ironing out its problems, Osbourne's madcap stunts were making headlines. Less than a year after biting off a dove's head, Osbourne was again in the news when, on January 20, 1982, he bit into what he assumed to be a fake bat a fan had tossed to him during a show in Des Moines, Iowa. The animal was quite real, however, and Osbourne was rushed to a nearby hospital after the show to undergo a painful series of rabies and tetanus shots. Osbourne proclaimed his ignorance, which did not placate the humane societies and animal-protection groups that tried to stop his shows in several U.S. cities, and his record label was swamped by letters of condemnation. Osbourne chuckled that he could not have bought better publicity. (The following year he donated $2,000 to the Society for the Prevention of Cruelty to Animals.)

In February, Osbourne made another public splash, this time by urinating in public at the Alamo. Texans were infuriated. The next time Osbourne would make the papers, he would be involved in a tragedy that would greatly alter his career.

The *Diary of a Madman* Tour was a hit. The stage show was lavish to the point of excess, the set designed to resemble the interior of a medieval castle, with drummer Aldridge perched at the top of a huge flight of stairs. Pigs' intestines and calves' livers were tossed at the audience as part of the show, and a midget, Little John (a.k.a. Ronnie), was unceremoniously "hanged." Critics called it a crude abomination, while Osbourne howled with glee. On the *Diary of a Madman* cover, he presented himself in a spooked house, surrounded by such demonic paraphernalia as a black cat and an upside-down cross hanging from one of the walls. Ozzy's face was caked with blood, and his wife Thelma was lying bloodied on a table covered in cobwebs. Not everybody appreciated Osbourne's sense of humor, though, and authorities in several towns tried—unsuccessfully—to ban his concerts.

On March 19, 1982, Osbourne and the band—Rhoads, Sarzo, Aldridge, and keyboardist Don Airey—were relaxing in Lakeland, Florida, before a show in nearby Orlando. The group's driver, thirty-six-year-old Andrew Aycock, was piloting a plane in which makeup artist Rachel Youngblood and Randy Rhoads were riding. Reportedly, Aycock tried to playfully buzz the band's tour

Osbourne hoists much-heralded lead guitarist Randy Rhoads during a show on his 1981–82 tour.

bus, but came down too low. The plane clipped the bus, tore through a pine tree, and exploded into a mansion. All three passengers were killed.

The tragedy should have put an end to the tour, which was scheduled to continue through June. Besides the musical loss, the emotional toll was heavy. Indeed, it would take Osbourne quite some time to get over the death of a protégé who was acknowledged as one of the most important new guitarists in rock. But just two weeks later, with Bernie Torme in Rhoads's place, the tour recommenced in Bethlehem, Pennsylvania. Osbourne finished the string of dates with guitarist Brad Gillis, a twenty-four-year-old who would find greater fame in 1984 with his band Night Ranger.

⮌⮌⮌⮌⮌⮌⮌⮌⮌⮌⮌⮌⮌

"Everyone has a certain amount of madness in them, otherwise why would they go to see people act mad onstage?" —Ozzy Osbourne

Osbourne continued to make still more news, divorcing Thelma in April and marrying his manager, Sharon Arden, in June, in Hawaii. Of course, Osbourne could not resist a little lunacy even at his own wedding, and so donned some vampire fangs for the occasion. He also shaved his skull after a binge in New Orleans' French Quarter, enabling him to shock the audience by whisking off his wig at crucial points in the show to reveal his bald pate.

On September 26 and 27, Osbourne, with Gillis, Aldridge, and Sarzo, who was making his last appearance before returning to Quiet Riot, recorded two shows at New York City's the Ritz for a double-album collection of old Black Sabbath tunes, including "Iron Man," "Paranoid," and other weighty chestnuts. It was a curious move, and one motivated by business considerations: Osbourne owed his label a live album, but refused to release tapes from the 1982 tour with Randy Rhoads so soon after his death. Also,

Osbourne knew that Black Sabbath was readying its own live LP, and was tickled by the thought of getting his out on the market first. He also claimed that he wanted the old material captured "the way it should be"—yet another dig at his former band.

Titled waggishly *Speak of the Devil*, with Osbourne on the cover spitting out blood and flesh, Osbourne's live opus did indeed beat out Sabbath's *Live Evil*. While his went gold, theirs peaked at #37, a respectable enough showing, but a disappointment nonetheless. It appeared as if Sabbath were snakebit, and tensions between Dio—a strongheaded artist—and Iommi and Butler led to both Dio's and Appice's leaving just prior to *Live Evil*'s long-overdue release, effectively hampering any chance of promoting the record with a tour. Black Sabbath's career was suddenly dark, and not by its own design.

Dio's departure from Sabbath was nearly as bitter as his predecessor's. Butler and Iommi charged that Dio had tried to sneak into the recording studio to boost the level on his vocals for the live LP; Dio responded by firing his own salvos at Sabbath. Though temporarily vilified, Dio was vindicated later that year with the launching of a highly successful solo career. He assembled his own band—Vinny Appice, bassist Jimmy Bain, and guitarist Vivian Campbell—and earned two gold LPs in his first two tries, with 1983's *Holy Diver* and the following year's *The Last in Line*.

At the time of Sabbath's splintering, Ozzy Osbourne might have appeared to have had the upper hand, but Randy Rhoads's death left Osbourne without a writing partner. There were also a number of personnel changes in Osbourne's bands following Rhoads's death. Through early 1985, Osbourne had worked with three bassists (Daisley, Sarzo, Don Costa, and Daisley again), three drummers (Kerslake, Aldridge, Carmine Appice, and Aldridge again), and four guitarists (Rhoads, Torme, Gillis, and Jake Williams, a.k.a. Jake E. Lee, a former member of early versions of Dio and Ratt).

It would take Osbourne until late 1983, nearly

two years after his last studio album, to issue *Bark at the Moon*, a transitional LP much in the same vein as *Sabbath, Bloody Sabbath* nearly a decade earlier, marked by a softening of direction on such songs as "You're No Different," Osbourne's response to those critical of his flamboyant image. Overall, he seemed, as per the title of one of *Bark*'s songs, "So Tired," and at thirty-five, ready again to take stock of his career.

Black Sabbath members, meanwhile, were forced to rethink their own direction. They had seemed to make a savvy professional move by coaxing Ian Gillan, the former lead singer for Deep Purple, one of Sabbath's few rivals during their early-Seventies heyday, to join. And Bill Ward had returned to drum on *Born Again*, its title promising more vitality than its music delivered. By the time Sabbath was ready to tour America, Ward had quit yet again, replaced by Bev Bevan, drummer for the Electric Light Orchestra and before that, the Move. It soon became clear that the post-Osbourne material lacked distinction and that the fans were still coming to hear the Sabbath standards. Immediately after the tour —on which the band traveled with three twenty-six-foot-high replicas of Stonehenge—Bevan and Gillan were gone, and Butler and Iommi were once again left to rebuild Sabbath. By early 1985, no definite arrangements had been announced, but one gets the feeling that they will not be buried alive.

Osbourne, who had tempered his criticism of his old band once it became apparent that his career was by far the more successful of the two, spent 1984 in much the same way, staying at his fifteenth-century thatched cottage in Staffordshire with his family, and working on material for his fifth solo LP. He also seemed determined to take better care of himself physically.

The one question never fully answered during Osbourne's lengthy career is, is he a shaman or a sham? To many, his pranks are merely a cover-up for his music, which has never really progressed and at times wallows in Seventies metal clichés. But his outlandishness does appear to be genuine and not the product of slick calculation. Besides, the publicity that it has generated has not always been favorable. Rock & roll is about extremes, so why do so many outside of heavy metal detest Ozzy Osbourne? Such rock & roll icons as Elvis Presley, John Lennon, Jim Morrison, and Jerry Lee Lewis each had their own peccadilloes, which only enhanced their legends.

The basis of Ozzy Osbourne's continuing popularity is that he has never behaved like a hypocrite. Most of his peers have either mollified their commitment to rock & roll or have rejected their past entirely. Not Osbourne. And that is what his audience respects the most. Osbourne still possesses a tenacious commitment to rock that you can believe. He says it well in his song from *Bark at the Moon*, "Rock 'N' Roll Rebel": "When it's all boiled down, and the day's at an end / I'll give you no bullshit, and I'll never pretend."

JUDAS PRIEST

⊏⊏ ⊏⊏ ⊏⊏

DEFENDERS OF THE FAITH

JUDAS Priest's career is a study in perseverance and a mirror image of heavy metal's own history. Formed amid the depressed and grimy industrial environment of Birmingham, England, in 1971, the band has survived a climb to the top that has been slow but deliberate. Often referred to as the "grandfathers" of heavy metal, Judas Priest's members—and particularly hellfire-screaming, leather-clad lead vocalist Rob Halford—have become the widely acknowledged spokesmen for the metal movement, or, as per their 1984 album title, Defenders of the Faith.

And it is a faith, a new religion, especially for the group's fans, who endow Priest's members with a power that is unusual even for rock & roll, a medium which has had more than its share of shamanlike figures over the years. Even the group's name, juxtaposing the title for a clergyman and the name of Christ's betrayer, suggests a redeeming yet forbidden presence. "It is a sort of power," says guitarist Glenn Tipton, "but it's not a case of wielding authority. You see, we just feel so strong on stage that people just naturally follow."

Is it the power of suggestion, then? "Exactly," says Halford, who shoulders most of the responsibility as the group's lyricist and frontman. "I don't think that people want to be told what to do, and I don't pontificate or lay down the rules. In fact, one of the greatest things that we've had going for us is that our audience is able to relate to us. They see us pretty much as themselves."

The members of Judas Priest spent their youths in a manner typical of Britain's working class. Guitarist K. K. Downing, who founded the group with bassist Ian Hill, was thrown out of school and out of his home when he was just fifteen. Born Kenneth Downing, he used the K. K. simply because "it sounded better and it just sort of stuck." Until Downing discovered music relatively late in his teens, he was disenfranchised from those around him. "Nothing interested me," he recalls, "not even music."

Growing up poor, contends Downing, was

largely responsible for imbuing the members of Priest with a strong determination to escape Birmingham, where fate offered them little better than a factory job. That fighting spirit is still heard in the group's music. Of those early experiences, Downing says, "That's what hardens you, that's what helped us stick to the grindstone over the years; it taught us to appreciate what we had."

The lot of those who still reside in Birmingham has not changed much. In December 1983, Priest returned to its hometown to give two emotion-charged Christmas shows. Upon his return to the States, Halford observed, "The problems that were there—especially the unemployment among the young people—are still very dominant. Yet there's a tremendous sense of belief in the city, just like what I see when we tour the less fortunate areas of the States. I still witness that striving, that desire to make something of oneself, which is an attitude largely associated with heavy metal."

Halford's boyhood was also poor, though less tumultuous than Downing's. He remains close to

his parents. Growing up, Halford was always intrigued by the arts, and even now believes that had he not wound up fronting a rock band, he might have become involved in theater. And he tried, though he only got as far as becoming the lighting designer for the Wolverhampton Grand Theatre. In 1971, he was recommended by an acquaintance to Hill and Downing, who contacted the vocalist even though, aside from singing with a local outfit called Lord Lucifer, he had no professional singing experience.

"I arranged to meet him at his house," recalls Downing, "to see what he looked like and what he was into. There was some nineteen-fifties American singer on the radio—Doris Day, somebody like that. And Rob started singing, adding harmonies to two or three records that came on the air, all the while just puttering about the house. It

Posing with a vengeance: Judas Priest's Dave Holland, Glenn Tipton, Rob Halford, K. K. Downing, and Ian Hill. Priest's look and hard-driving rock style are the essence of heavy metal.

was apparent that he had a great voice and real musical ability."

The band that the burly Halford joined then included Downing and Hill (who later married Rob's sister) and original drummer John Hinch. Shortly before the recording of its first album, the group enlisted guitarist Glenn Tipton, who had been playing Birmingham in a succession of rival bands. There was some reluctance to add a fifth member, partially because the group was not sure it wanted to split the little gig money it earned with another musician. But having seen Tipton play numerous times, they were all convinced that the move would prove beneficial.

Priest was signed to Gull Records, a small subsidiary of Decca, and in 1974 released *Rocka Rolla*, produced by Roger Bain, who had produced fellow Birminghamptons Black Sabbath's first three LPs. The influence most clearly reflected on this debut LP was that of Sabbath, with Halford's lyrics creating a similarly doom-laden tone that was further expounded upon on the next album, 1976's *Sad Wings of Destiny*, released in the United States on Janus Records. Selected apocalyptic song titles included "Epitaph" and "Victim of Changes." Musically the band was still in its infancy, and its sound was a bottom-heavy pastiche of white-noise clichés and generally sluggish rhythms. Like so many other hard-rock bands of the period—Scorpions, Rush—Judas Priest was simply not ready.

Several crucial changes took place in 1977. Drummer Alan Moore, who had replaced Hinch for *Sad Wings*, took leave from the group, initiating a period in which Priest was drummerless and had to rely on such session men as Simon Phillips, a dextrous player hardly thought of as a metal masher but who is best known for his work with Jeff Beck, Roxy Music, and the Who's Pete Townshend. More important, the group made the decision to leave Gull Records, for it had become quite clear to them that the small label's limited resources in distribution and promotion were hindering the band's progress. Priest signed with CBS Records and released *Sin after Sin* in April 1977. Produced by former Deep Purple bassist

Roger Glover, it maintained the lyrical course of the previous records, with "Starbreaker" and "Sinner." However, it was noteworthy for the band's hilariously misguided rendition of Joan Baez's paean to Bob Dylan, "Diamonds and Rust," a cover that was as audacious as it was out of character.

Judas Priest embarked on its first major U.S. tour that June, and while the music was still in the process of refinement, the live show and overall image were becoming increasingly theatrical, focused, and stylized, highlighted by Halford's dramatic, forceful presence. Bedecked in black leather, silver studs, and motorcycle cap, and carrying his trademark black riding crop, the singer would strut menacingly across the stage, working himself into a frenzy until he seemed thoroughly possessed with spreading the heavy-metal gospel, presiding as he did over a show that had almost spiritual overtones. In a sort of sacrament, Halford would beat his clenched fists in the air, while the guitar tandem of Tipton and Downing would cross their instruments over their heads, forming a skewed crucifix that was unnerving in its visual intensity. The band's U.S. trek climaxed with two shows opening for Led Zeppelin at the Oakland Coliseum in late June.

❖❖❖❖❖❖❖❖❖❖❖

"I don't think that people want to be told what to do, and I don't pontificate or lay down the rules."
—Rob Halford

The following year Priest placed its first album on the American charts, *Stained Class* (which featured new drummer Les Binks), trespassing on the Top 200 for three weeks and getting as high as #173. Hardly impressive, but coming at the crest of the soft-rock movement, this was at least a hopeful sign.

In 1979 Judas Priest scored its first hit single in the U.K., the Top Ten "Take On the World" from *Hell Bent for Leather*, which in the States nearly

entered the Top 100. The group's uncompromising stance, songs about working-class defiance, and Halford's black-garbed hellion image created some degree of confusion. Coming in the middle of the punk boom, the group's attitude and image seemed as akin to that movement as to heavy metal. In New York City, on a ten-week 1979 tour, Priest played the Mudd Club, usually regarded as a bastion of punk and new wave. The show was packed, with even pop artist Andy Warhol in attendence. Still, critics—who were then in the thrall of their fascination with British punk—failed to recognize that Priest's similarities to punk, thematically and politically, far outnumbered their differences, and wrote them off.

Perhaps the reason Priest was relegated to the heavy-metal legions was the fact that it was ardently heavy metal in terms of music and its performance, featuring its then somewhat unique two-lead-guitar attack. Tipton and Downing helped introduce to hard rock the concept of colead guitaring, later adopted by such tandems as Iron Maiden's Dave Murray and Adrian Smith, and Def Leppard's Steve Clark and Pete Willis (later replaced by Phil Collen). Tipton and Downing have such similar styles and biting, metallic sounds that it is difficult to tell their solos apart. For the record, that is Tipton soloing on "Living after Midnight" (from *British Steel*) and "You've Got Another Thing Comin'" (from *Screaming for Vengeance*), while both play lead on "Love Bites" (from *Defenders of the Faith*).

"It's so subtle that even I can't describe the difference," admits Tipton. "I've heard Rob describe it by saying that I tend to play the more melodic stuff, and K. K. plays the wilder stuff. But that's not really accurate, because on many of our songs the very opposite is true."

When the two are onstage, they cut striking figures. Tipton, with his long brown hair, provides a visual counterpoint to the more impetuous

This late-Seventies—and slightly shaggier—Priest lineup consisted of drummer Les Binks, K. K. Downing, Rob Halford, Glenn Tipton, and Ian Hill.

Downing, who with his blond pageboy cut looks like a youthful knight from the Middle Ages. Together, they are perfect foils for Halford's overwhelming stage presence. Can two guitarists develop telepathy—the ability to instinctively know when and what the other is going to play—through practice, or is it a process that evolves on its own over a period of time?

"I think it's just something that you get into after years of playing together," Downing speculates, to which Tipton adds, "It took us a couple of albums to find our style together, and we've been developing it ever since."

In addition to developing a playing rapport, guitar teams tend to establish a camaraderie offstage as well as on. Maiden's Murray and Smith go fishing together when the band is off the road. Def Leppard singer Joe Elliott describes guitarists Collen and Clark as "the terror twins." Likewise —and somewhat out of keeping with their public image—Downing and Tipton can often be found on opposite sides of a tennis net. These personal relationships no doubt come in handy, particularly for lead guitarists, a breed that boasts an unusually high percentage of egomaniacs. But with Priest, when it comes to deciding who will solo on what song, democracy prevails. After the basic tracks of an album are recorded, Tipton and Downing will divide their solos equally. "It's all quite amicable," Downing contends. And unlike Scorpions, who painstakingly detail in their liner notes the precise credits for each and every guitar solo, Tipton and Downing prefer to keep their fans guessing, though with *Defenders*, they did relent.

The beginning of the Eighties brought with it a challenge for heavy metal, still considered by many critics, radio station programmers, and the general public to be a noisy, if not totally mindless, anachronism from the previous decade, and a genre that would prove unable to adapt to changing musical tastes.

Priest, with new drummer Dave Holland, formerly of the British band Trapeze, met that challenge with 1980's *British Steel*, a landmark metal album that pointed the way for Eighties hard-rock groups. The Tom Allom–produced LP featured concise songs whose aggression was only heightened by their brevity, best evidenced by "Breaking the Law" and "Living after Midnight," which clocked in at under three minutes and four minutes respectively. This new approach flew in the face of metal convention, and proved that a guitar-showcase band, of which Judas Priest was certainly one, did not have to sacrifice its power by cutting time off its songs. That it was a modern heavy-metal album was not an accident. "We set out," says Halford, "to get away from the almost archaic heavy-metal approach that people had tagged us with to a certain extent. It was probably the most direct album we've done, very raw but very communicative."

British Steel was clearly a turning point. The years of struggling had finally paid off, and on this album Judas Priest emerged as an unusually mature band, sure enough of its talents to practice a degree of musical and lyrical restraint, neither a common virtue in heavy metal. Priest's members are experts at dynamics, a musical device often overwhelmed by the noise and passion of most

Following pages: The key to former Black Sabbath lead singer turned solo star Ozzy Osbourne's success is his ability to revel in heavy metal's macabre aspects while retaining the affection and trust of his many fans. In late 1984, after he had undergone treatment for drug and alcohol abuse, Osbourne spoke honestly of his plight in the press and on television. Still, Ozzy will be Ozzy: His stage show remains one of the most elaborate and outrageous anywhere (55, 56, 57). ⊂⋑ In many ways, Judas Priest's members set the standards for both metal's sound and its style; for that reason, they are regarded as heavy metal's elder statesmen. Lead vocalist Rob Halford forsook a career in theater to join the band, but his sense of the dramatic is still put to good use. Halford—shown here on the Metallian set in 1984 (58-59) and with his Harley-Davidson cycle (62)—popularized chains and leather, while colead guitarists K. K. Downing (60) and Glenn Tipton (61) evolved into what is certainly the best known and most accomplished metal guitar team.

metal bands. In Priest's hands, dynamics intensify the drama of such songs as "The Hellion" and "You've Got Another Thing Comin'" (*Vengeance*), "Metal Gods" (*Steel*), and "Love Bites" (*Defenders*), the arrangements perfectly setting up Halford's riveting vocals. Even in concert, where it is too easy to drown any sense of moderation in a flood of pumping adrenalin, Priest will often cruise at a steady pace—with Tipton and Downing playing muted chords that sound like a train just chugging out of the station—before racing to a climax of shrieking guitars and exploding rhythm.

British Steel broke Priest in America and was its first LP to go Top Forty. The group took to the road, and as its popularity escalated, so did the stage show, one of the most elaborate and darkly ostentatious in rock. Even before the band could afford its gigantic sets and the Harley-Davidson Lowrider cycle Halford makes his grand entrance on, Judas Priest had a very definite visual image in mind. Back then, with the exception of Kiss, who was most often regarded as bubble metal, little thought was given to a deliberately cultivated look. The advent of rock video changed all that and has since made the metal look truly cliché. And as a result, current metal bands strive to create stage sets as visually arresting as the ones Priest had used years before.

"I think Priest were the first band to develop the look of the leather and wearing studs and chains," claims Halford, who would frequent sex shops that carried S&M gear, to augment his cache of bondage paraphernalia. The singer, whose arrival is usually announced by the clanging of heavy hardware accessories, has added so many chains to his evening attire that, he says with a laugh, "One day they'll have to bring me out in a wheelbarrow."

Halford's trademark fashion is only a small part of Priest's attempts to visualize the music. The awesome stage show, however, is not meant as a subterfuge. Like many metal bands, Judas Priest believes that fans pay a lot of money for a ticket and deserve a real show. But there is always the danger that once you present an extravaganza,

fans' expectations will increase until the band is forced to bring out the Marines and a cast of thousands. Again, videos—wherein some groups are presented amid the most grandiose sets imaginable—contributed to this. And more than a few bands eventually sink under the weight of a garish production, proof again that metal fans do listen to and care about the music over almost everything else. On its five-month 1984 American tour, Judas Priest performed on a seventeen-foot-high set that was presided over by the Metallian, a deco-style Sphinx-like mythological beast the group invented for the *Defenders* LP. Out of the darkness, with only the Metallian's eyes illuminated, Halford emerges. The effect is dramatic and true to Priest style, one the group contends is really an expression of their individual personalities.

While hordes of imitators don a Priest-like persona like so many yards of chain, only to revert to their everyday demeanor once the lights go up, members of Priest pretty much continue to look and dress in real life as they do onstage. "We don't live in two different worlds," Tipton emphasizes. Halford, who most strongly personifies Judas Priest's image, argues that for fans who cherish the group's mystique, knowing what goes on after the show may not add anything to their enjoyment of the band and its music. "I think that people are content to see the show and listen to the records." This attitude contrasts sharply to those of other groups, like Motley Crue and Van Halen, to name only two, whose offstage excesses are not merely reported but glorified. Even after Priest's many years of popularity, many find Halford's reserved demeanor and articulate manner surprising. After a performance, you can find the band members slumped in their dressing room, their hair matted with perspiration, their bodies drenched with sweat.

From all appearances, Judas Priest hardly seems to live up to the Satyricon-like after-show legends that surround most metal bands. "Some bands do different things, don't they? They go into the dressing room and start punching the walls. Me, I usually go straight to the shower and

scream a bit more. It's a very quiet sort of fifteen to twenty minutes. It's as though we've purged ourselves or gone through fire—which is pretty close, with all those lights blasting down," says Halford, who claims to lose as much as ten pounds during each show.

One of the perennial problems for rock & rollers of all stripes has been the inability to equal in everyday life the intense exhilaration of being onstage. The resulting tension often leads to destructive behavior. Priest, however, lives on a fairly even keel, a fortunate state of affairs Halford attributes to the group's having been together for so long. "We're able to cope with all the things that come our way."

Things became considerably easier for Judas Priest after the release of 1982's *Screaming for Vengeance*. After eight tries, Priest finally netted its first platinum album for sales of over one million copies. Despite the album's title, however, the group was harboring no grudges against those who had failed to believe in them: managers, record-company personnel, hostile press, the radio industry's conservative nay-saying programmers. And surprisingly, there was no bitterness in the sweetness of success that had been so long denied. As Halford says, "We've never looked back in this band."

Following *Vengeance*'s late-summer release, the band began its U.S. tour in Bethlehem, Pennsylvania. ("Judas Priest in Bethlehem," Halford mused. "I suppose it proved to be some sort of blessing from above.") While smashing attendance records in nearly every city it played on the 110-date trek, Priest noted the album's progress. It eventually hit the Top Twenty and stayed on the charts a little over a year.

The growing crowds on the post-*Vengeance* tours were made up mostly of younger fans, a development that is atypical in rock & roll in general, where musical styles and tastes often fall

K. K. Downing and Glenn Tipton comprise the most widely imitated tandem guitar team in metal, exchanging solos and phrases almost intuitively.

within strict generational lines. While the influx of younger fans pleases them, both Halford and Tipton admit it is a puzzling statistic that hard-rock audiences are almost always comprised solely of teenagers. This, despite the fact that many of these fans' idols are at least in—and sometimes a decade beyond—their early thirties.

"I'd really like to play to thirty-year-olds," admits Halford, who became one in 1981. His theory is that when it comes to heavy metal, there is an energy that is directed at and can be felt more strongly by a younger audience. "But," he adds, "it can cut across a wide spectrum of ages. I think that's one of the unique qualities of heavy metal, unlike new wave, which was essentially a very youth-oriented commodity. Our audience may start at fifteen, sixteen, but it also includes some people in their thirties. They may not be sitting down in front, but they're probably back there in the shadows."

ᴃᴃᴃᴃᴃᴃᴃᴃᴃᴃᴃᴃ

"The worst thing groups can do is to go with the stock formula. I don't think there is a formula in heavy metal, or ever has been."
—Rob Halford

———

Also adding converts to the Priest call was the group's exposure on MTV. Their videos for "Hot Rockin'" and "You've Got Another Thing Comin'" were played regularly. The latter best epitomizes Priest's message and style. Amid a dark, futuristic set, shots of the group performing in the green-laser-lit darkness on a black platform alternate with scenes of a fearful, conservative businessman, in trenchcoat and bowler à la Magritte, who is trying to escape some unseen force. As the music builds to a crescendo, the shots tighten until Halford's power becomes almost palpable. His fist pounding the darkness in time with the bass drum, Halford seems omnipotent and god-like. Indeed, so great is his wrath that he wills the

businessman's head to literally explode. It is the title's threat—in a song that is basically about social injustice—realized in dramatically surrealistic fashion. It is perhaps the quintessential heavy-metal video.

One repercussion from having gone platinum was that the group members' personal incomes were now high enough to put them at the mercy of Britain's stringent tax laws, forcing Halford to become a tax exile in the mecca of allergy and sinus sufferers, Phoenix, Arizona. As Halford once explained, he eschewed the United States' twin music capitals, New York City and Los Angeles, for the simple pleasure of being able to swim in his own pool on Christmas Day. Another more positive benefit of success was that Priest could now afford more creative freedom; they could probably reissue 1981's *Point of Entry* and make it a hit. That album remains something of a sore spot with the band; an attempt at progressive metal, it sold disappointingly. Its lack of acceptance demonstrated why most bands—including bands outside heavy metal—are often reluctant to release material that substantially deviates from their preceding—and successful—work.

"I don't think everyone understood it," Tipton says cautiously of *Point of Entry*. "Personally, I think it was the most original heavy-metal album I've ever heard; we're really proud of it."

Point of Entry is especially interesting in that its lyrics divert from the standard heavy-metal themes. "I'm sure people get tired of hearing me scream about demons and death and destruction all the time," Halford said at the time. "There's always that tendency in heavy metal to have that kind of stylized writing because the words usually don't mean a great deal."

However, Halford still contends that heavy metal is the most difficult rock music to write, because of its built-in limitations. But how do you avoid repetition in a music that is inherently repetitious? "It is difficult," says Downing, who with Tipton and lyricist Halford comprise the group's songwriting team. "It's very easy to write a melody, but melody and heavy metal don't always go hand in hand. We've been able to widen our

limits to a degree. But you've got to be heavy, aggressive, and powerful, which is a pretty tall order. There's a lot of material we've written that we never could use for Priest because it would be considered too lightweight."

Certainly none of that material appeared on 1984's *Defenders of the Faith*, a rough-and-ready, back-to-basics LP that capitalized on the growing militancy of the heavy-metal audience. The front cover was graced by the Metallian—which looked like one of the Blue Meanies from the Beatles' 1968 feature-length cartoon *Yellow Submarine*, only with horns and a more fearsome snarl. (The beast was designed by artist Doug Johnson, also

responsible for the screeching, Rodan-like creature on the cover of *Vengeance*.)

According to the legend on the back of the LP, the Metallian stalked those who still possessed their hearing, for, it warned solemnly, "Only those who keep the faith shall escape the wrath of the Metallian." The Metallian's identity? Master of All Metal—nice work if you can get it.

In keeping with that theme, *Defenders* contains several healthy arguments for the joys of high-decibel brain damage: "Rock Hard Ride Free" urges metalheads to "rock hard ride free all your life," while the album-ending "Heavy Duty"

Rob Halford and Glenn Tipton onstage. Unlike some metal acts, Priest uses its stage show to augment the music, not act as a subterfuge.

sounds its passionate clarion call: "Let's all join forces / Rule with an iron hand / And prove to all the world / Metal rules the land."

The music on *Defenders* reflects its rebellious stance, with few concessions to FM-radio standards. Priest had not recorded an album this vicious since *Hell Bent for Leather*. The melodiousness that had typified the band's Eighties albums, however, was somewhat lacking, except on the antinuclear statement "Some Heads Are Gonna Roll" ("If the man with the power can't keep it under control") and on the salacious "Eat Me Alive," an uncharacteristic bit of sexual bravado for this bunch ("Lunge to the maximum / Spread-eagled to the wall / You're well equipped to take it all"), usually more concerned with extolling metal's virtues than with regaling listeners with tales of sexual conquests.

The recording sessions for this album were accompanied—for the first time in Priest's career—by pressure. The group now found itself in a position where it was forced to best or at least equal the success of its last album. Another pressure was that to resist the temptation to repeat the winning formula, an all-too-common chain of events that has robbed many a rock band of its edge. "The worst thing groups can do," acknowledges Halford, "is to go with the stock formula, although, personally, I don't think there is a formula in heavy metal, or ever has been. We've always looked to progress from record to record."

That, ultimately, provides the explanation for Priest's longevity, unequaled by any act in heavy metal except Black Sabbath and Ozzy Osbourne. Not that in those years, Halford, generally a quietly confident sort, has not experienced moments of self-doubt along the way, particularly during the late Seventies, when Priest's fortunes looked grim. Accepting the reality that the odds were against their making it took time.

"We've done it the hard way," he says reflectively, "which we don't regret." Is there an easy way? "I don't think so."

Priest on the set of its "Heading out to the Highway" video. The band's clip for "You've Got Another Thing Comin' " is perhaps the quintessential metal video.

S C O R P I O N S

⊂⊟⊂ ⊟⊂⊟

BREAKING THE BARRIERS

THERE is nothing particularly unique about Scorpions from a musical standpoint; they have no gestalt or overriding philosophy; and it has been only since 1982—eleven years into their career—that they have become internationally known. But Scorpions are significant in hard-rock history for being the first metal band from a non-English-speaking country to have popularity in the West.

Scorpions' success—one platinum and two gold albums, plus a well-earned reputation as a frenetic live act—helped blaze the transatlantic trail for other bands, not only from Germany, but from all over Europe. Surprisingly, for a group whose image and sound so clearly typify the heaviest metal, Scorpions' impact has not been relegated solely to other hard-rock bands. Musicians of all genres followed their example, and among those who came to prominence in 1983 and 1984 were Nena, a German new-music quintet that had an international hit with the antinuclear "99 Luftballons," and Falco, an Austrian disc jockey

who scored with the quasi-rap hit "Der Kommissar," both of which were released in English and German versions. Another German act to gain some degree of recognition outside the homeland was Accept, a metal band whose U.S. debut, *Balls to the Wall*, sold moderately.

"We opened the doors for them," Scorpions founder, leader, writer, and colead guitarist Rudolf Schenker says proudly in his halting English. "I still think, though, that for our music, it sounds pretty silly to sing it in German; it sounds much better and more natural in English." "Anyway," adds singer Klaus Meine, "English is the number-one language—you can go anywhere in the world and everybody speaks it. We want to go all over the world and be understood."

On "Bad Boys Running Wild" from 1984's *Love at First Sting*, when Meine sings, "Bad boyz vunning vild / zo you bedder ged oud uv de vay," the threat of violence so common to heavy metal pales, taking on the tone of a nagging warning from a Miami Beach retiree. But despite these

occasional—and unintentionally humorous—fumbles with the English language, Meine and Scorpions still deliver a highly charged, guitar-heavy sound that is the essence of heavy metal. Meine's operatic vocals, Matthias Jabs and Schenker's screaming guitar breaks, and drummer Herman Rarebell and bassist Francis Buchholz's workmanlike rhythm section all combine in a tornado of sonic fury. Yet Scorpions are distinguished from many other metal bands in that their songs are often strongly melodic. And, for a group that traces its influences back to the instrumentally self-indulgent late Sixties, Scorpions shed their predilection for long-winded jamming fairly early. Their streamlined compositions put them at the forefront of the Eighties' metal style, and they are much emulated by such newer and younger bands as Queensryche, Dokken, and Heavy Pettin'.

Though weathering years of hard work and disappointment seems par for the course in heavy metal, Scorpions' story is truly one of beating the odds, not the least of which was the fact that they hailed from Germany. World War II may have ended twenty years before seventeen-year-old Rudolf Schenker first began playing the electric guitar, but international prejudice against the German people continued. And though Germany, particularly the port city of Hamburg, had long been a second home to such early-Sixties British acts as the Beatles and the Searchers, aside from the Rattles—a German group whose popularity never crossed the borders despite the fact that they sang in English—Germany had yet to export one significant, internationally recognized rock & roll act.

Still, rock & roll, and especially heavy metal, has long enjoyed a strong following in Germany, a nation split in two, with West Germany separated from the dreary reality of the Communist Bloc nations by a guarded stone wall and a heavily

Mid-Seventies Scorpions, essentially a merger of original band members Schenker (far left) and Meine (center) and the group Dawn Road. Uli Roth is second from right.

patrolled border. To its young, who had grown up in an economy still reeling from the aftermath of the war, rock & roll's music and lyrics represented the ultimate freedom. The camaraderie that rock & roll inspired among its fans was particularly strong and the enthusiasm with which young German teens received their idols bordered on violence. Even in the otherwise sedate Fifties, a live appearance by a rock & roller like Jerry Lee Lewis or Bill Haley often sparked full-scale rioting. To this strong audience identification, heavy metal added the dramatic, dynamic swells of volume and crashing waves of sound, a highly emotive musical approach that harks back to the work of nineteenth-century German composer Richard Wagner. Generally, German metal fans tend to be more demonstrative than their Western counterparts, at concerts often chanting their heroes' names in a rhythmic, frenzied, almost religious manner. But through most of the Sixties and early Seventies—or until heavy metal's early-Eighties resurgence—German rockers were more often spectators than participants.

"Germans would be told that they couldn't play rock & roll," recalls Rudolf, a tall, mustachioed man with clearly Nordic features, who is generally regarded as Scorpions' leader. "People would call it 'Kraut rock.'" And of course, part of the problem was the German language. Even though some German-language records—like the Beatles' German "I Want to Hold Your Hand" ("Komm, Gib Mir Deine Hand")—were well received, they were regarded as novelties. On the whole, the language's harsh, militaristic cadence worked against, rather than with, rock's kinetic, flowing rhythms.

Through the Sixties and Seventies, when American and British rock & rollers were appropriating every conceivable style, from blues to country, most German acts gravitated toward instrumental-dominated, classically influenced progressive rock and synthesized rock, the area in which German artists have made some note-

After a decade and a half of hard work, Scorpions finally cracked the American market. Their early-Eighties success inspired other German artists.

worthy contributions. In 1970, the group Can, comprised of six German students, two of whom had studied under avant-garde composer Karlheinz Stockhausen, recorded *Monster Movie*, a primitive but inventive montage of sounds that stressed texture over structure, an approach that was consistent with the musical and technological experimentation of the period. Can was an early proponent of trance music over dance music, and its work inspired the next generation of innovative young bands who formed the vanguard of the technopop movement and would themselves prove influential in some very surprising ways.

The best known of the early technopop bands was Kraftwerk (the name means *power plant*), whose "Autobahn" is an aural automobile trip that incorporates the Beach Boys' "Fun, Fun, Fun" celebratory sensibility in lyrics that float over a droning melody. Interestingly, Kraftwerk was also one of the first bands of the prevideo age to adopt a uniform and look—in their case, a short-haired, clean-cut style that more than suggested the Nazi Youth. Coming when it did in 1974, amid the mellow-rock craze and the early days of the disco boom, "Autobahn" was truly ahead of its time, yet it managed to hit the Top Five. Similarly, Kraftwerk's 1981 album *Computer World* was a predecessor to another trend, and enjoyed a second life as a backing track for break dancers and rappers. Other German synthesizer bands included Amon Duul II and Tangerine Dream, the latter of which would go on to compose movie soundtracks. On the whole, though, German rock that did become known outside the homeland was best characterized as mechanical, experimental, sterile. In this environment, heavy metal's savage drum beat —bludgeoned out of cannoning acoustic drums rather than electronic percussion's robotic *tick-tick-tick*—and caterwauling guitars were ecstatically received.

Though Schenker, who was born on August 31, 1948, was inundated by music from his earliest years, he didn't begin playing the guitar in earnest until 1965. His father, a construction engineer, played the violin as a hobby, and as a child, Schenker would pretend to be conducting the orchestra coming over the radio as his parents danced together in the living room of their Hanover home.

In the Fifties, when German radio began airing records by Elvis Presley, Chuck Berry, Jerry Lee Lewis, Bill Haley, and others, Schenker's interest shifted from the music his parents enjoyed to American rock & roll. Later, British exponents of the same sound—the Beatles, the Yardbirds, and the Pretty Things—further impressed him; the first single he ever bought was the Pretty Things' "L.S.D."

"I remember being amazed by the fact that here were these young guys with guitars. 'Oh, that's interesting, you can play along with other people and make music.'" Suddenly the guitar that had languished in Schenker's bedroom became the object of his doting attention. As he grew older, Schenker frequently made the sixty-mile trip to Hamburg, where he would go to see the legendary bands that were then playing the Star Club, the popular beer hall where the Beatles honed their craft in the early Sixties. Even today Schenker claims his songwriting is most influenced by John Lennon and Paul McCartney.

When Rudolf decided to form his own rock & roll band, he recruited his first member without even leaving the house: his brother Michel, born January 10, 1955. Rudolf had started teaching Michel to play guitar when the latter was nine. "I'd play him classical pieces and tell him, 'You try to play the melody of the cello, and I'll play the rhythm.'" So rapid was Michel's progress that when he later joined Rudolf's fledgling Scorpions in 1971 at age sixteen, he became the group's lead guitarist, relegating his older brother and teacher to rhythm guitar.

Years earlier, around the same time that Rudolf was frequenting the Hamburg clubs, Klaus Meine was also there observing the British rockers. A diminutive, curly-haired singer also from Hanover, Meine had fronted a local act called the Mushrooms. "I began singing very early, when I was about eight or nine. I remember that I was very excited the first time I heard Elvis Presley. We had a few singers in Germany who'd try to copy the American rock & rollers like Elvis and Little Richard, but what a difference!" Though Meine is best known for his lusty, full-throated screams, he still harbors an affection for the dovetailing harmonies of the Everly Brothers and the Beatles.

⊏⊐ ⊏⊐ ⊏⊐ ⊏⊐ ⊏⊐ ⊏⊐ ⊏⊐ ⊏⊐ ⊏⊐ ⊏⊐ ⊏⊐

"I began singing very early, when I was about eight or nine. I was very excited the first time I heard Elvis Presley. We had a few singers in Germany who'd try to copy the American rock & rollers like Elvis, but what a difference!"
—Klaus Meine

Meine's musical career had come to a temporary halt when he was drafted into the German army. After his less-than-distinguished hitch ended in 1969, he returned to Hanover, where he met the Schenker brothers and coaxed Michel to form a band with him. That group, Copernicus, rehearsed in a basement studio; practicing next door were Rudolf and the first version of Scorpions. Rudolf, curious to hear his younger brother's band, dropped by and was so impressed with the group that he wanted to work with them. Meine and Michel disbanded Copernicus to join Rudolf in the new Scorpions.

This lineup—the two Schenkers, Meine, bassist Lothar Heimberg, and drummer Jurgen Rosenthal—recorded their debut album, *Lonesome Crow*, in 1972 for the tiny Brain label. They promoted the record with some small tours as the warm-up act for British groups like Chicken Shack (which included Christine Perfect, later McVie and later of Fleetwood Mac) and UFO, an early British metal band.

Lonesome Crow is a good representation of the band's early style, and remains a popular import album in the United States. Recorded in producer Conny Plank's studio, the songs on the album reveal traces of Led Zeppelin, the Yardbirds, and early Fleetwood Mac, all blues-based rock influences that would be heard in Scorpions' songs throughout their career. For a small-label debut, the record was received relatively well in Germany, and the group was understandably optimistic about its future. Later that year, on a Scorpions/UFO tour of Germany, Michel subbed for UFO guitarist Mick Bolton, playing the opening set as a Scorpion and then headlining with UFO, a band that could be both ferocious and sophisticated, a rare combination for heavy metal back in those days. Within the year, Scorpions' career had fallen into a holding pattern. And Michel, who was beginning to come into his own as a young heavy-metal guitar star, left his brother's band to assume the lead role in the more established and internationally known UFO. Soon after, he anglicized his name to Michael. At this time he spoke no English and had to have his wife translate for him. This language barrier was a problem that would haunt Schenker in the future.

Of that time, Meine says, "We nearly broke up. Everything had been looking so good for us, and then—boom!—Michael left and it was like we were finished." But Rudolf, who had been doubling as the band's manager in addition to being its primary songwriter and rhythm guitarist, showed for the first of several times the steely determination that would pull Scorpions through this crisis and others in the years to come. Rather than give up, he again overhauled the band's personnel. He convinced members of another Hanover band, Dawn Road—lead guitarist Ulrich Roth, bassist Francis Buchholz, and drummer Wolfgang Dziony—to join him and Meine in Scorpions.

In 1974 this new lineup recorded *Fly to the Rainbow*, which like its next three studio LPs—*In Trance*, 1975; *Virgin Killer*, 1976; and *Taken by Force*, 1977—sold well enough, but showed signs of the band's confusion in its direction. Roth's Jimi Hendrix obsession led him to write material that often took off in free-form flight, while Rudolf Schenker's songs clung to a more compact, standard verse-chorus format. The result was a metal mishmash. On the positive side, though, Scorpions' personnel problems seemed to have abated. Over the next several years, only the drummer changed. Dziony left after *Fly to the Rainbow* and was replaced by Rudy Lenners, who quit in 1977 because of a heart ailment. His spot was filled by Herman Rarebell, a native of a small German town near the French border. Rarebell had just returned to Germany from London, where he had spent six years looking for music work but mostly had to settle for such menial jobs as washing dishes and cleaning toilets at London Airport.

Over the next few years, Scorpions continued slugging it out, touring and recording, their big break seeming to loom forever on the horizon, just out of reach. By 1978, though, everyone in the band was butting heads with Roth, who felt that Scorpions' direction was becoming alarmingly commercial. Increasingly, Roth's own compositions became little more than vehicles for his rambling guitar explorations, and tensions within Scorpions mounted to the point where Roth would refuse to play on Schenker's more conventionally structured songs. That year, during the tour that produced the live *Tokyo Tapes* double album (recorded over two nights at Tokyo's Sun Plaza Hall), Roth abruptly quit to form his own band, Electric Sun. He has kept a relatively low profile ever since, finally emerging with an album under his own name in 1985.

Once again, Rudolf took charge. He is an unusually selfless musician who downplays his guitar work and prefers to take pride in his songwriting, the very thing that drove Roth from the group. "I see myself more as a composer," he says. Unlike many hard-rock guitarist/writers who seem to write songs only for the sake of connecting their favorite guitar riffs together, Schenker writes for the lead voice. His approach —unusual for heavy metal—is best evidenced on such tuneful yet heavy Scorpions tracks as "Loving You Sunday Morning" and "The Zoo." Meine and Rarebell supply the lyrics; as Rudy once admitted, "I can't even write a postcard."

Though the band knew it would persevere without Roth, his departure started another spell of bad luck. The group's American label, RCA, dropped them, claiming that Scorpions would never crack the U.S. market. Ironically, RCA had played a part in limiting the band's potential audience by releasing only *Fly to the Rainbow* and a best-of collection, and never allowing Scorpions to tour the States, an oversight that nearly ended their career. In fact, Scorpions did not tour stateside until 1979, a year later, and then they were opening for such acts as Ted Nugent, Aerosmith, Journey, and AC/DC. But Schenker was determined to prove RCA wrong. After auditioning 170 guitarists, some of whom he claims were "big names," Scorpions chose Matthias Jabs, a boyish-looking twenty-one-year-old Hanover native. While Jabs had been aware of Scorpions, he was not particularly a big fan, though he'd played in an amateur band with Ulrich Roth's younger brother, Johann. During his stint with Scorpions, Jabs and Rudolf developed a fairly traditional division of labor between lead and rhythm guitar.

"Michael is a really great player —he's a star—but even if he wanted to play with us today, we'd never bring him back into Scorpions again."
—Klaus Meine

Twelve weeks after bringing Jabs on board, Rudolf received a phone call from Michael, who announced that he had finally quit UFO. During his five years with the British group, Michael, who had been catapulted to stardom at the tender age of seventeen, had grappled with drug and alcohol problems. In 1977, right before a major U.S. tour with UFO, he had disappeared for two months. Band members had come to fear that Michael—who UFO lead singer Phil Mogg describes as a "Jekyll-and-Hyde character"—had been abducted by or had run off to join a religious cult. All the time, Michael had been hiding in

Germany, where he was drying out and trying to remain undiscovered for fear his bandmates would try to woo him back to UFO before he was ready. Despite his problems, Michael had proven himself one of metal's freshest talents, particularly on the eclectic 1977 album *Lights Out*, which includes a version of the L.A. psychedelic group Love's "Alone Again Or." But Michael felt that the atmosphere in UFO was simply wrong for him, and his problems with the English language only added to his difficulties. He asked Rudolf if he could rejoin Scorpions.

"For me, there was no question," says Rudolf, and the other members agreed. Jabs, who had been in Scorpions only about three months, was told he was being replaced by Michael. An introverted young man who seems to find his voice in the guitar, Jabs admits that being let go then stung. But he was also relieved in a sense, for the *Lovedrive* sessions had been fraught with pressure.

Though welcomed back to the fold, Michael still had not resolved the problems that had plagued him in UFO. And musically, it was soon clear that his phenomenally fast and very dominating lead-guitar style did not fit. For Schenker, who excels in situations where his dense sound has no competition from other lead or melody

Singer Klaus Meine's operatic vocal style has become Scorpions' trademark. He and Rudolf Schenker have worked together since 1969.

Overleaf: Scorpions' energetic metal choreography: Francis Buchholz, Rudy Schenker, Klaus Meine, and Matthias Jabs.

instrumentalists, Scorpions' two-guitar format soon proved frustrating. "I got fed up playing lead breaks with somebody else," he says, despite the fact that that "somebody else" was his own brother. When Michael began missing dates on a 1978 European tour, the others felt they had no alternative but to replace him with Jabs.

"Our musical direction really came together then," says Meine. "From then on, it was a five-piece *band*, not a band with a star guitarist. Michael is a really great player—he's a star—but even if he wanted to play with us today, we'd never make a move like that again. And even Rudolf will tell you the same thing."

Michael has since gone on to a moderately successful career as the leader of the Michael Schenker Group. In November 1983, Rudolf and Meine joined Michael onstage at London's Hammersmith Odeon for an emotional encore of the UFO hit "Doctor, Doctor." "I love to play with my brother," says Rudolf, adding that he hopes one day the two will be able to record an album together. "But not in Scorpions."

At the heart of all great heavy metal is the lead guitar. Unlike Michael Schenker, Jabs is a deft and flexible guitarist who can work his solos into the songs. Jabs is also known for his ability to make concise musical statements, a talent that is necessary in the newer, condensed metal of the Eighties. His presence helped Rudolf further refine his writing style, and since he was still young, Jabs developed his guitaring with Scorpions' music. Though Jabs's and Rudy's styles work together, the difference between them is striking. Schenker's technique, derived from the blues rock·he grew up on, is emotive and full of dynamics. Jabs, while a more technically oriented and proficient player, is an unusually discriminating flash guitarist, letting the songs determine when he unleashes his display of pyrotechnics. His blistering four-bar rampage on Scorpions' first U.S. hit, 1982's "No One like You," is one of the most head-turning stunners in all of hard rock.

To their increasingly powerful music, Scorpions added lyrics all about the heavy-metal staples—sex, women, and more rock & roll. Both *Lovedrive* and 1980's *Animal Magnetism* had made the American charts, the first Scorpions studio LPs to do so, and on its early U.S. tours, the band consolidated its record success by establishing itself as a wild live act. Their performances would climax with Jabs and Schenker hoisting Meine on their shoulders to form a human pyramid, or Jabs, Schenker, and bassist Buchholz writhing on the stage floor while playing their guitars. The overwhelmingly positive reception they received on these early U.S. tours, and the first stirrings of what became known as the heavy-metal revival, seemed to indicate that Scorpions had—at last—arrived.

Then came what Meine describes as "the worst time in my life." As the band was settling down to record its ninth album, *Blackout*, the singer developed nodes and a polyp on his vocal cords. After surgery and a few weeks' convalescence, Meine was assured that he would regain his fire-breathing intensity. But when he gamely tried to lay down some vocal tracks, Meine could muster only a fraction of his usual volume. His voice was completely frayed. Meine underwent another operation, and in all, Scorpions lost seven months of precious work time.

More serious than that, Meine's confidence was shattered. Normally glib and excitable, he was reduced to communicating to the others with hand signals. He became discouraged, then depressed, convinced his career was finished. So sure was he that his singing days were over, at one point he told Schenker to find another vocalist. Schenker, a man of few words, was characteristically direct, telling Meine that Scorpions would wait for him, but that he had to do all he could to get his voice back. "There was no way I could quit," Meine says.

A Viennese throat specialist who treated opera singers cared for Meine. With the aid of an electric massaging device, Meine was finally able to complete *Blackout*, as well as a hugely successful eight-month world tour. To this day, he frequently wakes up in the morning and anxiously tests his voice. "I'll go like this—" Meine clears his throat and glides effortlessly up a scale "—and then I'll say to myself, 'Mmmmm . . . yeah, it's still there.'"

Finally released in the spring of 1982, *Blackout* broke the American Top Ten, became Scorpions' first gold (and, in 1984, platinum) album and contained "No One like You," one of the few heavy-metal songs to crack the Top Forty. Perhaps the most important element in the LP's success was the emergence of Jabs as a new guitar deity. On previous albums, he'd been intimidated by having to follow in Michael Schenker's and Ulrich Roth's footsteps, and so was reluctant to assert his own artistic views. And the difference in ages— Jabs is the youngest Scorpion by seven years— made his move to the forefront even more difficult. But by the time the group recorded *Blackout*, Jabs had changed his attitude and simply played what he wanted to play. In addition, the brown-haired guitarist is clearly the group's sex symbol, his youthful good looks and winsome, quiet smile in stark contrast with the rest of band's tougher look.

With the success of *Blackout*, the group had a large and dedicated following. In fact, so enthusiastic was one fan that he tossed a glass jar containing three live, deadly scorpions onto the stage in St. Louis. The jar broke on impact, and despite the efforts of several brave road crew members, none of the namesake pests was recovered. Luckily, most fan enthusiasm was restricted to more conventional displays.

But though by 1982 Scorpions' future seemed assured, things were still far from stable. In early 1983, drummer Rarebell went to Switzerland for treatment to combat a drinking problem. Since the group had already booked time at Abba's Polar Studios in Stockholm, Sweden, to work on *Love at First Sting*, they brought in former Rainbow drummer Bobby Rondinelli. The British music press soon picked up on rumors that Rarebell was about to be fired. The Scorpions, however, never

intended to replace Rarebell; in fact, when they reassembled at producer Dieter Dierks's Cologne, West Germany, studio, they made so many alterations to the original tapes that Rarebell drummed on every single track of the finished album anyway.

With increased exposure through radio and touring, "Rock You like a Hurricane" hit the Top Sixty. A major factor in the single's success was the video that accompanied it. While the band sweated over its instruments in a single-minded frenzy, wicked-looking semiclad women in torn leather reached through the bars of the band's cage and appeared to be literally bending the steel, trying, one presumes, to get their hands on the boys. The sex angle was nothing new for Scorpions; their next video, "I'm Leaving You," was based on the premise that after one look at the Scorps' black leather and muscle-T-shirt outfits (not to mention a few receding hairlines), a team of young Middle American female softball players became a hungry horde of hotel-room-crashing groupies. *Love at First Sting* peaked at #8 on the album chart and launched another hit, the uncharacteristically poignant ballad "Still Loving You." Finally, in 1984, Scorpions toured the U.S. as headliners.

> **"We never think of changing members. Being in Scorpions is like being married. We're still in love with one another."**
> **—Klaus Meine**

In spite of their success and the fact that they are now the biggest band in rock history to come from Germany, the members of Scorpions have never forgotten the long, tough road they traveled together. "We never think of changing members," says Meine. "Being in Scorpions is like being married," he laughs. "We're still in love with one another."

RUSH

ELEVATING FROM THE NORM

WHILE other hard-rock acts toil dutifully within the hard-rock framework— in which certain musical values are accepted, others vehemently rejected—Rush is always iconoclastic. By its twelfth studio album, 1984's *Grace under Pressure*, the band hardly sounded like the metallic trio it had been at its inception. In place of brittle, screaming guitars were complex webs of synthesizers, owing more to the new-music bands of the Eighties than to the Led Zeppelin–inspired British blues-rock its members were nurtured on. In contrast, when such veteran metal groups as Kiss and Judas Priest tried to variate from their established directions well into their careers (with *The Elder* and the *Point of Entry* LPs, respectively), their audiences unequivocably rejected their attempts at something new, and their next albums found them back pursuing their original course—if anything, more conservatively than before. But Rush's creative free-spiritedness has generally been accept-

ed by its audience, one of the more sophisticated in hard rock. Why? Maybe it is because they recognize Rush's commitment to experimentation— and above all else, because the Canadian trio executes its concepts so well.

The thinking man's hard-rock band? It is a description Rush drummer/lyricist Neil Peart could live with. The group's lyrics espouse a philosophy of self-initiative that could be likened to that of one of Peart's favorite authors, Ayn Rand. It is a theme common to heavy metal through the years, but in Rush's and Peart's hands, it is much more eloquently expressed. And it is an ideology that has guided Rush throughout its decade-and-a-half career.

Rush was formed in Toronto, Canada, in September 1968 by childhood friends Alex Lifeson, an aficionado of classical guitar, and bassist Geddy Lee (born Levy), both fifteen. Joining them were drummer John Rutsey and, for a brief time, a keyboardist/guitarist named John Lindsey. In

Rush's early days, Led Zeppelin served as its inspiration, and the trio played local high schools as a copy band, essaying the best of Zep, Cream, and the other hard-rock bellwethers of the time. The music had little to distinguish it outside of its volume, which got Rush fired from one club because the waitresses could not hear the beer orders.

Historically, Canada has never been a cradle of significant rock & roll activity, probably because it's only been recently that original music has been encouraged there. Such notables in pop-music history as Neil Young and Joni Mitchell were Canadian born, but in the mid-Sixties they migrated to California, where the club scene was much more conducive to creativity. The Band got its start backing rock & roll singer Ronnie Hawkins, a transplanted Arkansan, in the late Fifties, but would not come into its own until after relocating to Woodstock, New York, in 1966.

Most of the groups whose popularity tran-scended the Canadian border have been hard-rock acts: the Guess Who and Bachman-Turner Overdrive, from Winnipeg; Triumph, from Toronto; Loverboy, from Calgary. Bars were for drinking, not for showcasing musical acts, and hard rock moved the most beer.

Many Canadian bands were so conditioned by the prevailing system of the bars that they did not begin writing until relatively late in their development. Rush's Lifeson and Lee began collaborating on songs early on, though they had not shed their Zeppelin affectations by the time of their first album, issued on their own independent Moon Records label in 1974.

Rock archaeologists searching for the group's influences could listen to only the opening cut, "Finding My Way," and acquire a complete understanding of the group's gestalt. Lee, possessor

The thinking man's hard-rock band: Always iconoclastic, Rush used metal as a base from which to move in a variety of musical directions.

of a shrill, shrieking voice much like Robert Plant's, indulges in some impromptu yelps: "Yay yeh!" "Ooh yeh!" and nearly every other patented Plantism. Despite the obvious references to the Zeppelin singer, Lee's vocals were refreshingly gutsy, unlike the more incantory style he would later adopt as the trio's music matured.

In general, this early version of Rush played with less obvious intellect than the band would in later incarnations. Lifeson played with a grittier tone in those days, and as the lone featured instrumentalist, he was afforded much opportunity for soloing, which he executed with Jimmy Page—like panache, combining fast, fluid phrases with dramatic chordal work.

At this time, the group's focus was on instrumental showmanship, and both side-ending songs were seven-minutes-plus excursions into jamland. "Here Again," a heavy blues, sounded like

Rush's Geddy Lee, Alex Lifeson, and Neil Peart: Though portrayed as serious, they opened shows on their '84 tour with a recording of the "Three Stooges Theme."

Led Zeppelin's reading of "Since I've Been Loving You" from their third album, and the LP's closer, "Working Man," included some improvisatory jamming à la Cream.

While the music suggested Zeppelin, and even the riffy hard rock of Lynyrd Skynyrd, the band's photos on the album's back cover make it clear that the members of Rush were not content to be viewed as conventional hard-rockers. With drummer Rutsey garbed in a glittery jacket, Lifeson in an elaborate ornamental necklace, and Lee wearing a surplus of bracelets, they seemed to be positioning themselves as Yes-like mystics, though their music mostly failed to back up that self-perception.

Rush sold several thousand copies as an import in Cleveland, which led to the group's signing with a major American label. The LP entered the album chart in September 1974 but hardly grazed the Top 100. It remains a competent and at times exhilarating album, marred only by Lee's "In the Mood," in which he feels compelled to adopt an uncharacteristically swaggering Lothario persona. Considering that Lee, with his stick-straight, long black hair and his prominent nose, was never the prettiest of rock stars, it evokes a few chuckles.

The members of Rush were musicians first, rock & roll stars fourth, and they never attempted to cultivate an image. "If there is an image for this band," Lee would say even after the trio had achieved international stardom, "it comes from the music." They have never adopted the customary heavy-metal look; in fact, the only leather on stage is their guitar straps. Their refusal to be trapped into one style has been reflected over the years in their musical philandering.

Before recording its second album, Rush fell out with John Rutsey and took on Neil Peart, a drummer from nearby Hamilton whom Lifeson had heard playing with a semipro band in one of the area clubs. Tall and rangy, with a cool intelligence that has frequently been mistaken for arrogance, Peart had traveled to England in 1970

in search of work, but he returned to Canada disillusioned with the music business, and settled into a routine of working a day job and playing drums at night.

Peart had heard of Rush but had never heard its album. Lifeson had seen him play around town and was impressed enough to ask him to join, and Peart, eager for some full-time work, immediately accepted.

**"Without wanting to sound too pretentious about it, we don't consider ourselves to be on a higher plane than our audience, so we don't feel we have to 'play down' to them."
—Neil Peart**

What Peart brought to the group was apparent with "Anthem," the lead-off track to Rush's second LP, *Fly by Night*. A remarkably dexterous drummer who would become one of the most acclaimed percussionists of his generation, Peart led the band through some insistent machine-gun snare-drum volleys, with Lee and Lifeson following him. Rutsey had been an efficient but rudimentary player, and being a three-piece band, Rush needed another mainspring.

The track then evolved into the type of Zeppelinesque hard rock that typified *Rush*, but Peart's playing lent the group a whole new dimension, and his ability to take on the most demanding time signatures spurred and expanded Lee and Lifeson's songwriting, for they were no longer restricted to conventional hard-rock rhythms.

Peart, an avid reader, also helped direct the group lyrically, and on "Anthem" he set the tone that would be identified with the group throughout its career. "Know that your place in life is where you want it to be," he preached. And, borrowing a sentiment from Ayn Rand's *The Virtue of Selfishness*: "Live for yourself, there's no one more worth living for."

Hard rock has always celebrated the self, even

though its audience seems to have a more desperate need to assimilate into the heavy-metal tribe than fans of other types of rock & roll. Peart, on the other hand, celebrates the self-made individualist as opposed to the mere individual. Not surprisingly, his rigid philosophy has often aroused critical ire, some of which, however, has been extremely wrongheaded. Peart is not, as some critics claim, a fascist, but merely, he contends, a believer in the individual.

"Sometimes you find yourself being complicated for the sake of complication, which doesn't always make for good music. The one element often lacking in our music was feel."
—Geddy Lee

Since Geddy Lee must voice the drummer's thoughts, it is important that both he and Peart agree on the lyrics. "Usually, I'm pretty much in sync with Neil," says Lee, "but there are times when I don't grasp the point he's trying to make. When that happens, we talk it out, and by just twisting some phrase, everything's realigned, and it all works out."

Peart's writing is often historically minded, and his "Beneath, Between, & Behind," for example, is about both America's freeing itself from the yoke of British imperialism in the 1700s and its problems in the wake of the 1974 Watergate scandal. "The principles have been betrayed," Lee intones sadly, "the dream's gone stale." But the track is hardly anti-American, and ends with an optimistic "Let hope prevail."

Two songs on *Fly by Night*—which peaked on the U.S. charts in the spring of 1975 at #113 but went gold in Canada—that best illustrate the band's split personality at the time are the title track—Rush's closest thing to a hit single, classically structured and unusually concise—and "By-Tor & the Snow Dog," its first recorded attempt at a rock epic. Like many of Rush's mid-

Seventies songs to come, "By-Tor" is written in several movements, a composing technique frequently employed by Yes ("And You and I," "Starship Trooper," "Close to the Edge"), to whom Rush would frequently be compared. A disjointed, convoluted tale built around ancient mythology, it fails to resolve itself, but points to the direction of Rush's next record, *Caress of Steel*.

With *Caress*, also released in 1975, both Peart's lyrics and the music became even more complex. Song lengths expanded, with Peart detailing not only vignettes but such story-songs as the lengthy "The Necromancer," which reintroduces Prince By-Tor. There's no question but that the band is taking itself seriously. The lyrics are printed in Gothic typeface, and look as if Peart had chiseled them onto two tablets of stone. And even a potentially humorous, self-mocking title such as "I Think I'm Going Bald" turns out to be a sober reflection on mortality. But for all its ambitiousness, ultimately *Caress of Steel* is one of Rush's least-focused albums, with nary a memorable full song to be found. It also fared the worst commercially, stalling at #148 and falling off the album chart within just six weeks. In Canada, however, Rush had already established itself and was awarded a Juno (Canada's Grammy) as Most Promising New Group.

Had Rush commenced its career either five years earlier or later, it probably would have ended right there. But in the mid-Seventies, financially secure record companies gave acts two or three albums on which to develop before canceling contracts. With no spectacular success to date, Rush settled down to the task of recording their fourth—and what may have been their last—album. Neil Peart remembers being extremely cognizant of the importance of this LP. "At the time, people were telling us we couldn't do this or that, that we had to write a single, and that we *had* to compromise, blah blah blah. But Pink Floyd

Drummer Peart joined the band in 1974, in time to record *Fly by Night*. He doubles as Rush's lyricist, espousing a philosophy of self-determination.

didn't have to do that. Frank Zappa didn't have to do that."

As it turned out, neither did Rush. *2112* was the group's most unconventional album to date. The first side was a twenty-minute epic in seven parts, replete with overture. Peart's most elaborately constructed piece, "2112," takes place in an oppressive society ruled by the Federation, headed by the priests of the Temple of Syrinx. They control everything so that one "never need to wonder how or why. . . . What a nice, contented world," they rejoice.

In the third movement, "Discovery," the hero of "2112" finds a guitar beneath the cave in which he dwells. After plucking tentatively at the instrument, he quickly escalates his playing into a cacophony of electric-guitar chords. He excitedly rushes to tell the priests, but they destroy the instrument because it represents freedom of expression. The hero retreats to his cave, despairing and saddened, and falls into a deep sleep in which he dreams of an oracle who leads him to another city, one in which man's spirit is permitted to flourish. Instead of inspiring him, the dream only frustrates the hero and drives him to contemplate death. The epic ends with the line "I don't think I can carry on," followed by an abrupt stop to the music. And as "2112" ends with a dramatic "Grand Finale," one wonders about the hero's fate.

Though it is as impenetrable as it is impressive, *2112* was a success, coming as it did during the height of progressive rock's popularity. *2112* became the group's first album to crack the Top 100, reaching #61. By 1981 it had sold over one million copies.

Rush had reached a definitive stage in its evolution, and the band celebrated with its next album, the double-record live set *All the World's a Stage*, recorded in June 1976 at Toronto's Massey Hall and containing material from all four of their albums. "This album, to us, signifies the end of the beginning," the members wrote in the liner notes, "a milestone to mark the close of chapter one in the annals of Rush."

Chapter two opened with 1977's *A Farewell to Kings*, on which Rush further explored the art rock touched upon on *2112*. Songs now were more delicately structured, but what separated this band from the one on *Fly by Night* and *Caress of Steel* was the change in the texture of its sound, particularly Lifeson's guitar. Though now using more crystalline, chimelike tones, Lifeson's playing was every bit as powerful as the more conventional metallic sound of the past.

On the intro to the opening title track, Rush assumed the roles of medieval minstrels, with Lifeson playing a beatific pattern on an acoustic guitar (one could imagine the blond-locked Lifeson sitting cross-legged on the stone floor of some drafty sixteenth-century castle, playing a lute or a dulcimer), while Peart added orchestral bells. Another track, "Madrigal," was just that, also with its roots in olde English music.

Thematically, however, *A Farewell* did not vary all that much from *2112*, only here it was an evil king, rather than some scheming priests, as oppressor, "beating down the multitudes and scoffing at the wise." The struggle between good and evil plays heavily in Rush's songs, even those not penned by Peart, like Lee's "Cinderella Man."

As it had on *Fly by Night*, the group juxtaposed its affection for longer, arranged pieces with its growing melodiousness. "Closer to the Heart" became Rush's first single to chart (#76, 1977), while capping the album was its most adventurous and musically demanding exercise to date, "Cygnus X-1." With lyrics about the black hole, it posited that it was not merely a hole of death, but rather "the astral door" leading to fantastic new discoveries for mankind. Musically, it hurtled through its ten and a half minutes like a satellite through outer space. "Cygnus" left the listener gasping for breath; in all, a fast, furious ride.

Peart has long entertained a fascination with the cosmos and with space travel, most fully explored on "Countdown," from 1982's *Signals*, for which the group was able to acquire from NASA actual tapes of voice transmissions between ground control and the space shuttle. For their video of the song, they incorporated footage of the launch, which they were personally invited down to Cape Canaveral by NASA to witness.

The subsequent *A Farewell to Kings* Tour drew well over one million people, and in June 1978, Rush earned its second Juno, for Best Group of the Year, an honor they would receive again in 1979. The LP charted at #33 and set the course for Rush's next album (following the rerelease of their first three LPs as *Archives*), late 1978's *Hemispheres*, an important album in Rush's history not so much for what it contained, but for what it represented: an end to their second era.

Hemispheres, like *2112*, had as its centerpiece a side-long suite, "Cygnus X-1 Book II/Hemispheres," an eighteen-minute sequel to the previous LP's final track. There were only three other compositions on the album: "Circumstances," "The Trees," and "La Villa Strangiato," a nine-and-a-half-minute instrumental that meandered through no fewer than twelve movements and was accurately subtitled by the band "an exercise in self-indulgence."

"With that album," Lee says in retrospect, "we felt that we'd done as much as was possible with the long-song format." Rock & roll was undergoing a massive upheaval at the time of *Hemisphere*'s release, and Rush was undeniably influenced somewhat by the burgeoning punk/new-wave movement's ethos of a return to shorter, more pointed songs. And more significantly, by this time, FM radio was gradually adopting more stringent programming policies, no longer airing lengthy tracks as it once had.

For the band members themselves, the more focused direction they would debut on 1980's *Permanent Waves* had more to do with changing attitudes on their part than with appeasing radio programmers. Following *Hemispheres*, by which point Rush had built up an impressive musical vocabulary, the band did not feel as compelled to prove its proficiency through difficult, drawn-out songs. Reflecting on that period of experimentation, Lee says, "Sometimes you find yourself being complicated for the sake of complication, which doesn't always make for good music." The

band realized, says Lee, "that one element often lacking in our music was feel."

The music on *Permanent Waves* was radically different, simpler and sparser, with Lifeson's guitar played down in favor of Lee's synthesizer work, giving the band an exciting new instrument with which to work. The LP title was an ironic reference to the new wave—the band was neither lauding nor criticizing it, merely implying that quality music is a permanent wave unaffected by musical fashion. The ultimate irony, reveals Lee, is that the band found that "working in a shorter framework, which we used to think was the easy way out, isn't really easy at all."

> **"It seems that as we've grown up, the music around us has gotten simpler and simpler, so that even though we keep getting better at what we do, everything around us is *legitimizing* us."**
> **—Geddy Lee**

Rush's members may have unwittingly tailored their sound to better suit radio, but they were hardly attempting to ingratiate themselves onto programmers' playlists. The album-opening track, "The Spirit of Radio," was an indictment of radio's antiart stance. Peart, in the past, had railed about restrictions placed upon music in his fantasy pieces such as "2112"; now it was taking place for real. Musically, the song exemplified the new Rush, so well versed in musical styles that within its mere five minutes, the band shifts stylistic gears several times, moving from blazing hard rock to a coy, reggae-ish verse in which Peart paraphrases from Paul Simon's "The Sounds of Silence:" "For the words of the profits are written on the studio walls . . ."

Ironically, Rush's invective against radio was also the very song that garnered it extensive airplay, and *Permanent Waves* went all the way into the Top Five, selling well in excess of one million copies and hitting #3 in the U.K.

The members of Rush were now cast in the unlikely role of superstars. Other progressive-minded bands like Yes and Genesis had already attained massive popularity, but Rush was still unusually imageless. Fans flock to the group for its musicianship. They admire Lee for reaching his impossible high notes, Lifeson for his digital dexterity, and Peart for his flailing around the kit. Onstage, the band is tame by most standards, largely due to the enormous musical responsibility each member shoulders: Lee is usually held captive at the microphone, where in addition to singing and playing bass, he works a set of bass pedals. And as the group got more heavily into keyboards with its Eighties albums, Lee spent more and more time positioned behind a bank of synthesizers. Lifeson also stays put, concentrating on meticulous solos and fills. And as seen from the audience, Peart is merely a head bobbing up and down in a revolving sea of drums and cymbals.

As the band's popularity increased, Rush's members were suddenly inundated with one aspect of fame they had rarely experienced before: their audience's growing interest in their personal lives. It became such a problem for Lee—of the three probably the most intensely private—that he was forced to vacate Toronto for the city's outskirts. "My home life was havoc," he says. "People wouldn't leave me alone, and I had no peace of mind."

The majority of Rush's fans respect the band's wishes for privacy, Lee says, "but there's always a fringe that doesn't understand that an artist's responsibility is to perform well. And that's where it ends."

As the group's lyricist—and particularly as a writer of uncommonly deep songs—Peart receives the bulk of the fan mail, much of it from zealots who believe they have discovered the "message" behind his songs, many with cryptic pseudo-religious connotations. At one point, Peart was considering starting a Flake of the

Bassist Geddy Lee: He and guitarist Alex Lifeson formed Rush in Toronto in September 1968. Led Zeppelin served as their initial inspiration.

Week Club based on some of the mail from those who wanted the drummer to conspire with them in their bid to save the world.

In the aftermath of John Lennon's assassination in 1980 by a mentally unbalanced fan, Peart reluctantly admits that the letters from the kooks and the crackpots now take on a somewhat different meaning. "It's an unfortunate situation that I know to be true. But you can't let it stop you from doing what you do or being what you are or feeling what you feel."

Peart expressed his feelings about the stardom *Permanent Waves*' success brought with it in "Limelight," a song off the followup, 1981's *Moving Pictures*. It was a rare personal statement, and one he had not made since the band's earliest days. "One must put up barriers," Lee sings on Peart's behalf (though probably speaking for himself as well), "to keep oneself intact," a partial explanation of why the drummer was often attacked by the press for his seemingly aloof, detached manner.

Another line from the song addresses that perception: "I can't pretend a stranger is a long-awaited friend," a reference to the ceremonial back-slapping and glad-handing that regularly follows rock concerts, among the hapless band members and suited-and-tied record-company executives who know the group as little more than the reason they are able to vacation in the Caribbean this year. Or the members of the media who often seem more intent on striking up a long-term friendship than in conducting professional interviews.

Moving Pictures further aided Rush's commercial climb, hitting #3, going platinum, and remaining on the charts for over a year. One reason why was Lee's altered vocals: There was barely a trace of his trademark keening voice on *Pictures*, with Lee instead writing songs to accommodate his husky lower register. Ultimately, it was a more emotional style. Lifeson, too, changed his sound, utilizing the more processed, phased sound favored by the Police's guitarist, Andy Summers. Lifeson was relying more and more on rich, chordal work, while his infrequent solos became increasingly dissonant, almost jazzlike in their phrasing.

Just as it had with 1976's *All the World's a Stage*, Rush issued a live LP to mark the end of yet another stage in its career. Nineteen eighty-one's *Exit . . . Stage Left* is an excellent chronicling of the previous seven years, beginning with its cleverly concocted cover, which reprises images from the nine album covers before it: the band logo from *Rush*; the owl from *Fly by Night*; the painting that adorned the *Caress of Steel* cover, carried by the same two movers from *Moving Pictures*; the marionette from *A Farewell to Kings*; the dapper gent from *Hemispheres*; the model from *Permanent Waves*; and the nude figure and the red pentagram from *2112*. Except for "A Passage to Bangkok" (from *2112*) and "Beneath, Between, & Behind" (*Fly by Night*), *Exit* was comprised exclusively of post-*2112* material and was awarded gold-album status; at the same time, *2112*, *All the World's a Stage*, and *Moving Pictures* were certified platinum.

Nineteen eighty-two's *Signals* was as much a continuation of *Moving Pictures* as it was a departure. Keyboards figured yet more prominently in the band's sound, with Lifeson being relegated to more of a support role. Lyrically, Peart seemed to be softening somewhat; his words to "Subdivisions" were unusually sympathetic toward teenage social outcasts. "Nowhere is the dreamer or the misfit so alone . . . in the high school halls, in the shopping malls. Conform or be cast out."

The music was marked by increasingly kinetic rhythms and an overall richer but darker-hued sound. "New World Man" became the group's first bona fide hit single, scaling the Hot 100 all the way to #21, but sounding more like the Police than the Rush of a few years before. Guitarist Lifeson, who had spent the past year listening to such groups as the synth-dominated Ultravox, even adopted the new look from Britain, sweeping his blond hair over his eyes. The album went to #10 and sold platinum.

Despite its popularity, *Signals* created some backlash among the fans who were first attracted to Rush because of its guitar-heavy focus and thrashing rhythms, or by the larger-scale albums of the mid-Seventies. Lee mused before *Signals'* release that it might alienate the more "hard-core heavy-metal freaks," and he was right.

There is a certain irony in the fact that Peart and Rush stress individuality more than probably any other hard-rock group, while the audience they are reaching is the one most concerned with protecting the status quo, often rejecting change. "It's astonishing just how conservative young music fans can be," the drummer marvels, adding, however, that Rush is unusually fortunate in that respect.

All artists have to tread the fine line between remaining aware of their audience's expectations and compromising their own artistic integrity. In Rush's case, it is a line that the band has rarely considered, Peart claims.

"Without wanting to sound too pretentious about it, we don't consider ourselves to be on a higher plane than our audience, so we don't feel we have to 'play down' to them. We like to think that the things we find interesting and enjoyable, our fans will, too."

But if segments of their audience found fault with *Signals*, so did the band. Peart, for one, calls the album "restless and schizoid," comparing it to the early albums of each Rush period, searching for an identity.

With the next album in the "series," 1984's *Grace under Pressure*, Rush took equal steps forward and backward. Lifeson's playing was beefed up and much more conspicuous than it had been on *Signals*; Lee continued to work out more on synthesizer; and for the first time in its career, the band went with a new coproducer, Peter Henderson, over longtime associate Terry Brown.

Though its lyrical outlook was bleak, with many of the songs concerned with an inevitable nuclear peril, *Grace under Pressure* was a supremely confident album. The band seemed much more comfortable with its direction. Most noticeable were the songs' rhythms, which, for Rush, were unusually straightforward.

Peart, by this point, had also matured considerably as a lyricist, his writing more concise but filled with more imagery than before. He points to "Red Lenses" as a prime example of his new, simplified technique, saying, "That song has fewer words than a lot of my other songs, but it took me longer to write. Although it seems to make no sense, it was a lot of trouble to get that exact combination of nonsensical phrases." What it comes down to, he continues, is no longer feeling required to explain every detail of his songs, but being able to allow for different interpretations or simply create a mood.

Rush's increased confidence was evidenced on their 1984 tour, on which they seemed determined to debunk the notion that they were a self-serious, almost dour band: The trio took the stage to the "Three Blind Mice" theme from the Three Stooges, and at one point in the show had a song introduced by Count Floyd—a composite late-night television Dracula and borscht-belt comedian character from the TV comedy show *SCTV*—projected onto the backdrop. (In 1982, Lee had sung on the Top Ten comedy record "Take Off" by *SCTV*'s fictional Canadian talk-show-host brothers, Bob and Doug McKenzie.) The band's show makes the most effective use of background visuals of any group with the possible exception of Devo or Pink Floyd. Rush's visuals embellish without distracting. For "Red Barchetta," a Peart song about a high-speed drive in an antique car, the audience is taken for a whirlwind cruise along a colorful videogame highway. For "Subdivisions," Rush's video depicting teenage alienation —filmed at a Toronto high school—is projected onto the screen. Peart's lyrics, so full of detail and imagery, lend themselves well to video—ironic in that Rush, with its decided lack of an image, is the furthest thing from a so-called video band. And—more irony—without having to resort to overblown productions, its videos are among the most effective, in terms of representing both the band and its songs honestly. And this helps make Rush's live show unusually provocative, well paced, and multidimensional.

Grace under Pressure became Rush's fourth consecutive platinum studio album, but immediately following its release, Geddy Lee questioned

how much longer the trio—one of the most stable units in rock & roll, generally not the most stable of businesses—would continue. Ten years into their career, they had become one of the most influential bands in all of rock & roll, but not in terms of spawning dozens of imitators. Quite the opposite. Few bands, it seems, have picked up on Rush's lead, a fact that Lee finds difficult to explain:

"It all sounds the same now; heavy metal hasn't really gone anywhere. It seems like anyone can pick up a book and go, 'Hey, let's learn how to be a heavy-metal band: Get lots of amps, have lots of explosions, dress up, and use those same four chords while singing about rock & roll.'"

The lack of competition has benefited the group, however, he adds, laughing. "About our technical prowess . . . It seems that as we've grown up, the music around us has gotten simpler and simpler, so that even though we keep getting better at what we do, everything around us is *legitimizing* us!"

As Rush's music changed, so did guitarist Alex Lifeson's role. In their more song-oriented music of the Eighties, he uses rich chordal work for a less cluttered style and a cleaner sound.

AC/DC

BACK TO BASICS

IF Judas Priest are the defenders of the faith, then Australia's AC/DC are the keepers of the flame. No other hard-rock band—not even Priest—has so tenaciously resisted the trends. Ten years into its career, AC/DC's sound has changed not a jot since the beginning; the last cut on its most recent album is nearly identical in sound and spirit to the first track the group ever recorded.

Over the years, other heavy-metal groups have adapted to several conventions: making elaborate concept rock videos, for example. But not AC/DC, whose only concessions to that phenomenon have been a handful of hastily assembled in-concert clips. When most metal groups relied on state-of-the-art records, spending longer and longer periods of time in the recording studio to perfect their sound, AC/DC countered with its rawest, crudest LP to date, 1983's *Flick of the Switch*, purely as a reaction to what the members saw as just another futile trend. The band members still refuse to conduct a soundcheck before concerts, staunchly believing that spontaneity is the key to playing rock & roll, an attitude that would have any producer or record-company exec reaching for his Rolaids.

The group's vision of rock & roll is unequivocably intractable; to lead guitarist Angus Young, the heart of AC/DC, change or progression is tantamount to treason. Young, who when the band started in 1973 dressed up in a natty schoolboy's outfit to accentuate his youth, has not abandoned the costume even though he is now well into his twenties. And when he talks about rock & roll in his confused medley of accents (he was born in Scotland, raised in Australia, and now resides in Holland), Young divides the music into two categories: rock & roll (heavy metal) and disco (everything else).

Critics have both praised and damned AC/DC for its single-mindedness. What some call dedication to the form, others consider artistic myo-

pia. In terms of its stressing rock's basic values— grating guitars, yowling vocals, a wallop of a beat, and plenty of sex—AC/DC has frequently been compared to the Rolling Stones. But to Angus Young, even *they're* not pure enough: "They've always been concerned with fashion; we're not."

Angus was just four years old when his father moved the ten-strong Young clan from Glasgow, Scotland, to Sydney, Australia, in search of work. Angus (born March 31, 1959) and Malcolm Young (born January 6, 1953) were the youngest of the family, and were exposed to rock & roll before they entered their teens. Their brother Alex played in a band, and another brother, George, twelve years older than Angus, was a member of the Easybeats, Australia's leading pop group from 1965 to 1970 (they achieved worldwide success with "Friday on My Mind," in 1967). Because the Easybeats toured outside of Australia so frequently, Angus rarely got a chance to see his brother play. "It didn't really influence me that

much," he recalls, "because I wasn't playing seriously at the time, and besides, my parents were trying to keep us back," no doubt believing that one rock musician in the family was enough of a scarlet letter to bear. But by age five, Angus had already started dabbling with a banjo.

It was his older sister Margaret who proved more influential, by making tape cassettes of Fifties rock & rollers such as Buddy Holly, Fats Domino, Chuck Berry, and Elvis Presley, and Sixties British acts such as the Yardbirds, the Beatles, and the Rolling Stones, the latter three of which profoundly affected Malcolm, who might be even more provincial in his attitudes toward rock & roll than Angus. "I especially liked the Yardbirds," he remembers fondly, "because they were tight, energetic, there was a lot going on,

The band today: Cliff Williams, Malcolm and Angus Young, Simon Wright—who replaced Phil Rudd in 1983—and Brian Johnson, who joined in 1980. A decade after its debut, AC/DC is still ignoring the trends.

and it seemed like a *band*, not just a lead guitarist with some backup musicians."

Mr. and Mrs. Young's hopes that their two youngest sons would enter respectable fields were dashed early, when both brothers left grammar school, Angus at fifteen. He briefly became a sweeper and a typesetter, but it was apparent that he and Malcolm would follow in their older brother's footsteps. Malcolm had already played with several Sydney bands, biding time till his brother was out of school.

In 1973, Australia was as barren culturally as its outback country is physically. Other Australian acts such as the highly successful Men at Work, whose early-Eighties fame owes a great debt to the example set earlier by AC/DC, frequently comment on how until the late Seventies, little national pride existed. Later, the country would become a source for award-winning films and a

The late Bon Scott. "Bon was like a pied piper," Angus Young says of the singer, "very easygoing, with a magnetic personality."

parcel of new-music (INXS, Eurogliders) and heavy-metal (Australian Crawl, Heaven) acts. But at the time that Angus and Malcolm Young decided to form a band, Australia's contributions to popular music were few, and banal: the Bee Gees, Olivia Newton-John, and Helen Reddy.

"There was very little rock & roll going on in those days," says Angus. "It'd all gone to disco or whatever; radio had forsaken the kids."

The two brothers formed an early band with an anonymous rhythm section and a singer named Dave Evans. One of their roadies was a tattooed Scot, from the town of Kirriemur, Bon Scott (born Ronald Belford), who was so enamoured of rock & roll and its lifestyle that he would do anything to be around a rock band, including haul equipment in and out of dingy pubs for little pay. He had previously been a singer/drummer for some amateur r&b bands and had worked as a chauffeur, which was his first position with the Young brothers. As it turned out, Scott had a frontman's charm and a gin-soaked voice that well matched Angus and Malcolm's primal rock & roll material. Eventually, Evans left, and Scott joined the band, which they dubbed AC/DC. Coming in the midst of the glitter-rock period, with its flamboyant ambisexuality, AC/DC was a controversial name, but according to Angus, its origin was simple and quite innocent: It was suggested by Margaret, who had seen it inscribed on a vacuum cleaner.

⊂⊐⊂⊐⊂⊐⊂⊐⊂⊐⊂⊐⊂⊐⊂⊐⊂⊐⊂⊐⊂⊐⊂⊐

"A lot of people got offended by us. I mean, you turn on your TV set and see something like us . . ." —Angus Young

The lone exposure for Australian rock bands came by way of the country's pubs. Though Angus was just fifteen at the time, there were no laws restricting entry, just against purchasing liquor. Beer flowed freely in the pubs, where working-class men would gather immediately after work. By the time bands were ready to come on, Angus

recalls laughingly, "they'd already been there for about eight hours, steaming drunk. If they couldn't find a woman, it was, 'Well, then, I'll go hit that guy in the mouth.' If they didn't like you, they'd throw beer—glasses and all—at you."

Fortunately for AC/DC, who after a series of interim bassists and drummers settled on Mark Evans and Phil Rudd, both of Melbourne, its boozy, bluesy hard rock worked well in the hot, sweaty atmosphere and further lubricated the audience, usually packed to the rafters and just waiting for some tanked-up bloke to start a fight. Scott also proved to be an ideal frontman for such incendiary surroundings, able to regale the drinkers with tipsy patter and lewd stories.

"Bon was like a pied piper," Angus Young says fondly of the singer, who died in 1980. "He'd go up to complete strangers on the street, and he had this way about him that would win them over completely, as if he'd known them all his life. He was very easygoing, with a magnetic personality."

Angus, who was thirteen years younger than Scott, "always looked up to him." Essentially, he says, "I grew up in this band," and both Scott and Malcolm looked after him, though Angus was equally protective of his older brother.

While many of the hard-rock bands that would excel in the Eighties were undeveloped in their early stages, AC/DC had its image and direction pinpointed early on. The group made good use of Angus's young years, with the band's image that of incorrigible juvenile delinquents. The cover to its first album, 1976's *High Voltage*, featured Angus, with a suitably demented expression on his face, dressed in his brown Ashfield Boys' High School outfit, with tie, short pants, white knee socks, sneakers, and brown cap with a large *A* on its front. The gimmick had been suggested by a drummer in one of Angus's pre-AC/DC bands, who was tickled at the idea of an adolescent guitar star. The gimmick worked; the gimmick stayed.

In February 1975 four tracks were released

Overleaf: AC/DC circa 1979, the year they broke in America with *Highway to Hell*: Malcolm Young, Cliff Williams, Phil Rudd, Angus Young, and Bon Scott.

prior to *High Voltage* that were indicative of AC/DC's future direction. With no Australian role models to speak of, the group looked to England and especially America for inspiration, and found it in the same source as had the Rolling Stones: the blues. The music's simplicity and grittiness appealed to them as musicians, as did the fact that it was easy to play. And the frequently lascivious lyrics, with their coy (and sometimes not so coy) sexual references and innuendos, were of equal attraction. One of the quintet's first releases was "Baby, Please Don't Go," a 1944 Joe Williams composition that had been covered in 1967 by the Amboy Dukes, a Detroit group whose guitarist was Ted Nugent, for whom AC/DC would open years later. "I'll be your dog," Scott implores wickedly while the band churns out a locomotive blues-rock run, "kiss you way down here."

Scott's ability to weave a ribald tale was evident on other early AC/DC tracks, rereleased in 1984 as part of the five-song EP *'74 Jailbreak*. Both "Jailbreak" (which came out in 1976) and "Soul Stripper" could be right out of the pages of a Mickey Spillane thriller. In the former, Scott relates the story of a friend given sixteen years in prison for the murder of a man whom he'd seen bedding down his woman. He escapes from jail, but "with a bullet in his back." Though AC/DC's songs are often antiwoman, men are the victims in Scott's songs, usually written in the first person. In "Soul Stripper" he is taken by a tempting vixen, who teases him, seduces him, and then, in the throes of passion, plunges a knife into his back.

Heavy metal has often been accused of being misogynistic, and it's a recurrent theme in AC/DC's early songs, many of them so X-rated it's surprising their albums did not come wrapped in brown paper. On *High Voltage*'s "The Jack," a staple of the band's early live shows, Scott uses card-game metaphors for describing a girl with a sexually transmittable disease. When the band performed "The Jack," with its sinuous bump-and-grind blues beat, in the pubs, Scott would twist the irony around, actually pointing to girls at the front of the stage, proclaiming, "She's got the Jack"; the unlucky girls would run screaming from the club.

"Whole Lotta Rosie," from 1977's *Let There Be Rock*, is about a girl from Tasmania who weighs nineteen stone (266 pounds) but "when it comes to lovin', she steals the show." Scott's tone is biting, almost mocking on this one. At times he seems as confused about the opposite sex and his sexual identity as the group's name. In a song like "She's Got Balls," he craves the same haughty quality that he loathes: "She's got ability / Gonna make a man outta me." The chorus of "She's got big balls" is sung by the band in mock-deep voices, as if they had just been injected with steroids.

AC/DC toured incessantly during this period, limiting Scott's world view to that of dressing rooms and bedrooms. Many of his songs concerned the rock & roll life, both lauding and ridiculing it. A 1975 song, "Show Business," is a humorously wry assessment of the "glorious" life the band was leading in its early days, set to a slow blues shuffle. "Why don't the businessmen ever learn to pay?" he laments. And even on the one level on which the dispirited rocker can succeed—sexually—the singer brings home a groupie after the show, but "No use, man, you're worn out to the bone."

Scott's songs about the road to stardom alternated between self-pity—"Ain't No Fun (Waiting round to Be a Millionaire)"—and self-determination. *High Voltage*'s opening track, "It's a Long Way to the Top (If You Wanna Rock 'n' Roll)," smashes the rock-star myth while announcing the arrival of a future contender: AC/DC.

But the image most often portrayed by the band and most often exploited in its music is that of bad boys, though frequently it is so obvious it's not threatening. *High Voltage*'s back cover features "letters" written to the band members: one from an outraged father ready to initiate a lawsuit against drummer Rudd for breaking his drumsticks over his daughter's head; one to Scott from an impressionable teenage nymphet, asking what it was that lurked inside his leather trousers; another to Angus and Malcolm's mother from a school authority complaining about her sons' behavior. Etc.

AC/DC's nose-thumbing rebellion is immortalized in the first album's "Rock 'n' Roll Singer," in which Scott snarls his contempt for society as viciously as Johnny Rotten and the Sex Pistols did with their anarchic "God Save the Queen," out around the same time. "You can stick yer nine-to-five livin' and yer collar and yer tie," he brays, "you can stick yer moral standards, 'cos it's all a dirty lie."

The band romanticized their unsalvageable souls on "Bad Boy Boogie" and "Problem Child," contemporary blues songs that owed a debt to Willie Dixon's "I'm Your Hoochie Coochie Man." Many of the black blues songs of the Thirties and Forties were written from the perspective of being born into a life of hell and hell-raising, and Scott's opening line to "Bad Boy Boogie," "On the day I was born . . . ," could have been lifted from a number of blues classics.

Musically, AC/DC referred to the Rolling Stones on much of *High Voltage*, its sound pivoting on a churning rhythm section, with only Angus's squealing Jimmy Page–influenced blues-rock solos and Scott's voice rising out of the mix. Many of AC/DC's songs would begin with just Angus's guitar playing stuttered chords before the rest of the band fell in behind him, then letting loose with full, ringing chords on the chorus, for which the band shouted out the lyrics—never harmonizing, not even singing along with Scott, but shouting, like a gang marching to a rumble.

High Voltage was an instant hit in Australia, but then, in a country searching desperately for some rock credibility, any Aussie band probably would have fit the bill. AC/DC was not received favorably outside the homeland. The non-Australian release entitled *High Voltage* contained cuts from their second Down Under LP, *T.N.T.*, in addition to some *Voltage* tracks. In the United States, AC/DC was categorized as a group of punks, since the heavy-metal movement was at its

nadir, and they received some of the most derisive criticism ever aimed at a band. "A lot of people got offended by us," Angus admits. "I mean, you turn on your TV set and see something like us . . ."

⊏⊐⊏⊐⊏⊐⊏⊐⊏⊐⊏⊐⊏⊐⊏⊐⊏⊐⊏⊐⊏⊐⊏⊐

"When Bon died, it was like losing a brother. Malcolm, Bon, and I had good times together; we were very tight with one another."
—Angus Young

Often missed was the group's naughty sense of humor, at its best on two tracks from a 1976 album, *Dirty Deeds Done Dirt Cheap*. For years, this was the "missing" AC/DC LP. It wasn't released in the States until 1981, by which time the group had acquired international fame and a new lead singer.

On the title track, Scott portrays a sort of romantic hit man selling his services. Your high-school principal trying to seduce you? Your boyfriend or girlfriend two-timing you? For instant retribution, call Bon Scott. Scott was a master of double entendre, best evidenced on another 1976 cut, "Big Balls," in which he plays an upper-crust member of the bourgeoisie—the very type he sneers at in "Rock 'n' Roll Singer." His voice dripping with sarcasm, Scott mockingly sings in a "proper" accent, "It's my belief that my big balls should be held every night."

With 1977's *Let There Be Rock*, AC/DC first cracked the U.S. charts, going to #154 in the late summer and following it with their first major American tour. If Scott was the main focus on record, Angus stole the show live. He rooster-strutted back and forth onstage as if his genitals had been hot-wired, his head bobbing up and down continuously, as if perched on a spring. "That's just my way of keeping time," he explains. "I do it quite naturally." And in reply to the question most often asked of him: "No, I don't get dizzy."

But he does get hurt, often cutting and bruising himself, though he claims not to feel the pain till after the show. Young's onstage mania is an outgrowth of his preshow jitters ("I'm always nervous before a show"); he usually paces the dressing room like a prisoner awaiting his execution. When the show is at its climax, Angus leaps atop one of the roadies, who gallops through the crowd while Angus strums his cordless guitar, surrounded by a phalanx of guards trying to protect him from the fans grabbing and groping for his skinny, sweaty frame.

For all of Scott's cockiness, the sexual frankness of AC/DC's lyrics was mostly tongue in cheek, for with the exception of Scott, AC/DC was about as repugnant a band as there ever was, a fact they capitalized on, as had the equally unsavory Stones a decade earlier. One of the highlights of their set was, and still is, Angus's mock striptease—more tease than strip, actually—dropping his trousers midway through the set. There was nothing remotely sexual about him exposing his pitifully skinny buns; it was just a prank. Even by the time of AC/DC's Eighties success, the group's audience was almost predominantly male, and the atmosphere at its shows was one of locker-room camaraderie—a night out with the boys.

To capitalize on the live show, the followup to their 1978 album *Powerage* (#133) was *If You Want Blood You've Got It.* By this time, Mark Evans was gone from the band, replaced in 1977 by Englishman Cliff Williams, who had won the job over fifty other bassists the band had auditioned in London. The LP's cover was in typically poor taste, showing Angus, impaled by his own Gibson SG guitar, lying dead and bloodied on the back of the jacket, with the instrument's neck protruding from his back. *If You Want Blood* demonstrates the band's live strengths—particularly Scott's charismatic stage presence—as well as its in-studio detriments—how constricted they apparently felt while recording.

Exactly two months after the death of Bon Scott, on April 19, 1980, AC/DC officially named singer Brian Johnson as his replacement.

One highlight is "Let There Be Rock," which the band stretches out for over eight minutes. The song comprises AC/DC's own book of Deuteronomy, as Scott proclaims, backed by an accelerated beat and a wall of white noise: "In the beginning, back in 1955 . . . the white man had the schmaltz, the black man had the blues." And God said: "'Let there be sound,' and there was sound. . . ." And in the end, but of course, He probably surveyed what He had done, and it was good and loud.

By 1979 AC/DC was a high-profile act in Australia and Europe, but not in America, where *If You Want Blood* had reached only #113. Their music was far too crude for FM radio, which at the time would air only the more refined and more highly produced hard-rock bands, such as Boston and Aerosmith. And lyrically, AC/DC was still too seamy.

The breakthrough came with 1979's *Highway to Hell*, which was curious since there was little to distinguish it from its predecessors, except that it was the first AC/DC album for which the band did not use George Young and fellow former Easybeat Harry Vanda as producers. This time Robert John "Mutt" Lange was in charge. It seemed that they had effectively laid the groundwork with their first four American LPs and extensive touring as an opening act, and were now ready to reap the benefits. The album's title track became the group's first hit single, reaching #47 and helping boost the LP's sales beyond the one-million mark. On its summer U.S. tour opening for Ted Nugent, the band played Madison Square Garden, where the audience leaped onto its chairs the moment AC/DC hit the stage, only to topple like dominoes when the hot, sticky air and the blasts of volume from the stage became too much. The band's momentum was such that even Jeane Dixon could have accurately predicted that 1980 would be a banner year for them.

But on February 19, 1980, Bon Scott was found dead in the back of a car on a London street. Always a hard drinker who, according to Angus,

"lived each day to the fullest," he had choked to death on his own vomit. The band was devastated by Scott's passing at age thirty-three. "When Bon died," Angus recalls sadly, "it was like losing a brother. Malcolm, Bon, and I always had good times together; we were very tight with one another."

Following Scott's funeral in Australia, Malcolm turned to his brother: "Well, what do you want to do? Do you want to work?" Together they had already written the bulk of the material for the next album, and the only way to cope with Scott's death, Angus contends, was to immerse himself in the band that he, Malcolm, and Scott had started nearly seven years earlier.

They auditioned lead singers, most of whom merely imitated Scott's delivery, not at all what AC/DC was looking for: someone compatible yet original. The only singer who met those requirements was Brian Johnson, a burly thirty-three-year-old ex-car roofer from Newcastle, England, and the son of a retired British sergeant major. He had sung with a British band called Geordie, and a fan in Chicago who had heard the album recommended him to AC/DC. Johnson possessed none of Scott's charm, but had a range and a fullness to his voice that Scott never had.

The band regrouped at Compass Point Studios in the Bahamas, but the sunny, delightful environment could not shake the overall dark mood of the band, making *Back in Black*, released just five and a half months after Scott's death, AC/DC's most fascinating record.

No mention is made of Scott directly, but his presence haunts nearly every track. The opening "Hells Bells" begins with the tolling of a bell as swirling, ominous guitar lines rise from the mix before the band lurches into its patented thundering rhythm. Images of Satan and hell had permeated such past AC/DC songs as "Hell Ain't a Bad Place to Be" and "Highway to Hell," and Scott's songs often sounded like modern-day Robert Johnson laments of having a hellhound on his

Angus Young's schoolboy getup was the brainchild of a drummer in a pre-AC/DC band. The gimmick worked; the gimmick stayed.

trail, but a good percentage of the songs on *Back in Black*—the cover of which was a pure flat black with embossed black lettering—seemed resigned to the fate that befell the group's former singer.

"We've never tried to judge people's taste. We just do what pleases us; in fact, we've generally done the opposite of what's supposed to sell records." —Angus Young

Most eerie of all is the cryptically titled finale, "Have a Drink on Me," neither a celebration nor a condemnation of Scott's death by misadventure. It is fitting that for a band that seems to have taken very little seriously during its career, death—even that of a close friend—would not escape similar treatment: "Don't worry 'bout tomorrow, take it today / Forget about the check, we got hell to pay"—the credo by which Bon Scott lived and died.

On the title track, which was a Top Forty hit, Scott's sexual braggadocio is applied even in death, as its main character comes back from the dead, proclaiming, "I got nine lives, cat's eyes. . . ." Johnson had his own singing style, but his lyrics fitted right into the band's stylistic themes. He likens a boxing match to a torrid sex session on the album's other hit, "You Shook Me All Night Long." The singer's range is remarkable. Just when you are marveling at the high notes he hits on the chorus's melody line, he leaps up another couple of notes on a doubletracked harmony part. If Johnson was lacking in any area, it was in terms of stage presence, stumbling about the stage like a woozy prize-fighter, trying to keep his cap propped on top of his head. At least he did not try to come across as a sex idol—most of the time he just leaned back on his haunches, gripped the mike tightly, and screamed.

Johnson, and the band, received almost unanimous support from the audiences on their 1980 world tour, making the new vocalist's maiden tour much easier than he had a right to expect. Besides the fact that here was a band obviously on its way to the top, there was also the audience's acknowledgment that the band had suffered a major emotional blow. That AC/DC was back as strong as ever gave these shows a heightened sense of drama, beginning with Johnson tolling a huge two-ton liberty bell that descended from the ceiling for the show-opening "Hells Bells."

"I remember the first date we played on that tour, in Europe," says Angus. "The audience had been waiting and waiting for us to go on, and when we finally did, there was this incredible, ground-shaking roar. We really felt their support, and it was extremely gratifying."

Back in Black sold five million copies and went to #4, by far the most successful of AC/DC's six albums. By early 1981, the group was so popular that its label, Atlantic, released *Dirty Deeds Done Dirt Cheap*, which had been fetching between fifteen dollars and eighteen dollars among ardent fans as an import item. The band was against the release at first, worried that consumers would not realize that it was a five-year-old album by a band that had undergone two personnel changes. But after Atlantic agreed to put a disclaimer on the LP and to discount it by ten percent, the band agreed to its release. So vast was AC/DC's popularity that *Dirty Deeds* sold nearly as well as *Back in Black*, still in the Top Ten at the time of *Deeds'* release, and streaked past the one-million mark after just ten weeks.

Returning to Australia, the band was greeted with incidents of violence, marring several shows. One concert was described by the local press as "the loudest, wildest, and most violent rock event ever." In Melbourne, a second performance was almost canceled after a series of vicious fights broke out at the first, and several fans had to be hospitalized after violence that occurred during a show in Sydney. On a more positive note, the band was awarded four years' worth of accumulated gold and platinum records, including posthumous plaques for Bon Scott.

For their next album, AC/DC took two months

in the studio, an unusually long time for them. *For Those About to Rock We Salute You*, released at the end of 1981, became AC/DC's first Number One LP, probably based more on the group's momentum than on the album's actual content. The title track was a statement of solidarity between the band and its audience, as well as a gesture of thanks for the support shown during the *Back in Black* Tour. It was also unusual for a rock anthem —slow, somber, and heavy, instead of the typically charging rhythms used for most rock calls to arms. "Stand up and be counted," Johnson intones in his high, shrill voice, "for what you are about to receive," as if handing out holy communion. On its lengthy U.S. tour, during which AC/DC headlined New York City's Madison Square Garden for the first time on December 2, the band even sounded a cannon salute.

It would be nearly two years before the band released *Flick of the Switch*, something of a troubled album. Producer Lange, who had established himself as a hard-rock hitmaker with AC/DC, Def Leppard, and Foreigner, was swamped with production offers and at the time was busy working with the nonmetal group the Cars. So AC/DC, for the first time, produced themselves, with some assistance from the "Dutch Damager" and the "Gorgeous Glaswegian," a.k.a. the group's former production team of Vanda and Young.

Further adding to the apparent eroding of stability was the departure of drummer Phil Rudd shortly before the band was to go on tour. Rudd, who at twenty-nine had had enough of the road and retired happily to Melbourne, was replaced by twenty-year-old Simon Wright. He had been on the dole in Britain and had contemplated abandoning his music career, when he answered an ad in a British music paper placed by an anonymous band—which turned out to be AC/DC.

The *Flick of the Switch* album contained all of AC/DC's classic elements, but for several reasons, most notably the thin production sound and a paucity of strong material, it seemed flat. The album went only gold, and many auditorium seats on the band's American itinerary were empty. But whereas other groups might tear out their hair worrying about the downturn in sales and might consider returning to their winning formula, AC/DC seemed nonchalant.

"We've never tried to judge people's taste," contends Angus. "We just do what pleases us; in fact, we've generally done the opposite of what's supposed to sell records."

For one thing, the band has refused to get any more involved in the rock-video craze than to allow it to be taped while performing. The only AC/DC clips to receive significant exposure on MTV were "For Those About to Rock We Salute You" and "Put the Finger on You." The band remains suspicious of music video. Brian Johnson refers to it as little more than "a new toy" and grumbles about "these five-minute mini-epics with a cast of thousands."

Commercial sense would also probably dictate a change in Angus Young's schoolboy shtick, which perhaps has grown old and lost its credibility after a decade, even though Angus, who stands a mere five feet four inches, looks ageless. Typically, Young shrugs off such a suggestion, and that is pretty much the way he has helped direct the group's career. Besides, he insists, the idea that it no longer reflects him is completely wrong, even though Angus is married, admits to painting and puttering around the house when he's not on the road, and is a soft-spoken teetotaler.

"I wouldn't do it if I felt it looked silly," he says. But will his audience accept a grown-up Angus Young?

"Well," he replies, "I've been waiting to grow up for a long time now. I'm still waiting."

VAN HALEN

LIKE THERE'S NO TOMORROW

HEAVY metal, more than any other form of rock & roll, is a populist music that not only speaks to its fans but frequently for them as well. Van Halen, who hails from the sedate Southern California town of Pasadena, is metal's most potent populist movement. In the realms of rock & roll hero worship, few bands have been the objects of such intense adulation as Van Halen, heavy metal's ambassadors of good times. Onstage, the four-man group relies on the chummy rapport projected by its effusive, good-humored, wise-cracking lead vocalist David Lee Roth as much as the phenomenal talent of its lead guitarist, Edward Van Halen. Every movement needs a slogan, and Van Halen's ranks right up there with the best of them. As the band is fond of saying, "There's a little Van Halen in everyone."

"We are part of the audience," contends drummer Alex Van Halen, Edward's older brother by

two years. "It wasn't too long ago that we were sitting out there, watching other bands." And there seems to be no barrier between the two. In concert, Roth will regularly halt songs in mid-flight to hoist his ever-present bottle of Jack Daniel's in a toast to the crowd—even if the majority of his fans are still weaning themselves off soft drinks. And the blond-haired, green-eyed singer loves to crow, "It's great to be here with fourteen [or twenty-five or fifty] thousand of our closest friends." Not everybody makes his buddies cough up fifteen dollars a shot to come over and party, but Van Halen's fans do not seem to mind this small contradiction any more than any other group of fans. Van Halen is their band and its remarkable success—six platinum albums in six tries—has propelled its members to a level of stardom and wealth few of their fans—or their show-business contemporaries, for that matter—can identify with. Yet this band-fan camaraderie

still thrives, as Roth and Company regale them with songs celebrating the heathen pleasures that befit a quartet of young Californians.

Despite his outrageous public persona, David Lee Roth is a product of Middle America, born on October 10, 1955, in Bloomington, Indiana, the son of an eye surgeon. His family moved to Massachusetts, then to Chicago, before settling in Southern California. Diagnosed as hyperactive by the family doctor at age six, Roth knew early on that the stage was his calling. "I just wanted to be in show biz," he recalls. "I wanted to make music and sing and dance, tell jokes and stories, make ya smile, make ya cry—" then, with his natural comic timing, he adds, laughing, "—and charge you $8.50!"

At Pasadena's Muir High School, Roth was a chronic class cutter. Dean of Men Jim Storms recalls that Roth would escape outside with an acoustic guitar and hold court under a tree, performing for other AWOL students. Roth later confessed, "I was just one of the fuck-ups."

But while Roth earned only average grades, he was generally recognized by his teachers as being very bright. Marvin Neuman, who taught Roth's guitar class at the school, says his student was not pursuing a music career at the time, "but I pretty much got the impression that he would because nothing else seemed to interest him." The shaggy-haired Roth's attention was taken up by his amateur band, the Redball Jets. "The name alone should indicate how authoritative our sound was. The music was garbage, but what a good time!"

At the time, Roth's crosstown competition was another local band called Mammoth, a hard-rock

Alex Van Halen, David Lee Roth, Michael Anthony, and Eddie Van Halen around the time of their 1978 album debut.

trio led by the Van Halen brothers, who had emigrated to Pasadena from their native Nijmegen, Amsterdam, with their parents in 1968. "We had some family that had moved to L.A.," recalls Alex, "and they always wrote us letters about the beautiful weather and the ample opportunities. So, taking a gamble, our parents sold everything and we moved."

Sons of a professional musician father, Jan Van Halen—who played clarinet on "Big Bad Bill (Is Sweet William Now)" from the band's *Diver Down* album—Edward and Alex began studying classical piano when Alex was eight and Eddie was six, still living in the Netherlands. "We were seriously going to train to be concert pianists," said Alex, "but then the Beatles and the Dave Clark Five came along, and so it was goodbye, piano." Alex took up guitar and Eddie, drums, on a kit he bought with money earned from a paper route. The two soon switched instruments, and Eddie eventually purchased his first "real" guitar, a Teisco Del Rey from Sears Roebuck.

The Van Halens assimilated into their highschool environment better than did Roth, attending Pasadena High School, not far from Muir. "They were well-liked kids," recalls Chuck Barrick, principal in charge of activities at Pasadena High, who would hire the brothers' band for school dances. "Their individualism really stood out; you could tell they were going places."

After graduating, the Van Halens did begin going places, albeit close to home, in what Eddie has laughingly called "the premier backyard party band of Pasadena." During Mammoth's early shows they played mainly jamming vehicles and note-for-note renditions of Cream and Black Sabbath tunes, with Eddie trying gamely to sing lead. Roth quit his Redball Jets to join the more serious (and more talented) venture, followed by Michael Anthony, born June 20, 1955, and bassist for another local outfit, Snake. Mammoth played all over the Pasadena–Los Angeles area, accepting any job they could get: wet T-shirt contests, supermarket openings, beach-ball parties, and other modest dates. Their repertoire, which Anthony once estimated approached three hundred songs, encompassed the expected white hard rock, but also the black funk of James Brown and the Ohio Players. Whenever possible, the group would sneak in one of their Eddie Van Halen–David Lee Roth compositions, generally one per forty-five-minute set, of which it played five a night—no breaks—two dozen nights in a row. As Mammoth moved up beyond the amateur ranks, Gazzari's on Hollywood's Sunset Strip (for $75 a night), L.A.'s the Starwood Club, and a biker's bar where they once witnessed a knifing in the audience, became their regular haunts. At Gazzari's it opened for name recording acts such as Nils Lofgren, Santana, UFO, and Sparks, and by 1976 it was able to draw three thousand fans to the Pasadena Civic Auditorium. Clearly, Mammoth was on to something big. "They'd sit in their vans," recalls L.A. disc jockey and impresario Rodney Bingenheimer, who booked acts for the Starwood, "and they'd always say, 'Maybe someday we'll get to play the big halls.'"

It was at the Starwood that the group was dis-

Following pages: When Scorpions finally did break in the United States, it was the result of constant touring and a grassroots following inspired by their powerful live show. Here are Scorpions guitarists Rudy Schenker (left) and Matthias Jabs (right) supporting singer Klaus Meine in a human pyramid formation (111) and the three taking their bows before an enthusiastic crowd (112). A band that seems far removed from the metal mold, Rush still claims a large and devoted audience that appreciates drummer Neil Peart, guitarist Alex Lifeson, and bassist Geddy Lee (114-115) for their musicianship and intelligence. Here, group founders and Toronto schoolmates Lifeson and Lee onstage (113). AC/DC's Angus Young is his group's founder, spokesman, and visual focal point (116, 117). Though Angus claims to suffer from preshow jitters, armed with an electric guitar and clad in his schoolboy uniform, once onstage, he proceeds to tear the house down.

covered by Gene Simmons, the flame-spitting bassist for Kiss, then at the pinnacle of its success. What impressed Simmons almost as much as Roth's affable onstage presence and Eddie's undeniable talent was the group's sheer audacity. At the time there was really no so-called heavy-metal scene anywhere in the United States, least of all in trendy Los Angeles, where the whole music community was jumping on the punk, pre–new-wave bandwagon. "They were totally confident in themselves," says Simmons, whose own band had always defied both critical and cult tastes to become one of the most popular bands in all of rock. "And the audience loved the pants off them."

Simmons had come to the club to see headliners the Boys. After the set, he went back to Mammoth's cramped dressing room and offered to produce a demo tape. The next day Simmons and the group went to Village Recorders, where they cut thirteen or fourteen tracks. Simmons was also partially responsible for the group's changing its name to Van Halen. "I was afraid of that name," he admitted. "I asked the guys if they weren't worried that [naming the band after Eddie and Alex] was going to cause an ego conflict. I suggested Daddy Longlegs, then Virus, then Rat Salade, the meaning of which is lost in the dim recesses of time. . . ."

Within weeks, Simmons brought Van Halen to New York City's Electric Lady Studios, the recording complex Jimi Hendrix built for himself shortly before his death in 1970, to finish up the tapes. These tapes were, according to Simmons, of semimaster quality. Yet despite his recommen-dation, Simmons could find no one—including his own management firm—even remotely interested in Van Halen. After several unsuccessful pitches on the group's behalf, Simmons gave them the tape and wished them good luck. Ironically, the very songs countless record-company pundits had rejected would comprise the bulk of Van Halen's first two platinum albums.

But just a few weeks later, in a scene that could have come from a Hollywood script, one evening in 1977, Warner Bros. President Mo Ostin and producer Ted Templeman caught Van Halen's show at the Starwood and signed the group backstage that very night. In just eighteen days, Van Halen had its eponymously titled debut LP completed. *Van Halen* remains the group's definitive record, introducing all the elements that would be reiterated on its next four releases. Songs like "Runnin' with the Devil" and "Jamie's Cryin'" had the thundering bottom of most hard-rock outfits but also featured a melodic sensibility that was generally foreign to heavy metal. Roth's voice —more notable for its randy-dandy charisma and inflections than its actual singing ability—was topped by Anthony's keening high harmonies. Harmonies in hard rock?

But the band's centerpiece and what caught the ear of most critics was Eddie's guitar histrionics. He instantly established himself as the most technically advanced and original player since Hendrix. Van Halen, who producer Templeman once praised as the "best guitarist alive," possesses a style that is an amalgam of what has come before him but is peppered with his own techniques, among them his frequent use of har-

---

Preceding pages: **With something for everybody, it's not surprising that Van Halen is the most popular band in hard rock today. Even backstage, lead singer David Lee Roth cops the perfect pose (118); onstage, he is rock's premier showman (120-121). Lead guitarist Eddie Van Halen (119) is still rewriting the book on electric guitar. For their 1984 tour, Van Halen erected one of the biggest sets on any stage (122-123). ⊂⊒ From its name to its ten-foot-tall rotting corpse mascot Eddie (shown here in an earlier incarnation, 125), Iron Maiden seemed obsessed with metal's Satan-and-death shtick. In fact, though, Maiden's songs are clearly anti-Satan and explore a range of topics—like nuclear war and civil rights—that should not be ignored. Its 1984 release, *Powerslave*, was inspired by Egyptian mythology (124) and the subsequent tour was the band's greatest success to date. Left to right: Steve Harris, Nicko McBrain, Bruce Dickinson, Dave Murray, and Adrian Smith. Maiden lead singer Bruce "Air Raid Siren" Dickinson (126).**

monics, distortion, and especially his famous two-hands-on-the-neck style. Other guitarists would so obviously try to copy the technique that in Mammoth's bar-band days, Eddie would play with his back to the audience so that would-be rivals could not see how he did it. For a metal guitarist who claims to be unversed in scales and theory—despite his piano training—Van Halen plays with an unusual amount of musicality, often tossing classical motifs into his live solo spots, as well as a rare degree of sensitivity and wit.

"I just wanted to be in show biz. I wanted to make music and sing and dance, make ya smile, make ya cry—and charge you $8.50!"
—David Lee Roth

After winning the Best New Talent award from *Guitar Player* magazine in 1978, he was voted Best Rock Guitarist for five consecutive years. Perhaps part of what fuels his playing is the years spent as a self-described loner, years when he would lock himself in his room, practicing and writing. Today, when Van Halen takes the stage, he becomes as extroverted as Roth, bounding about the set and leaping off the amplifiers. His enthusiasm is not an act, simply an unabashed display of his zeal for playing. His guitar has truly emancipated him and his joy is real. "If I couldn't play guitar," he once said, "I'd be pumping gas."

Van Halen, presaged by the release of a single, the band's volcanic version of the Kinks' "You Really Got Me," came out in February 1978 and eventually sold over five million copies, despite the fact that metal was still in its dormant stage. The band was further aided in gaining an audience by the fact that the late Seventies were still a prime time for mega-tours and large arena shows, a trend that would end abruptly with the 1979 gas crunch. Concurrent with the album's release, Van Halen embarked on its first major tour, as the opening act for Journey and Montrose. In no time, Roth established himself as one of rock & roll's premier showmen, with his onstage acrobatics—back-wrenching flips, turns, splits, and spins—and his quotables quotes, including his prophecy, since fulfilled, that Edward Van Halen would become the "first guitar hero of the Eighties."

Van Halen comfortably embraced its new status and a larger-than-life image. For a stadium show before a crowd of 62,000 in Anaheim, California, they leaped from an airplane to parachute into the arena as fans screamed their approval. And by year's end, they had been booked on a tour with metal legends Black Sabbath, where, much to the elder band's chagrin, Van Halen consistently upstaged the veteran headliners night after night.

Observers may have been puzzled by Van Halen's quick rise to fame. After all, Van Halen's music and image were pretty obvious. And that was just the point. "We felt that the music was accessible to a lot of people," Alex says, "and that if we could do it in the Los Angeles area, we could do it anywhere."

Nineteen seventy-nine's *Van Halen II*, again presided over by Templeman, was recorded in even less time than its predecessor, six days. There is little to distinguish it from the debut, except for one truly ill-conceived cover—a dinosaur stomp version of "You're No Good," a Linda Ronstadt hit—and the band's most successful attempt at combining hard-rock energy with pop songwriting, "Dance the Night Away," which bolted up the charts to #15. *Van Halen II*'s sales quickly eclipsed those of *Van Halen* (though by 1984 the debut did exceed its followup's sales by two million copies), changing their status from upstart rookies to major-league band. On April 8, 1979, Van Halen commenced its second world tour, this time traveling with a twenty-two-ton, 10,000-watt sound system, and 444,000 watts of

Roth kicks it up onstage. A product of Middle America, the wise-cracking singer believes he was destined to become a star.

offer their services to journalists and photographers in hopes of gaining entrée into a room. Where some groups might at least pretend to exercise some discretion, Roth simply sighed, "This is never-never land. It's like being Hugh Hefner." And the rock-star image could be played to the hilt. In a widely publicized incident, prior to a concert at the University of Southern Colorado in Pueblo, the band demolished a dining room, a bathroom, and a dressing room, all because they spotted some brown M&M candies in a dish—a violation of a rider to the group's contract. Total damages: $10,000.

ᴄᴇ ᴄᴇ ᴄᴇ ᴄᴇ ᴄᴇ ᴄᴇ ᴄᴇ ᴄᴇ ᴄᴇ ᴄᴇ ᴄᴇ ᴄᴇ ᴄᴇ

"Edward and I were seriously going to train to be concert pianists, but then the Beatles and the Dave Clark Five came along, and so it was goodbye, piano." —Alex Van Halen

But rooms were not all that got damaged on this tour. In March, Roth fractured his hand in a fight with a disco fan in the Starwood parking lot, and in April, one month into the nine-month 1980 Invasion Tour, he was charged with inciting a crowd to "light up" during a Cincinnati show, allegedly violating an Ohio fire law. He was freed on $5,000 bail, and three months later the charges were dismissed. In late May, Roth broke his nose after executing one of his patented twelve-foot leaps and hitting a low-hanging lighting rig during a performance for Italian TV. Roth was flown back to the United States for medical treatment and advised to relax for two weeks. The next night he was back in Europe and the show was on.

By 1980, with three platinum albums and sold-out world tours behind them, Van Halen was a full-fledged phenomenon. It was a band whose four separate and distinct personalities were tal-

ented, witty, and likable. And though this sort of congeniality was generally alien to metal, Van Halen was the first group since the Beatles to so completely charm its audience, and sometimes even its critics. Roth was the flamboyant sex symbol, singing and wise-cracking with a perpetual leer. Around this time he let it be made public that he had taken out an insurance policy with the respected firm of Lloyds of London to protect him against paternity suits. With his all-American good looks and leonine mane, the pursed-lipped singer struts about the stage like a peacock. While leather-and-studs still stand as the heavy-metal uniform, Roth sports absurdly garish costumes, allegedly of his own design: tight pants, revealing shirts, and brightly colored scarves tied around literally everything. His wardrobe's piece de resistance, however, is a pair of tight pants, which, except for a strap running up the middle of the seat, are totally seatless, and which Roth wears au natural.

Women in the audience react exactly the way Roth would like, especially when he rips off his shirt to reveal a chest full of muscles, the product of a fanatical devotion to physical fitness that seems totally at odds with the debauched lifestyle he advocates and claims to practice with zeal. Perhaps it is because heavy metal has yet to produce enough male sex symbols to meet the demands of the relatively new influx of female fans or because Van Halen's songs tend to portray women as desirable but likable, while other metal bands seem to sing only about evil dominatrixes or all-service bimbos. But regardless, Roth is the recipient of unadulterated love—and lust. Girls in Van Halen's audience ogle Roth as if he were a star in Chippendale's revue and often return his lewd suggestions from the stage with naughty invitations of their own.

By contrast, Eddie Van Halen appeals more to the men, who most respect and appreciate Van Halen's guitar antics. Eddie exudes a boyish zeal that is directed exclusively at his guitar. The

Overleaf: "It's great to be here with fourteen thousand of our closest friends," Roth loves to crow. Van Halen's rapport with its audience remains unparalleled.

crowd's applause either goes unnoticed by him, so engrossed is he in the pleasures of the fretboard, or inspires an extreme attack of embarrassment, an unusual response from an acknowledged guitar master.

His brother Alex spends most of the set hidden behind his gargantuan drum kit, which includes four bass drums, two of which support even more drums. Alex emerges every now and then, jumping down to the front of the stage to accept the applause, to play the *de rigueur* drum solo, or to smash the flaming gong erected behind him. Alex, who is now married, previously shared with Roth the wildest aspects of the rock & roll lifestyle that he and Roth both enjoyed and lampooned at the same time. The backstage area of the Van Halen entourage at the '83 US Festival bore this sign: Van Halen Trail—No Virgins, Journey Fans or Sheep Allowed.

Finally, there's Michael Anthony, like Edward, more comfortable with his role as a musician than as a rock & roll star, at least offstage. The short and burly Anthony portrays an almost thuglike character onstage, often punching his bass with his fist instead of plucking the strings. During his bass solo, he throws the instrument to the ground from the catwalk that spans the stage, leaps down, and jumps and stomps on his bass as it protests by emitting grinding, wall-shaking sounds. The crowd, predictably, goes nuts each time Anthony performs this slightly amended version of Pete Townshend's guitar-smashing routine.

By 1980, Van Halen could afford to bust up dressing rooms and instruments, prompting many to question if the band's original premise had not been eroded by fame. It is the same dilemma the Rolling Stones and nearly every other long-lived and successful rock & roll band have faced: How do you maintain your street credibility when you live on Easy Street? Has money changed Van Halen? "Aw, it ain't changed shit," replied Roth. "Money doesn't change people; experiences change people. This band is seven years old now, and we've had tremendous success. And so far, everybody is *regressing*, maybe as a reaction to that success."

Another reaction to that success was to steer away from the proven formula of the first three albums. Van Halen did not seem to be contriving a new direction, but it was surely trying to answer the question of whether or not it was capable of progressing. And unlike before, other heavy-metal bands—many inspired by Van Halen—were coming up through the ranks. Where there was once a heavy-metal void, there was now competition, new bands that were just as hungry, just as determined to make it as Van Halen had been. In May 1981, *Fair Warning* was released, one month after Eddie Van Halen married actress Valerie Bertinelli in Los Angeles. *Fair Warning*'s songs were less structured—that was intentional—and less focused, which was not. Though it went platinum, it marked a significant drop in sales, and while Van Halen's ten-month tour was predictably successful, all did not augur well for the band's future. Had its songwriting talents dried up?

The following year's *Diver Down* did not provide any disclaimer to that possibility: Clocking in at a mere twenty-nine minutes, five of its twelve songs were written by other writers, including another Ray Davies tune, "Where Have All the Good Times Gone?" Was it a real question, a tip of the hat to their early days, or a further indication that creative atrophy had set in? These doubts were temporarily assuaged by the album's reception: It charted at #3 and spawned the band's first hit single in three years, a spirited cover of Roy Orbison's 1964 chart-topper, "(Oh) Pretty Woman," minus an entire section of the bridge because, as Roth later giddily pointed out, he had simply forgotten to learn all of the words.

For the first time, Van Halen cut back on road work, touring for "only" five months, from July to December. There was no skimping on the technical end, however, with a crew of seventy required to keep the show on the road. The eighty-date Hide Your Sheep Tour, which began in Augusta, Georgia, reportedly grossed $10 million. The

"If I couldn't play guitar," Eddie Van Halen once admitted, "I'd be pumping gas." His onstage enthusiasm is no act; his zeal for playing is genuine.

tour's only slip occurred when Eddie suffered a hairline fracture of his right wrist after some horsing around midway through the jaunt and had to play the remainder of the dates with his injured hand in a cast.

Nineteen eighty-three was a critical year for Van Halen. After five albums, it was time for them to take stock of their future direction and a much-needed respite from the road. Following the end of a South American tour in February, Roth went on a six-and-a-half-week expedition into the Amazon jungle with a group of non—music-business cronies dubbed the Jungle Studs. (Future plans include scaling the Himalayas.) The only live date the band played was the US Festival in San Bernardino, California, for which they were paid a reported $1.5 million, or approximately $17,000 per minute onstage, putting Van Halen in the *Guinness Book of World Records* as the world's highest-paid group. But an even more important fact emerged as the result of their appearance. Tickets for the festival's Heavy Metal Day (which Van Halen headlined) outsold tickets for the day that industry experts predicted would attract the biggest crowd—David Bowie's first stateside appearance in five years. The upset helped set the stage for the full-fledged heavy-metal revival to come.

By now, however, it was no secret that the extent of the disparities between the garrulous Roth and the introverted Eddie Van Halen had become serious. For years, observers had been speculating as to whether Roth's basic sensibilities and artistic impulsiveness were not hampering the more musicianly Van Halen. Indeed, it was hard to envision any other guitarist of Van Halen's caliber still playing in such an irreverent group. For the first five years of the band's career, Eddie would scoff at the suggestion that he might do a solo album. But there were also times when he brooded, wondering whether or not, despite all the applause, the fans really got beyond the volume and the flash and appreciated the musicality of his performance. With work on the sixth LP

delayed, the guitarist sought fulfillment elsewhere, playing on a mini-LP with Queen guitarist Brian May, *Star Fleet Project*, and contributing the landmark guitar solo to Michael Jackson's "Beat It."

> **"Money doesn't change people; experiences change people. This band is seven years old now, and so far, everybody is *regressing*, maybe as a reaction to our success."**
> **—David Lee Roth**

This second performance proved to be of more value to Jackson than to Van Halen. In discussing Jackson's *Thriller*—at over 35 million copies sold, the largest-selling album in history—it is important to realize that upon its release in December 1982, there was little reason for anyone to expect that its sales would eclipse Jackson's previous album, 1979's eight-million-seller, *Off the Wall*. Long before Michaelmania, the Jacksons had produced a number of black hits, not all of which crossed over to the pop Top Ten, the result of a de facto color line that permeated FM radio and was carried over to the first national all-rock-video cable-television network, MTV. There is no question that radio's eagerness to play the "Beat It" single and MTV's decision to air the accompanying video were influenced by Eddie Van Halen's participation in the record. So elated was he at the chance to essay some other style of music that he never asked Jackson to pay him (and Jackson never did).

But amid all the excitement over Van Halen's contribution, Roth was remarkably unimpressed. "What did Edward do with Michael Jackson?" the usually easygoing Roth asked rhetorically in late 1983. "He went in and played the same solo he's been playing in this band for ten years. Big deal! Big change! As far as flexing his musical creativity, I ain't heard anything different." Whether Roth's comments reflect his true feelings

or are just the product of his natural inclination toward hyperbole, this was faint praise for the man he was the first to title a guitar hero. At the very least, they do spell out a very clear difference of opinion, and around this time rumors of an impending breakup were heard.

As it turned out, Eddie Van Halen's most creative and adventurous playing would appear on the group's next album, *1984*, released on December 31, 1983. And even more surprisingly, Eddie would not perform it on a guitar. On two tracks, "Jump" and "I'll Wait," Eddie played synthesizer, a brave test of the Van Halen audience's loyalty. The risk paid off, as "Jump" became Van Halen's first Number One hit and set

a precedent for other heavy-metal acts. Hard rock has traditionally been a guitar-oriented music, and by the early Eighties, keyboard textures had become associated with other types of music, particularly European technopop. Later in 1984, other metal bands, encouraged by Van Halen's lead, began adding keyboards to their sound, making "Jump" a quietly influential track in hard-rock history.

Van Halen's overall impact on hard rock has not derived from any one song, or even from its musical contributions in general. The group's

Bassist Michael Anthony was the last member to join the Van Halen brothers and Roth, who were then known as Mammoth.

greater influence has been in attitude. Van Halen is, in Roth's words, "the world's best-paid bar band." Roth takes great delight in the fact that nearly every aspect of the band's career has gone against the prevailing wisdom of the record industry, beginning with its early hard-rock success in the punk era. Roth once recalled a record-company A&R man telling him bluntly that the band did not stand a chance unless it aligned itself with the burgeoning new-wave movement. After its initial success, the band was even more determined to control its destiny and was soon provided with the financial resources to do just that. Van Halen's 1981, 1982, and 1984 concert productions were the largest ever taken on a continental tour in rock history.

"You have to take an active part in it," says Roth of the stage show, album covers, and videos, all things the group still controls from conception to production. Their participation seems to have had the greatest effect in rock video, where they actually had the least experience.

The band's first self-produced video was for "(Oh) Pretty Woman." A disjointed narrative did little to enhance the song, but the video's biggest problem was the fact that it featured midgets and a transvestite, both of which MTV considered sufficiently offensive to ban the tape (though given the normal sex-and-violence fare the channel offers, it is difficult to see why). For "Jump," the band drew up storyboard-like cards, detailing every single shot. In an age of lavish budgets and epic concept videos—particularly in heavy metal—this was a home-movie job that showcased the band's hammy good humor. Essentially a live lip-sync job, it won an MTV video award for Best Stage Performance in 1984. Its followup, "Panama," which intercut live concert footage with silly scenes of the band flying across the stage on wires or happily tooling around L.A. in a convertible, also revealed a friendly charm even nonfans could not deny.

But it was "Hot for Teacher" that best encapsu-

Van Halen's flamboyant sex symbol. In 1980 Roth took out an insurance policy with Lloyds of London to protect himself against paternity suits.

lated the group's madcap qualities and smartass appeal, with the band members and their "doubles"—four adolescent boys who looked like a younger version of the group—portraying instigators in a junior-high classroom. These four are, of course, the teacher's pets, and from the looks of things, scantily clad teach is something of a pet herself, no doubt from the pages of *Penthouse*. In typically self-deprecating Van Halen style, the four real members stumble through a parody of Temptations–Four Tops choreography, and the video thunders to a close à la *American Graffiti* or *Animal House*, with each of the young Van Halenoids' futures described: Eddie is in Bellevue's mental ward, Alex is a suave gynecologist, Michael, a champion sumo wrestler, and David Lee, "America's favorite TV game show host."

Van Halen may technically comprise a money-making business, but they have yet to fall into the trap of fabricating bloodless corporate rock. Certainly, their personal lives have long ceased to bear any resemblance to that of their fans', yet a revealing measure of their popularity is the fact that this never arises as an issue with the band's audience or its critics. "I think the whole thing behind Van Halen is that it *is* the audience," says Roth. And, judging by the intense response the group's performances generate, it also follows that the audience—in its grandest fantasies—is the band. Van Halen may pander to its audience by Roth's patronizing stage raps or the way the group's eagerness to satiate its audience has probably restricted the band musically, but they have never isolated themselves, nor have they hidden behind a phalanx of technology or producers. Van Halen's members are in a small group of rock stars who are beyond pretension, who inspire their fans to believe that they can do it, too, who make everything seem so open and real that they become the friendly magicians at the birthday party who can show you how all the tricks are done but still never fail to surprise and delight. Even—or especially—as the four enter their thirties, they still give credence to the claim they made with their first album: Van Halen is its audience, a true people's band.

I R O N   M A I D E N

S Y M P A T H Y   F O R   T H E   D E V I L

IRON Maiden is one of the most literate of heavy metal's bands, as well as one of its most misunderstood and controversial. Its songs often quote from classic British literature and frequently derive their hellish imagery and foreboding themes from famous films and writings, including the Bible. Lyrically, Iron Maiden stands apart from other heavy-metal bands, never patronizing its audience with carefully designed teen-oriented songs, but presenting themes that draw from ancient history and mythology, sung with the empathy and world-weariness of those who may have actually witnessed the atrocities of war or the doomed flight of Icarus. The songs take on such nontraditional heavy-metal subjects as the plight of the American Indian ("Run to the Hills"), imminent nuclear apocalypse ("2 Minutes to Midnight"), and the horrors of war ("The Trooper"), and so delve into areas of social commentary more familiar to folk singers than heavy-metal screamers.

However, it is the band's songs about evil and Satan—which do comprise a significant percentage of its catalog—that have received the most attention and have elicited charges of Satanism, an accusation that has been leveled against many hard-rock acts, in nearly all cases undeservedly so.

Most responsible for Iron Maiden's lyrical bent is bandleader/bassist Steve Harris, who was born in London's impoverished East End. After reading his unnervingly graphic lyrics, one might expect him to be a composite of film director Ken Russell and writer Edgar Allan Poe. But Harris is a soft-spoken, thoughtful man who worked for a time as a draftsman and who continued to live with his grandmother long after Iron Maiden rose to international stardom. Harris jokingly theorizes that perhaps his quiet demeanor is due to his having been rendered half-deaf by his group's massive volume. "Why be loud? I can't hear myself anymore anyway."

Harris, whose arms are covered with tattoos and whose handsome face is framed by dark, wavy hair, grew up on the British blues-rock bands of the early Seventies, and as Maiden's most prolific songwriter, he composes songs designed to emphasize instrumental prowess and a dominant rhythm section. Harris did not take up the bass until he was seventeen, relatively late compared to most musicians. He had considered the drums—any rackety instrument would have sufficed—but wanted to be a songwriter, so he settled on bass guitar. By the age of twenty, he was playing in a local pub outfit, Smiler, with some older musicians who exposed him to such British bands as Wishbone Ash, one of the first to introduce the concept of colead guitaring; the early Fleetwood Mac; Savoy Brown; and the Pretty Things. On his own, he discovered Deep Purple and Jethro Tull, hard-rock groups who borrowed heavily from classical music, making for a dramatic, powerful combination, and Free,

who played a lean, bright amalgam of blues and rock & roll. Harris then began writing his own songs, juggling these disparate influences of dark and light.

In 1976 a friend of Harris's suggested he give a listen to a local guitarist named Dave Murray, and the core of Iron Maiden—the only two members who would weather the many personnel changes over the years—was formed. The blond-haired Murray, even shyer than Harris, was a devotee of Free guitarist Paul Kossoff, legendary for his emotional, economical blues licks. Of the two, Murray is the speedier player, with a style typified by rapid spirals of notes played with stunning fluidity.

The nascent Iron Maiden's first recording was an EP on its own Rock Hard Records label, *The Soundhouse Tapes*. It sold an impressive 5,000

Early Iron Maiden around the time of *The Soundhouse Tapes*: Clive Burr, Dave Murray, Paul Di'anno, Steve Harris, and Dennis Stratton.

copies in England and helped them procure a record deal with EMI. By this time the band included drummer Doug Samson and lead singer Paul Di'anno, whose look diverged from that of the others. Actually Maiden's third singer (Paul Day and Dennis Wilcox preceded him), with his leather jacket and unusually short hair, Di'anno resembled a young, lean Marlon Brando. During 1979 Samson was replaced by Clive Burr, and the group added a second guitarist, Tony Parson, soon ousted in favor of Dennis Stratton.

The eponymously titled debut was released just in time to benefit from the heavy-metal revival that was sweeping the United Kingdom in 1980. It *entered* the British charts at #4. But immediately afterward, Stratton left because of musical differences ("He was a good player, but he wasn't really into hard rock," Harris explains) and was replaced by a longtime chum of Murray's, Adrian Smith. Murray and Smith had played together in a pre-Maiden London outfit called Urchin, and before that were in street gangs together on the city's East Side.

With Smith, at least Maiden's two-guitar attack jelled better than it had before, the two often playing harmonies with each other. But there were still plenty of rough edges, as the band's abilities could not yet match its vision. The typical early Maiden song owed considerable debts to both Led Zeppelin and Black Sabbath, frequently opening with a foreboding guitars-and-bass intro before exploding into a section played so fast—in sixteenth notes, double the tempo of most hard-rock songs—that a listener might think he had his turntable set on the wrong speed. Harris played, and still does play, a dominant role in the band's sound, often supplying fleet-fingered melody lines in the style of Sabbath's Geezer Butler, while the guitars hammer away so furiously that their chords sound almost percussive.

Maiden's first two efforts also hinted at its progressive leanings, probably picked up from the arrangement-happy Tull, with a track's galloping beat interrupted at random by machine-gun accents (as on *Killers'* "The Ides of March") or guitar-drums duets ("Genghis Khan"). Fre-

quently the transitions were abrupt and clumsy, but the band members—purists all, who on the inner sleeve to 1983's *Piece of Mind* would stress, "No synthesizers or ulterior motives"—indulged in precious few overdubs.

A live five-song EP, *Maiden Japan* was issued and proved, if little else, how much a live-in-the-studio group Iron Maiden was. Recorded in Nagoya, Japan, on May 23, 1981, its in-concert version of the second LP's "Wrathchild" varied not a bit from the studio-recorded original. There was barely a trace of melody in these early songs, played with hard-core punk abandon.

What kept Maiden afloat commercially while its members were still defining their direction and leashing their tendency for overkill was their image. The name alone—taken from the medieval torture device consisting of a hollow iron statue in the shape of a woman and lined with spikes that would impale the trapped victim—connoted horror. And whereas such bands as Aerosmith and Starz had personalized logos or emblems, Iron Maiden actually had its own mascot: Eddie, the ten-foot-tall rotting corpse who has graced every one of its LP covers—as a coconspirator with the devil (*The Number of the Beast*), a lobotomy victim (*Piece of Mind*), and a Sphinx-like Egyptian god (*Powerslave*). With a name like Iron Maiden, the group wanted a suitably gory logo, and came up with the idea of Eddie the 'ed. In the band's earliest days, Eddie was simply a face painted on a backdrop behind the band, and would spit stage blood on cue. Eventually he evolved, so to speak, into a character in the show, "played" by members of the road crew. His horrifically ugly countenance has become nearly as popular among Maiden's fans as the band members themselves, though his presence no doubt undermines their credibility with anti-Satanist critics.

Shortly before the band was to enter the studio with its producer, Martin Birch (of Black Sabbath and Deep Purple fame), vocalist Di'anno suddenly decided he'd had enough of the band's demanding travel schedule and quit. To replace him, Maiden tapped Bruce Dickinson, a twenty-four-year-old born in Worksop, Nottinghamshire, who had been singing with the hard-rock outfit Samson. They could not have made a better choice. Di'anno had been immensely popular with the band's audience, but Dickinson was confident, even cocky, about his singing ability. He dabbled in theater while growing up ("I received my first newspaper clipping when I was ten, for playing the mole in *Toad of Toad Hall*") and brought the band a decidedly different image than had Di'anno; the singer's look was much less dashing than his predecessor's, with his straight, long brown hair and frequently several days' growth of beard. But Dickinson's voice and his thespian abilities also made him more effective at putting across Harris's image-filled, dramatic lyrics. "In Shakespeare," Dickinson recalls, "I used to get cast for all the evil parts."

That experience came in handy for his first trial with the group, the controversial *The Number of the Beast*. The album-opening title track begins with a recitation from the Book of Revelation, Chapter XII, verse 12.

> "Woe to you, O earth and sea, for the devil sends the beast with wrath, because he knows the time is short. . . . Let him who hath understanding reckon the number of the beast, for it is a human number; its number is six hundred and sixty-six."

A first-person account of a rendezvous with the devil that Harris was inspired to write after seeing the film *The Omen II*, "The Number of the Beast" is a nightmarish fantasy, *not* an endorsement of Satanism. But despite Harris's adamant claims, there are many who took literally such lines as "666, the number of the beast / 666, the one for you and me," causing innumerable problems for the band.

Strangely enough, though, Iron Maiden was "spooked" all during the LP's recording. There

Steve Harris, who was born in London's impoverished East End, is most responsible for Maiden's foreboding image and socially-conscious lyrics.

were mysterious power failures during the sessions that took place at London's Batter Studios, and instances of amps blowing up and radio interference. The most unsettling incident occurred when producer Birch was involved in a car crash, and the repair bill came to £666.

"I know that sounds like bullshit," grants Harris, who insists the stories are all true. "I've even had friends come up to me and say, 'Aw, c'mon, Steve, that's all crap, innit?'" Asked if he believes in psychic phenomena, Harris considers the question carefully before replying, "I'm not sure what I believe as far as that goes. But I do believe that there are things out there that are unexplainable; things that really do exist."

Harris insists, however, that not only is he definitely not a believer in Satan ("'The Number of the Beast' is an *anti*-Satan song," he points out) but that he is in no way antireligion, though he personally does not practice any particular faith. "I went to church when I was young," he remembers, "and though I couldn't get off on it at all, I don't knock people who are into it. It has its place." Harris clearly gets disturbed by the charges from conservative anti-Satanist groups who have made heavy metal and rock & roll in general the target of a modern-day witch-hunt, so convinced are they of the music's nefarious influence. As exasperated as it often makes him, Harris refrains from exhibiting any contempt for his accusers. "People fail to see the humor in a lot of what we do," he says in his defense.

Harris is correct. The alleged references to Satan in Iron Maiden's and other heavy-metal groups' music has been taken very seriously by some factions. In Arkansas, for example, legislation was enacted to legally muzzle—indirectly—or at least harass parties guilty of promoting Satanism. Arkansas Congressman Jack McCoy proposed legislation in early 1983 that would require that albums containing "backmasking"—backward Satanic messages recorded onto one of the twenty-four or more tracks—bear warning stickers.

Any backmasked record that failed to sport such a sticker could be confiscated.

The bill was introduced in January 1983 to the House Committee on Public Health, which passed it. Then it was sent to the House itself, which passed it unanimously, 86 to 0, thus putting the bill before the Senate Committee, which also passed it, although with an amendment that would make the crime a Class A misdemeanor. Finally, McCoy's bill was sent back to the House for concurrence, but was tabled.

McCoy, the father of two teenagers, says he was prompted to propose the bill after having been contacted by "quite a few of my constituents who felt they had a right to know backmasking was on a record when they bought it." McCoy did not name Iron Maiden outright—it did not seem as if he knew Maiden from Zeppelin from Beethoven—but he did give a roll call of some of the offending song titles. At the top of the list: "Stairway to Heaven."

In an earlier case, in California, State Assemblyman Phillip Wyman and Congressman Robert Dornan crusaded for a law that would require offending recordings to bear stickers warning consumers, "This record contains subliminal Satanic messages audible when played backward." Dornan and Wyman began their 1982 campaign after hearing Led Zeppelin's "Stairway to Heaven" (released in 1971), which they claimed contained "messages" glorifying Satan. Supposedly, when it's played backward, the listener can hear the singer extolling "my sweet Satan" on the final lines to the fifth verse: "Yes, there are two paths you can go by, but in the long run / There's still time to change the road you're on."

Zeppelin's most popular track seems to be a favorite target of anti-Satanists for several reasons, not the least of which is guitarist Jimmy Page's admitted interest in the occult. In the mid-Seventies, he bought a house formerly owned by the self-proclaimed Satanist Aleister Crowley. Called "the Beast" by his own mother, Crowley was something of a star and an embarrassment in occult and psychic circles during the Twenties and Thirties (he died in 1947). Among his several famous practices was that of "sex magic," in which he sought a higher level of consciousness through sex. And the album from which "Stairway" comes, Led Zeppelin's fourth, is technically untitled. Its inner sleeve is graced by four unexplained symbols, each presumably the symbol for one member of the quartet. One of these symbols reads Zoso; some people refer to it as Runes. Drummer John Bonham's symbol, for example, consists of three interlocking circles. While those with an interest in such things searched for the profound meaning to this mythological three-ring pretzel, singer Robert Plant once noted laughingly that it could just as easily represent the Ballantine beer emblem.

Ever since the Beatles' John Lennon discovered the eerie effect that could be achieved with backward tapes on "Rain" (1966), it has been a frequently used technique in rock recordings. Backward tape was at the root of the Beatles' 1969 "Paul Is Dead" controversy, in which overzealous fans determined that bassist Paul McCartney had been killed in a 1966 auto wreck, on the basis of some visual, but mostly backward-recorded clues. Among the strongest pieces of "evidence" was the "accident" heard in its entirety on "Revolution 9" from the 1968 double LP *The Beatles* (The White Album), and the message "Paul is dead, miss him, miss him, miss him," allegedly tacked on to the end of "I'm So Tired" from the same album. And then you have John Lennon's infamous muttering at the conclusion of a 1967 single, "Strawberry Fields Forever": "I buried Paul" (recorded forward). "*Cranberry sauce*," Lennon would later insist.

All of which points out the folly of those who attempt to decipher such "messages": With repeated listenings—and a mind bent on sussing out a particular phrase—it is posible to hear, or at least think you hear, whatever words you are looking for on any record. "My sweet Satan" from "Stairway to Heaven" actually sounds more like "Ma Swede stain" and "No sweat, Timmy." And since the mind does not automatically comprehend words fed into a mix backward (and few

would risk ruining a turntable to play a record that way), it stands to reason that any artist intent on distributing a Satanic message could much more effectively hide it in the mix forward.

Iron Maiden struck back at those combing its LPs for such demonic references, by intentionally delivering such a message on 1983's *Piece of Mind*. Between the tracks "The Trooper" and "Still Life," recorded backward, one can hear the message, which essentially says, "Don't mess with things you don't understand," followed by a tremendous belch.

ﻕﻕﻕﻕﻕﻕﻕﻕﻕﻕﻕﻕﻕ

"I'm not sure what I believe as far as things like psychic phenomena go. But I do believe that there are things out there that are unexplainable; things that really do exist."
—Steve Harris

But the issue of alleged Satanism goes beyond the backmasking controversy. Satanism has become a buzzword and, in extreme cases, the reason offered for actions that are nothing more than censorship. Rock & roll and its culture have been decried as inherently evil, "the devil's music," ever since its beginning (as was jazz in the Twenties). Rock-record burnings are not an uncommon occurrence (even a group as popular as the Beatles was the target of several such events), and, like book burnings, have been somewhat on the rise in the last several years.

That there seems to have been an increase in such activities in the Eighties is due more to the growing conservatism in the United States than to any sudden influx of "Satanic" hard-rock bands. In the Seventies, with such acts as Alice Cooper— whose stage show included the grisly decapitation of a doll—and Black Sabbath, there seemed to be in the general public's mind a clear distinction between what was real and what was fantasy (i.e., show biz). Teenagers have long held a fascination with death and the devil, and it was apparent that entertainers like Cooper were merely playing on (well, yes, exploiting) those fantasies. But it *was* clearly fantasy, and tongue in cheek at that. Just a year or two later in his career, Cooper could be found on the golf links with Bob Hope, or appearing on TV as a celebrity contestant.

But with the call to a return to so-called traditional family values—in many respects an overreaction to what some people view as the general permissiveness and rejection of those values during the Sixties and Seventies—the right has lashed out more vehemently than ever against rock & roll, and heavy-metal acts make a particularly easy target, because of the fervency with which their fans react and the degree to which the music is misunderstood and so open to "interpretation." Anti-Satanist groups have picketed outside several metal acts' concerts, particularly in the Bible Belt, and Maiden guitarist Adrian Smith admits to sometimes feeling apprehensive about stepping onstage.

One band that has been the target of such reactionary groups longer than Iron Maiden is Kiss. Their early- to mid-Seventies concerts were literally overrun by preteens—often accompanied by their parents. In addition, the group was the subject of two Marvel Comics issues and a prime-time animated cartoon special on NBC. Clearly, their fire-breathing and war-painted shtick was viewed by most people—and most certainly parents—as pure entertainment. Yet there is a vocal minority who, over a decade later, still believe that the quartet's name is an acronym for Kids in the Service of Satan. Not only do bandleaders Paul Stanley and Gene Simmons scoff at the charge, they have publicly denounced their accusers.

On Kiss's early 1983 American tour, it was greeted in Chattanooga, Tennessee, by protesters bearing ten-foot-tall crosses and by obscene phone calls and letters. Even in a cosmopolitan city like Montreal, under a photo of the group in one of the local newspapers blared the headline: Satanists.

"It's real interesting," Stanley observes, "that these people have no firsthand knowledge—most of them have never even been to see the show. I'm not afraid to go to their sermons, so it's pretty amazing that they're afraid to come see us."

When most heavy-metal groups do raise the name of the devil, they do so only because the personification of pure evil is an intriguing character who is of as much interest to writers of rock songs as he's proven for centuries to be to artists, novelists, playwrights, and composers. The vast popularity and durability of such works as *Faustus*, the works of Edgar Allan Poe, *Rosemary's Baby*, and *The Exorcist*, to name only a handful of thousands, are proof of Satan's appeal as the subject of entertainment. If Iron Maiden's, or any other rock band's, songs are dangerous (anti-Satanists claim they seek to and have the power to make youngsters susceptible to Satan's powers), then it would follow that every one of the tens of millions of people who saw *The Exorcist* risked their souls. In fact, they were frightened and entertained. But perhaps the most important fact is that the devil figures prominently in the blues and every other musical form that derives from it.

The basic point usually missed by the anti-Satanists is that most of the songs they condemn warn against rather than encourage evil. Motley Crue's "Shout at the Devil," for example, interpreted superficially by many as a pro-Satan song, equates the devil with any sort of human evil—politicians, for instance, is songwriter Nikki Sixx's claim—and urges that the devil be shouted at and cast out, not invited into its listeners' lives. Similarly, the *il cornuto* sign—made by raising the index finger and the pinky—often flashed by hard-rock groups is an Italian hand symbol that has come to mean, at least in America, a way to *ward off* the devil or the evil eye. And, frankly, by now it has become so synonymous with heavy-metal concerts (and, surprisingly, rapper Afrika Bambaataa) that its meaning is probably lost on the majority of the fans in the audience anyway.

Bruce Dickinson, who had sung with the British metal act Samson, replaced Di'anno shortly before Iron Maiden recorded 1982's *The Number of the Beast*.

In Iron Maiden's case, being linked with the Satanist movement both helped and hindered its career. No doubt there were some young fans sufficiently intrigued by the controversy to buy one or more of the group's albums; probably an equal number were disenchanted by the connection. The most disturbing consequence, from the band's standpoint, was that an inordinate amount of attention was paid to the devil angle rather than to the musical and other lyrical aspects of the band.

Certainly not every lyric Steve Harris has written betrays an obsession with the devil, though his is certainly a macabre and at times dreary vision. On *The Number of the Beast*, seven of its eight songs pertain to death. The one exception, "22 Acacia Avenue," is about Charlotte the harlot, the prostitute first introduced on *Iron Maiden*. But Harris writes of death in fine detail and with chillingly effective imagery. The soliloquy of a prisoner about to meet his maker, "Hallowed Be Thy Name," is sung by Dickinson (nicknamed "Air-Raid Siren") as if his very life hangs in the balance, and the band supplies an almost movie-soundtrack backing, opening with chimes striking the hour ("I'm waiting in my cold cell when the bell begins to chime / Reflecting on my past life and it doesn't have much time"). Dickinson puts the song across with a sensitivity and believability that suggests method singing.

"If the song is about somebody who's crazy," Dickinson says, "then you extend the part of you that's crazy." But method singing, he emphasizes, is not the same as method acting. "Acting is adopting another personality; what I'm doing is simply interpreting the song as it relates to me."

Dickinson's voice differs greatly from Di'anno's, who possessed an effective, terrifying growl, but an unusually low range, which he rarely pushed on record. His best singing can be heard on *Maiden Japan*, where the band's deafening volume pushed him to new heights. Maiden's new singer had such an expansive range that he

Dave Murray and Steve Harris cofounded Iron Maiden in 1976. The two met after a friend of Harris's suggested he listen to the Paul Kossoff—influenced guitarist.

was able to harmonize with himself by way of doubletracking, capping his phrases with a distinctive, sometimes shrill vibrato and providing the band with a new sonic weapon.

The Number of the Beast broke Iron Maiden in the United States, going as high as #33 on the album chart and becoming its first LP to go gold. In England it *debuted* at Number One. But their ten-month, 150-date world tour took its toll, with charter drummer Clive Burr leaving the band in December for much the same reason as had Di'anno. In his place, the band hired Nicko McBrain, who had played with the French group Trust, Streetwalkers, and Pat Travers. For the recording of their fourth full-length album, the band traveled to Compass Point Studios, on the island of Nassau, and this time they were not beleaguered by the types of problems that plagued *The Number of the Beast*.

"If the song you are singing is about someone who's crazy, then you extend the part of you that's crazy. What I'm doing is simply interpreting the song as it relates to me."
—Bruce Dickinson

Piece of Mind introduced the songwriting of Dickinson and Smith, who teamed up for three compositions, lightening Harris's load for the first time. Interestingly, there is not the dichotomy one might expect among the album's nine tracks, with the Dickinson–Smith songs nearly identical to Harris's, though the latter still tended toward more graphic imagery, as in his song "The Trooper," which begins with the line "You'll take my life but I'll take yours too / You'll fire your musket but I'll run you through." Harris's antiwar diatribe, again penned from the first-person viewpoint of the victim, was accompanied by a performance video intercut with haunting black-and-

white war footage. Though the music retained its muscle, many of *Piece of Mind*'s rhythms were slower than the frantic tempos of previous albums, giving the more accomplished Nicko McBrain room to embellish the music with kinetic fills.

Iron Maiden's *Piece of Mind* Tour, which ran from June through October, was characterized by little serenity, unfortunately. On the early part of the turbulent trek the band was plagued by numerous equipment breakdowns, which were especially troublesome since the new material was more technically demanding. Bruce Dickinson admits, too, that there was some attendant pressure from the fact that this was Maiden's first headlining tour.

Piece of Mind eventually went gold, capping the band's most successful year yet. But perhaps the group was growing weary of the constant controversy, for its followup, *Powerslave*, released in September 1984, eschewed the demonic themes so prevalent on previous LPs. Maiden was just trying to avoid being typecast, was Steve Harris's oft-repeated claim, but one has to wonder if the group itself was not getting bored with its own image. The theme for the new album was based on Egyptian mythology; Dave Murray had visited Egypt, and Harris and Dickinson were intrigued with Egyptian history.

Dickinson also contributed Maiden's antinuke statement, "2 Minutes to Midnight," which contains such frightening imagery as "The body bags and little rags of children torn in two / And the jellied brains of those who remain to put the finger right on you." And in a daring move, the band recorded an epic track, "Rime of the Ancient Mariner," its thirteen minutes and forty-five seconds oscillating from blazing hard rock to a moody, meditative instrumental section and back again, including a narrative taken directly from Samuel Taylor Coleridge's poem, a favorite of Harris's since he first read it in school.

In September Iron Maiden became the first Western rock & roll act since Slade to play in Poland, Hungary, and Yugoslavia. The band had been somewhat apprehensive about making the

trip, but it proved a success. Iron Maiden played to 120,000 people behind the Iron Curtain in six days. All the shows sold out, with an estimated 2,000 to 4,000 straining to hear the band from outside each venue.

Maiden was not invited to play Gdansk, where most of the trouble between the Solidarity Movement and the Communist authorities has occurred, but overall the band was treated extremely well. One haunting moment took place in Wroclaw, when the band played Folks Hall, built by the Nazis during their occupation in World War II, and which has as its keystone a swastika.

Maybe their goodwill trip to the Iron Curtain countries will help change the public's perception of Iron Maiden, certainly the most misinterpreted metal act since Ozzy Osbourne. In a music that too rarely addresses issues other than those of adolescence and high hormonal levels, or the typical celebration of heavy metal, Iron Maiden has a much more worldly, if morose, viewpoint and frame of reference. Musically Iron Maiden has added little to metal's vocabulary, but it has proved that hard rock can effectively wed the dramatic surges of volume with equally dramatic words. And Maiden achieves that with more success than probably any other hard-rock band.

Iron Maiden on tour in Poland. In September 1984 Iron Maiden became the first Western rock act to play behind the Iron Curtain in several years. The band played to 120,000 fans in six days.

D E F   L E P P A R D

H E A V Y   M E T A L ' S   H E A R T B R E A K E R S

HEAVY metal is not pretty, nor are many of its stars. Which is the way it should be. For a music so loud and aggressive, with lyrics that often speak of being a social misfit, it would be incongruous for that message to be delivered by a smiling, wholesome face. *Very* incongruous.

And seeing as how the heavy-metal audience is largely made up of male adolescents suffering through the passage into manhood, such a face would probably only inspire resentment (guys like that always get the girls *you* spend your days pining over to no avail) or skepticism.

For every metal band that adopts superhero stage wear and presents itself as a group of brave warriors, larger than life, there's the metal band that strengthens its bond with its audience by resembling the audience. For some teens, heavy metal provides escapism and comic-book fantasies set to a squealing, crushing, pounding soundtrack. And at that stage of teens' development, the ultimate fantasy is achieving the sort of

power and adulation of their rock-star icons, who look much like themselves (though a little better fed and more jowly). It eases the pain of being enslaved by parents, school, work, and a body that seems to act of its own free will, with hair that won't comb right and skin that explodes with pustules before the most important social occasions.

Teen idols? That's for the opposite sex to giggle and squeeze its knees together over. In heavy metal, ugly is almost synonymous with commitment. So how do you explain the out-of-the-box success of Def Leppard, a hard-rock quintet from England? Lead vocalist Joe Elliott, guitarists Steve Clark and Phil Collen, bassist Rick Savage, and drummer Rick Allen all have faces little old aunties just love to squeeze and exclaim over.

The answer? Good songs and musical chops, enough to win over the most cynical, stringy-haired, poorly complexioned, army-fatigue-jacketed headbanger. One of the reasons the group's third album, 1983's *Pyromania*, sold five million

copies was its unusual crossover appeal: guitar solos for the boys, guitar poses for the girls, and the advent of the rock-video age, from which Leppard benefited greatly.

Def Leppard's members hail from one of Britain's least glamorous cities, the steel town of Sheffield. While the rest of the Yorkshire and Humberside region is still painfully breaking into new areas of modern business, with unemployment rampant among the once prosperous textile and coal-mining industries, Sheffield thrives as a steel-making center famous for its cutlery.

"Tin cans, knives, forks—you name it," Joe Elliott says impassively in his thick, heavy accent. "If it's made out of steel, it's made in Sheffield."

But the city's industrial might leaves Elliott cold. For most of Sheffield's youth, the future is pretty well defined: They leave school and go to work in the mills, bring home their pay, and head west once a year to holiday in Blackpool. But Def Leppard's members never even had to consider

such a plight; their rise to fame started while most of the band members were still in their teens. Drummer Rick Allen, for example, was just sixteen when the group's debut, *On through the Night*, was released in early 1980. "I think that'd be soul destroying, working in a steel mill," he says, shuddering at the thought. "I've never had what you'd call a 'normal' job; I've never known what it's like to have to get up in the morning and go to work."

In 1976, Britain was whirling from the punk-rock explosion that toppled the rock & roll hierarchy in that country, and along with it, the ailing heavy-metal movement. The hard-rock acts of the day were either fading veterans going through the motions, such as Black Sabbath, or undeveloped rookies growing up on vinyl, such as Judas Priest.

Early Def Leppard: Pete Willis, Steve Clark, Joe Elliott, Rick Allen, and Rick Savage. Allen was just sixteen when the group released its 1980 debut.

Rick Savage, a guitar-playing Peter Frampton lookalike, and tiny guitarist Pete Willis were pupils at the Tapton Comprehensive School, and shared a love of heavy-metal outfits such as Led Zeppelin, Deep Purple, and Thin Lizzy, no matter how *outré* they were considered at the time.

Together they formed a group called Atomic Mass, with Tony Kenning on drums, Andy Nicholas on bass, and vocalist Paul Holland. They played one show at school, performing Purple's "Smoke on the Water" and other hard-rock staples, before breaking up when school recessed for the summer.

Savage and Willis took menial day jobs, Savage as an apprentice technician for British Rail. In late 1977, they were joined by eighteen-year-old Joe Elliott, a delivery-van driver who had originally tried out for the drummer's spot but took over the microphone when it turned out that no one else in the fledgling outfit could sing lead. Kenning (nicknamed Reuben) was the drummer, and in June 1978 Steve Clark became second guitarist, relegating Savage to bass. Clark, a blond-haired lathe operator who had begun playing when he was ten, grew up listening to such guitarists as Joe Walsh, Jimmy Page, and Angus Young.

The name change to Def Leppard came as the result of in-school daydreaming by Elliott, who, during art class, would draw up imaginary posters for imaginary concerts featuring imaginary bands. One such band was Def (originally spelled "Deaf")Leppard, depicted by a jungle cat with a hearing horn, and at first only Rick Savage even remotely liked it.

The group rehearsed its original songs and covers of tunes by Thin Lizzy and T. Rex in an old football building located next to the Sheffield United Soccer Stadium. They found some early supporters in their parents, who would receive a heartfelt thanks on the back of *On through the Night*, "for putting up with it."

"They supported us financially," Elliott explains. "Our moms and dads aren't rich or anything, but as much as they could help, they did, loaning us money when we needed it, like, for equipment. They'd say, 'We want it back when you can pay it back,' which we did. At first they were a bit dubious: 'Why don't you get a steady job,' that sort of thing. But even if we didn't get in from playing till six in the morning, they didn't lock the door on us."

Juggling both the band and school or work proved difficult, especially for drummer Rick Allen, who, when he joined the group in November 1978, was already a five-year veteran of playing in bands. By now, the group was working as many as five nights a week in area pubs, and Allen recalls falling asleep during his lessons more than once. When he decided to pursue music full-time, his parents actually permitted him to drop out of school at age fifteen, a full year short of Britain's legal age of emancipation. Allen remembers hiding in his house—which was just down the road from school—whenever the doorbell rang, for fear it was the authorities. A tutor was assigned to him, "but it got to be a pain," says Elliott. "Rick finally said, 'Ah, sod it, I'm not gonna bother.'" According to the singer, the school authorities futilely chased Allen all over the country.

Unlike the music business in America, in England groups could have success with independently produced records, a do-it-yourself ethic that originated with the punks. Leppard, with a modest amount of borrowed cash and an interim drummer named Frank Noone, recorded an EP, *Getcha Rocks Off*, which they marketed on their own label, Bludgeon Riffola. A true homemade job, the record had a cover printed by the company Rick Allen's mother worked for. Radio 1 disc jockey Andy Peebles was an enthusiastic supporter of Def Leppard and began airing the record on his nightly program, generating so much interest that it sold over 24,000 copies, impressive figures for the relatively small British market. There was major-label interest—Elliott claims that at one point eleven record companies were scouting the band—but at first no takers. Gigs in

Guitarist Phil Collen (right, with Elliott in the "Photograph" video) left the band Girl to replace original guitarist Pete Willis in 1982.

those days were at local pubs, often in front of what the band calls "Rent-a-Crowds"; i.e., the few friends it was able to round up. One time, in June 1979, an A&R rep from Arista Records traveled to New Brighton to see Leppard at a venue called the Grand Hotel. There were ten people in the audience; the man from Arista vanished before the set's end.

In August, Leppard signed with Phonogram Records, and within a few months was touring with the likes of AC/DC, Pat Travers, Uriah Heep, Sammy Hagar, and Ted Nugent, all comfortable and beneficial pairings. Without mentioning any names, Elliott notes that the young band occasionally encountered some resentment from veteran bands that had been painstakingly cutting a path to success for several years. Here was Def Leppard on the same circuit, and most of its members not even twenty.

Leppard's youth may have made other bands jealous, but it paid off in almost all other respects. The press rallied around them because of the obvious story angle, and the group struck a responsive chord in its record-buying peers, who by 1980 were desperately searching for the next great white-noise hope.

With *On through the Night*, produced by Tom Allom, Judas Priest's producer, they did not quite get it. In retrospect, the album is more impressive for showcasing the group's potential than it is for realizing it. The weakest element is Elliott's singing, which sounds thin, partially the fault of a thick, muddy mix in which guitars compete for space with the rhythm section and with Elliott. The singer now says he cannot listen to *On through the Night* "without getting completely drunk first."

But the album is a good indication of the band's song-oriented direction, which would define Eighties heavy metal and Leppard's impressive range. "Sorrow Is a Woman" is a poignant hard-rock ballad that opens with acoustic guitar; "Hello America" is an unusually tuneful uptempo rocker ignited by, of all things, a sweet-singing chorale. Most metal bands seem to incorporate harmony singing about as often as they do a

ukulele, particularly live, but Leppard has always boasted the most taut and intricate backing vocals in hard rock.

As with most metal, the bedrock of Lep's sound was provided by the guitars, with blitzes of surprisingly sophisticated riffing that came on like a siege. But the solos were woven into the songs, rather than allowed to intrude on them. *On through the Night*'s most successful song is "Wasted" (the fifth song the band ever wrote together), with its freewheeling solos by Willis and Clark and its sad tale of a possible teen suicide. Its title is deceiving, for the song is not just another paean to inebriation, but as much about wasted time as about wasted minds. Elliott, having been spurned by a lover, is drunk with self-pity and a good deal of cheap booze. When he laments, "I'm outta my head / I wish I was dead," the music cuts ominously. Did he?

Despite its flaws, *On through the Night* bowed impressively, reaching #51 on the album chart, and the group earned praise on its U.S. tour as a supporting act for AC/DC. With the hard-rock revival gearing up, their prospects seemed bright.

A series of setbacks, however, prevented Leppard from immediately capitalizing on that initial success: Unhappy with Allom's production of *On through the Night*, they decided to go with Robert John "Mutt" Lange for the followup. Lange had been largely responsible for AC/DC's recent commercial turnaround and was much sought-after. Work on Leppard's album, *High 'N' Dry*, was delayed for nearly six months because Lange was first committed to complete Foreigner's *4* album, which finished way behind schedule. Going with Lange was a risky decision: As proven as he was, the delay was sure to hurt the group's momentum, particularly in Britain, where fan allegiances can shift like the wind.

The band retreated to Sheffield and worked on songs and arrangements. The time proved not to be wasted, for their subsequent tightness as a unit enabled them to record *High 'N' Dry* in just a few weeks, and the LP was issued in July 1981, with a thank you to their audience "for your patience."

From the opening guitar chords of "Let It Go," the band's growth from *On through the Night* was startling, beginning with the sound: crisp and rich, with each instrument sharply defined. Then Elliott's voice comes in, and it's as if the band had hired a new vocalist, his voice evocative of the shrill, upper-register singing of AC/DC's Brian Johnson. The group had a major radio hit with "Bringin' On the Heartbreak," a slow but powerful ballad that demonstrated amply their newfound depth as musicians, being equal parts hard rock and blues. Elliott convincingly moans over the loss of yet another love, and Willis's solo is equally emotional, with sharp, biting notes that sting like bitter tears.

🐆🐆🐆🐆🐆🐆🐆🐆🐆🐆🐆🐆🐆

"I think that'd be soul destroying, working in a steel mill. I've never had what you'd call a 'normal' job; I've never known what it's like to have to get up in the morning and go to work." —Rick Allen

———

Most of *High 'N' Dry*, however, was uptempo and high-spirited. Apparently, while waiting for producer Lange, the group had plenty of time to hold strategy meetings over several pints of lager, for there are a couple of odes to demon alcohol. On the title track—about spinning your wheels while waiting for Saturday night—the singer has started boozing it up long before nightfall. And on "Me & My Wine," one of Leppard's least exceptional tracks—which, presumably, takes place the morning after—he says with false confidence, "I'm doing fine, just me and my wine," though you *know* he is lying. Leppard's celebration of alcohol, and their reputation as serious drinkers, was ironic, in light of the role it would play in altering their own history.

High 'N' Dry peaked at #38, a respectable showing, but not what the band had hoped for.

The delay had been costly, for in the six months Leppard was stranded without a producer, groups such as Judas Priest and AC/DC had established themselves out of the morass of metal bands that had begun emerging in 1979 as part of the British new-wave-of-heavy-metal movement. Album number three was crucial, and they knew it.

Overall the group had coped well with its success at such a precocious age. Both Elliott and Allen feel that their working-class backgrounds played a large part in preventing their egos from swelling. When the band members would return to Sheffield, they still lived with their parents, hardly the lifestyle of rock & roll legends.

But Pete Willis, just seventeen at the time, was having difficulty contending with the pressure, and his drinking became a problem. Having been together for several years, the band was at first reluctant to confront the guitarist. Finally, in 1982, Willis was ousted from the band he had helped found. His departure is a painful subject for the band, one which Allen broaches gingerly.

"When we first started breaking, everyone buckled down to the idea that this was the job that we had to do, and that if we stuck together, we'd be successful. Pete obviously felt overwhelmed by everything that was going on. We'd say to him, 'Pete, you know, you've got to get your act together.' It'd last for a day or two and then . . . I didn't really want to see the guy go, but we had no other choice."

With the band's third album also behind schedule, the news of Willis's sacking was taken as an omen that heavy metal's brightest young hopes might self-destruct before they ever achieved what was foreseen for them. A short time later, the band announced a replacement, guitarist Phil Collen, a London-born twenty-five-year-old who had played in numerous pub bands before joining a moderately successful metal act called Girl, with whom he toured England, Europe, and Japan in 1979.

The band had known of Collen for some time, and the fact that he had experience as part of a two-guitar lineup, as well as a flair for onstage posturing, made him a logical choice. Leppard

were just partially through recording *Pyromania*; with Willis, they had gotten only as far as laying down the songs' backing tracks. The album would not be ready for the pre-Christmas months—traditionally a prime time for LP sales—so the band would not be able to release it until early 1983. "We knew that with this album we were either going to sink or swim," admits Allen. "If this one wasn't really strong, we were going to fall by the wayside, because there's so much competition."

This time, however, the delay between records seemed to have a positive effect, and by the time *Pyromania* was completed, there was an air of anticipation about the album, a feeling that Def Leppard was ready to truly break. All during 1982, while Leppard was dormant as far as the public was concerned, renewed interest was suddenly shown in *High 'N' Dry*—thanks largely to MTV's airing of the band's in-concert video for "Bringin' On the Heartbreak." By November 1983, the LP had gone platinum, and in 1984 was rereleased with remixes of "Bringin' On the Heartbreak" and "Me & My Wine," both of which were given new video treatments with Phil Collen in the band.

Pyromania did not disappoint. If *High 'N' Dry* had demonstrated the band's maturity as musicians and a better recorded sound, *Pyromania* evidenced their improvement as songwriters, providing Leppard with three hit singles, something it had been unable to achieve with the first two albums. The first single, "Photograph," might just be the hookiest song in heavy-metal history, with a tuneful verse that gets knocked aside by a bridge strong enough to be a chorus for another hit song, which in turn gives way to the chorus, with its wash of delicate harmonies (credited to the "Leppardettes") and chiming guitars. Collen is given the spotlight, and instantly responds with a tortured solo that makes great use of mathematics, zigzagging against the well-anchored rhythm. "Photograph" made #12 in the early spring, and was followed by two more Top

On New Year's Eve 1984, Rick Allen crashed his car while driving in his Sheffield hometown. His left arm was severed, reattached, but later amputated.

Thirty hits: "Rock of Ages" (#16) and "Foolin'" (#28).

The former was a rarity: a rock anthem that succeeds, with an infectious, martial drum beat and nursery-rhyme lyric: "Rise up, gather round, rock this place to the ground / Burn it up, let's go for broke, watch the night go up in smoke." Elliott teases a bit before leading into the chorus, asking his bandmates, "What do you want?" They reply, en masse and determinedly, "I want rock & roll," and Elliott ad-libs such playful asides as "You betcha!" displaying more confidence and personality than ever before.

"I'm singing better than I ever have," he acknowledged after *Pyromania*'s release, "but I'm still not as good as I want to be." What he lacks in range, he makes up for in dramatic instinct: the protracted scream that caps "Photograph"; the staccato phrasing on "Foolin'."

Pyromania quickly vaulted into the Top Ten, and was kept out of the Number One spot only by Michael Jackson's world-record-setting *Thriller*. Leppard's heavyweight success was not due just to its improved songwriting craft; rock video played a crucial part in its sudden rise to superstar status. And that aspect of Leppard's fame comes down to their looks.

The band was not unaware of the rapidly growing influence video was having on the public, and so refined its image accordingly. When the video for "Photograph" first began airing on music-video channels, the difference in Def Leppard's look was startling: Elliott, always handsome but stocky and blunt featured, was suddenly a svelte rock idol with straight and lightened hair instead of his dark halo of curls. Steve Clark, too, had a new, more attractive hairstyle, and Phil Collen definitely lent the band some sex appeal.

But the focus was Elliott, who is shown leaping off the drum riser in slow motion, wearing a Union Jack T-shirt that by year's end would be associated more with him than with the mother country. A confusing hodgepodge of images, the "Photograph" video depicts, among other things, caged vixens desperately trying to claw their way out to get to the band, a Marilyn Monroe lookalike, and

some allusions to a murder. At shows on Leppard's March-through-September U.S. tour, at first as an opener for Billy Squier, then as a headliner for the first time, girls in the audience—an extremely high percentage for a hard-rock act—reacted much like young Beatlemaniacs or Durannies.

In "Rock of Ages" Elliott wields a lightsaber (which turns into an electric guitar) while rallying all within earshot to stump for rock & roll. The medieval costumes and set stem from heavy metal's constant affair with Gothic and medieval history, and really are more in keeping with such singers as Ozzy Osbourne and Ronnie James Dio than with Elliott, but why quibble over an undeniably successful video?

As they crisscrossed the United States with four truckloads of equipment, they stared wide-eyed at the *Billboard* and *Cashbox* charts, unable to fully grasp their meteoric rise in popularity. "We knew *Pyromania* was a good album," Elliott confides, "but we never expected to sell five million copies."

Comprehending how big the band had become was even more difficult for Elliott's parents, Joe and Cindy. "I'd phone them back in Sheffield," relates the van driver turned singing star, "and I'd tell them, 'We just did a gig in front of fifteen thousand.' They'd go, 'That's really good,' but they wouldn't really understand." As the tour was winding down that fall, the band members flew their parents across the Atlantic to witness first-hand Leppard's conquest of the States. After attending two shows in Los Angeles and two more in the San Francisco Bay Area, their folks still couldn't quite take it all in. "My mother told me that my dad spent the first hour just watching the audience—he'd never seen so many people, except at a football match back in England."

Joe Elliott's perfect year was nearly tarnished by a simple slip of the tongue, however. With just two weeks remaining on the American trek, the band was playing in Tucson, Arizona, and Elliott tried to fire up the audience by comparing it to the previous night's crowd in El Paso, Texas—"that place with all the greasy Mexicans"—thinking "greasy Mexicans" was an expression along the lines of "limey" and not realizing that his poor choice of words constituted a racial slur. El Paso, comprised of a large Mexican-American population, simmered for a few weeks, but by the end of the month the repercussions from Elliott's remarks were in full fury. Radio station KLAQ announced a boycott of the group's records, and DJ Bill Clifton of station KSET broke Def Leppard albums on the air in protest.

Informed of the uproar in Japan, where he and Collen were vacationing and doing interviews, Elliott immediately phoned KLAQ with an apology, which seemed to placate both the station and most of its listeners. But the local League of United Latin American Citizens (LULAC) called the apology inadequate and pressed for a nationwide boycott of Leppard records and merchandise.

Elliott donated money to several Hispanic charities and traveled to New Mexico for three days of public penance, though some citizens of El Paso bluntly told him not to bother coming to their city. The incident seemed to genuinely upset Elliott, who remarked ruefully, "I almost ruined my career with one word."

⊂⊐⊂⊐⊂⊐⊂⊐⊂⊐⊂⊐⊂⊐⊂⊐⊂⊐⊂⊐⊂⊐⊂⊐

"When we first started breaking, everyone buckled down to the idea that this was the job we had to do, and that if we stuck together, we'd be successful." —Rick Allen

That aside, 1983 could not have been a better year for Def Leppard, who continued touring into early 1984 in the Far East, causing them to amend the name of the tour from Rock till You Drop to Rock till You *Die*. Following its completion, Elliott recalls, laughing, he would get out of bed in the morning and say, "Good evening, everybody," so worn out were he and the band from the constant travel. The band's gross income for the year was reportedly $15 million, and it had sold ninety-five percent of its concert tickets.

Nineteen eighty-four was spent recording Leppard's fourth album, and after all the exposure they received the previous year—gracing the covers of scores of magazines—the low profile was deliberate. The band did give a hint that it would not stick to the successful format of *Pyromania*, however, with the surprising news that it would not work with Mutt Lange, but with Jim Steinman. Better known for his work with more bombastic acts such as Meat Loaf, for whom he was the principal songwriter, Steinman had worked with singer Bonnie Tyler, hard-rock popster Billy Squier, and the soft-rock band Air Supply. But by November, Steinman was out of the picture and Def Leppard was at work producing itself.

On New Year's Eve 1984, tragedy struck when Rick Allen crashed his car while driving in Sheffield. Allen was thrown from the vehicle and his left arm was severed. Though doctors reattached the arm during ten hours of surgery, it was later amputated due to infection. As of this writing, the group gave no indication as to whether it would replace Allen, either temporarily or permanently. After a year in which everything seemed to go their way, 1984 proved to be a hard one for Def Leppard.

Despite the tragic accident, Leppard is in the enviable position of commanding such a large audience—one that encompasses even nonmetal fans—that it can pretty much write its own ticket. The hard-core headbanger community regards the group's pop metal with some degree of disdain —probably because Leppard is the only group both they and their younger sisters can enjoy. Heaven forbid! But overall, the band's songwriting prowess, hard-rock sensibilities, and—with the rock-video phenomenon showing no signs of abating—good looks have given it the luxury of being one of the few heavy-metal acts to successfully break the heavy-metal mold.

Former delivery van driver Elliott has become a topnotch vocalist, his voice evocative of the shrill, upper-register belting of AC/DC's Brian Johnson.

QUIET RIOT
❧❧❧
ALL CRAZEE NOW

WHEN Quiet Riot's *Metal Health* topped the album chart on November 26, 1983, the hard-rock quartet from Los Angeles became the first metal band to reach Number One with its U.S. debut. Not even Def Leppard, Van Halen, or the mighty Led Zeppelin could lay claim to such a feat.

No one was comparing Quiet Riot to Zeppelin just yet—at the time, that was an honor/albatross reserved for Def Leppard—but there was a parallel in that *Metal Health*'s remarkable showing was as unexpected as that of Zeppelin's initial effort nearly a decade and a half earlier. Unlike Zeppelin, who eschewed singles for protracted album cuts, its debut coming at the height of the FM-rock-radio takeover, Quiet Riot had an instant advantage: a hit single, and a well-worn hard-rock cover version at that. "Cum On Feel the Noize" was a metal anthem written and recorded by the British glitter/hard-rock group Slade in 1973. While the original had rocketed to Number One in England, it had stalled at #76 in the United States.

But heavy metal ten years later was more singles-conscious in response to 1983-style radio, not nearly as daring as it had been a decade before. Quiet Riot altered the song very little from the original recording, merely changing the irregular drum beat of Slade's version into a charging, highly danceable pulse. Bolstered by a half-live, half-concept video in which a bewildered headbanger wakes up to find that his stereo has assumed monstrous proportions and that the bedroom walls are crumbling and quaking from the group's cacophony, "Cum On Feel the Noize" climbed all the way to #5 in the United States and went gold, making it the highest-charting hard-rock entry of the year and the only 1983 metal 45 to sell one million copies.

Just six months earlier, Quiet Riot was a struggling act that had peaked as a local attraction in L.A. They had recorded their debut LP with

Spencer Proffer, a producer with no hard-rock credits, simply because he was the best they could acquire. And, lead singer/group founder Kevin DuBrow notes wryly, they were not in any position to be that particular. When *Metal Health* was released in March 1983, the band seemed destined to be known solely for having provided the training ground for Randy Rhoads, the lead guitarist who went on to become a legend in Ozzy Osbourne's Blizzard of Ozz group until his death in a fiery plane crash in 1982. The band had also supplied Osbourne with bassist Rudy Sarzo, albeit temporarily. With the success of *Metal Health*, DuBrow became Quiet Riot's key figure— only fitting, since he had formed the band with Rhoads in 1975.

A tall, lanky six-footer with an almost comical, rubbery face, DuBrow grew up on such Seventies white blues-rock singers as Rod Stewart and Humble Pie's Steve Marriott, whom DuBrow claims most inspired him to begin singing. (In fact, in the wake of Quiet Riot's success, DuBrow would cite Marriott's opening for the band in El Paso, Texas, in 1983, as the biggest thrill of his life.) Though DuBrow's voice is not quite as elastic as that of Marriott, generally considered to be among the best wailers in rock & roll, he wields a similar freedom of expression, ad-libbing phrases like a lead guitarist.

From Stewart, DuBrow has always borrowed his stage persona more than any vocal traits. Like the rooster-haired solo star and former singer for the Jeff Beck Group and the Faces, DuBrow is not afraid to play the buffoon onstage, wearing black-and-white striped pants that your average self-respecting circus clown would disown. Throughout Quiet Riot's set, he mugs constantly, rolling his eyes until he looks like Dracula's spider-eating assistant Renfield. DuBrow will appear to

The second band to bear the Quiet Riot name was the first to make it a household word: Rudy Sarzo, Carlos Cavazo, Kevin DuBrow, and Frankie Banali.

have glimpsed Nirvana whenever lead guitarist Carlos Cavazo takes a particularly inspired lead solo, and even when Cavazo does not. Both he and the band share the same boozy onstage camaraderie that typified Stewart and the Faces, with DuBrow draping himself over Cavazo and bassist Rudy Sarzo, maniacally shouting encouragements in their faces.

**"There seems to be this rule that if you're a heavy-metal band, you can't smile onstage, that heavy metal is nothing but grinding teeth and a lot of sneers. A lot of the heavy-metal singers who try to be very macho onstage turn me off."
—Kevin DuBrow**

In general, Quiet Riot seems to have taken the Slade song "Mama Weer All Crazee Now" (its first single from its second American LP, *Condition Critical*) to heart, as the band's image is that of sheer lunacy. A constant presence on the group's LP covers and in its videos is the decibel-crazed madman whose face is hidden behind a Middle Ages–vintage metal mask. The victim's eyes and curly hair more than suggest that it may be DuBrow himself. The band's invitation to join it in its rock & roll asylum is not only good-humored, it's downright infectious.

DuBrow was eighteen and a part-time photographer when he first encountered Randy Rhoads, then just seventeen but already a technically adept player. In rock & roll, legends are often based more on image and offstage exploits than on actual musical impact, as exemplified by the case of Jim Morrison and the Doors. But Rhoads's reputation was cultivated almost exclusively on his abilities as a musician—ironically, the antithesis of his mentor, Ozzy Osbourne, with whom he

played after leaving DuBrow and Company in 1979.

Rhoads can be heard on Quiet Riot's two Japanese LPs and on Ozzy Osbourne's *Blizzard of Ozz* and *Diary of a Madman*. But even in that limited sampling of his music, his talent was unquestionable. Rhoads combined fretboard flash with an unusual musicality derived from his love of classical-guitar music. At the time of his death, he was furiously studying classical guitar, even though he himself was a well-respected teacher. In heavy metal, particularly when played live, it is easy for ax slingers to get away with displays of style over substance. Rhoads, however, had both.

Born December 6, 1956, Randall Rhoads died on March 19, 1982, when the small plane he was flying in crashed into a mansion. At the time, he was on tour in Florida with Osbourne, and the pilot of the plane had been buzzing Osbourne's bus as a prank. Years after his passing, acclaim for his guitaring has remained overwhelming. Even after finally having achieved the fame that he and Rhoads had sought together for so long, Kevin DuBrow finds his friend's memory on his mind quite often. "Randy Rhoads was the greatest guitar player that ever lived," DuBrow said just as *Metal Health* was climbing toward the top, "and I consider it a great honor to have been in a band with him."

When DuBrow met Rhoads in 1975, the blond-haired guitarist cut an intriguing figure; he was tiny, almost frail. "He had hair down to his waist and a thumbnail about four inches long," DuBrow recalls. "I thought to myself, 'No way can this guy play.' But I listened to him play on this teeny amp, and I thought that my head was being plastered against the wall."

The original Quiet Riot consisted of DuBrow, Rhoads, and two local musicians, bassist Kelly Garni and drummer Drew Forsyth. This lineup recorded *Quiet Riot* and *Quiet Riot II*, which were released in 1977 and 1978 on the CBS/Sony label

The not-so-quiet Kevin DuBrow, whose outspoken opinions of competing bands have not always won friends and influenced people.

in Japan. Essentially, these albums comprised the group's demo tapes, raw and, frankly, unimpressive—an evaluation DuBrow shares. "We grew up on those albums," he explains, adding that he is eternally grateful that neither has been released stateside. After *Metal Health*, those records would fetch up to fifty dollars apiece as collector's items.

In late 1977 Garni was dismissed from the band after an argument with Rhoads. His replacement

was Cuban-born Rudy Sarzo, who had emigrated to the United States when he was nine years old in 1961, shortly after the Bay of Pigs invasion. Sarzo began his musical career by playing in a Florida strip joint and pinballed his way across the country, working in a series of bands. He first saw Quiet Riot perform at L.A.'s Starwood Club in

Banali, Cavazo, and DuBrow: The latter started Quiet Riot in 1975 with guitarist Randy Rhoads, who defected to Ozzy Osbourne's band in 1979.

early 1977. Sarzo was astounded by Rhoads's playing and impressed with the band in general, yet he never rallied the courage to ask to join. Instead, he headed for the East Coast in search of musical-job prospects. After Garni left, DuBrow immediately located Sarzo and summoned him back west to join Quiet Riot.

☙☙☙☙☙☙☙☙☙☙☙☙

"When I met Randy Rhoads, he had hair down to his waist and a thumbnail four inches long. I thought, 'No way can this guy play.' But I listened to him play and I thought my head was being plastered against the wall."
—Kevin DuBrow

A single the band recorded from this period, "Slick Black Cadillac" (which was rerecorded for *Metal Health* five years later), sold an impressive 100,000 copies in Japan, even though the group had never toured there. In Japan, where youngsters have a seemingly insatiable appetite for rock & roll and a paucity of native rockers, even unsigned American bands can become stars. In Quiet Riot's case, it was "good looks and tight trousers," according to DuBrow, that launched them in the land of the rising sun. "We used to have promo pictures that made us look like the Bay City Rollers of heavy metal. Randy used to photograph like he was straight out of heaven, like a rock & roll Farrah Fawcett." Sarzo also added to the band's teenybopper visual appeal, with his dark shag-cut mane, eternally youthful face, and a unique way of playing his bass onstage. Rather than pluck the strings, he hit the body of his instrument with such force that the notes just sounded themselves. The band concluded that with this kind of appeal and vast overseas popularity, a U.S. record deal would be forthcoming.

But then the band found itself in the midst of the new-wave explosion of 1979, a phenomenon ignited by the success of another L.A. band, the Knack. That group's Beatles-modeled image and chart-topping debuts—*Get the Knack* (whose cover photo imitated that of *Meet the Beatles*) and "My Sharona" were both Number Ones—marked the beginning of a temporary but serious decline in nationwide demand for new metal acts, as record companies, more prone to bandwagon jumping than the most unprincipled politician, descended upon the City of Angels, signing up every white-shirted, skinny-tied power-pop act in town. The result was a plethora of releases, by the Plimsouls, Great Buildings, the Motels, Phil Seymour, 20/20, the Pop, the Cretones, and others. Any band that failed to adopt the British Invasion–inspired style was more or less assured a place as spectator—not a winner—in the record-deal stakes.

The local club scene, which revolved around such venues as the landmark Whisky a-Go-Go, the Starwood (Van Halen's old haunt), the Troubadour, and the Roxy, has always been somewhat chauvinistic. Each successful band seems to spawn a bevy of imitators—the Knack had their progeny; Van Halen had theirs; and after 1983, Quiet Riot had theirs. The circuit is often fragmented and militant, with the fans of one or two music styles inevitably intolerant of anything considered alien. And in 1979, despite being overlooked by the record industry, metal still thrived, at least in L.A. With the frustrating specter of hard times, the competition among L.A.'s heavy-metal bands—traditionally intense to begin with—became downright fierce.

"It had been pretty competitive between us and Van Halen until they got signed," recounts DuBrow. "Then we became the top dogs." One band trying to usurp Quiet Riot's throne was Snow, whose guitarist was Atlanta-born Carlos Cavazo, later to become the lead player for DuBrow's band. Before that, however, there was little camaraderie. In fact, when Snow once opened for

Overleaf: Upon Rudy Sarzo's (left) rejoining the group DuBrow in September 1982, its name was changed back to Quiet Riot, because "the spirit of the old band was back."

Quiet Riot, the audience expressed its displeasure by throwing pennies at them, an incident DuBrow still recalls with no small trace of glee.

But despite its seemingly invincible position, Quiet Riot's status as L.A.'s most up-and-coming band was not getting it anywhere. After most of the new-wave acts—including the Knack—slipped commercially with their second and third albums, the record industry moved to new hunting grounds.

During this most disheartening time, heavy-metal stalwart Ozzy Osbourne, engineering a comeback after a two-year sabbatical, offered Randy Rhoads a position in his band. With Quiet Riot's career indefinitely stalled, Rhoads accepted the offer. "He would have been a fool to pass it up," DuBrow says, "though at the time, I wanted to kill him." And not only did Rhoads leave then, but Sarzo also opted to quit, and Quiet Riot became, to quote DuBrow, "Quiet Nothing." Once in Osbourne's band, Rhoads convinced his new boss to hire Sarzo as well. Meanwhile, the other half of Quiet Riot, DuBrow and drummer Forsyth, called it quits. Being the group's founder and a close friend of Rhoads, DuBrow took the band's dissolution the hardest. A natural-born performer, DuBrow claims that had he never begun a career as a singer, he might have become a radio announcer or a porno star. To suddenly be without an outlet for his performing instincts left DuBrow more than a little shaken.

"I began to question if I was in the right business," he recalls. "I had always depended on Randy because he was such a great player, and I was really a pretty mediocre singer back then. It was only after Randy left that I improved." But DuBrow chose not to mourn Quiet Riot and plunged headlong into his next project, a band he christened with his own last name.

Despite DuBrow's proven commercial instincts and yowling vocals, his contribution to this new band—and later to the new Quiet Riot—was his commitment to heavy-metal music. While everyone else had shifted to power pop—either by choice or under duress—DuBrow held firm in his belief that music styles are cyclical and that heavy metal would one day return. As for trends, he says, "Stay with the one you believe in, and the chances are that the cycle will catch up to you."

His new band included Snow's Carlos Cavazo, a baby-faced high-school dropout with a conspicuous tattoo of a Flying V guitar on his right arm; bassist Chuck Wright (replaced briefly by Juan Croucier, later to turn up in Ratt, L.A.'s most popular 1984 heavy-metal entry); and Frankie Banali, a veteran drummer so anxious for stardom that he once belonged to five different bands simultaneously, in the hopes that one of them might make it. A talented song arranger, Banali was a longtime friend of Rudy Sarzo's. While DuBrow, just signed to Pasha Records, was assembling material for the first U.S. album, its ex-bassist was contemplating leaving Ozzy Osbourne. Following the death of Randy Rhoads just a few months before, Sarzo was losing his enthusiasm for being an Osbourne sideman.

In the fall of 1982, while on a break from the Osbourne tour, Sarzo returned to Los Angeles to play on a track that DuBrow had written as a tribute to Rhoads—penned while he was alive—called "Thunderbird." Sarzo decided that it was better to play with friends, unsuccessful though they might be, than work in the businesslike atmosphere of Osbourne's group. Besides "Thunderbird," Sarzo completed nearly half of the DuBrow album in one day of recording.

Before Sarzo left Osbourne, he played a final date with the Blizzard of Ozz at New York City's the Ritz on September 27, one of the two shows recorded for the double live set *Speak of the Devil*, the only Osbourne album on which Sarzo actually performed. "I was never really fulfilled musically," he explains. "For two years I did little more than play Bob Daisley's [his predecessor] bass lines. But I put up with it because I was playing with Randy—that was ninety percent of my reason for being there. After Randy died, there was no more reason for me to stick around. After that, it just wasn't the same again."

On *Speak of the Devil*, Osbourne's in-concert tribute to his days as lead singer of Black Sabbath, Sarzo merely reproduced Sabbath bassist Geezer Butler's original lines. As creatively limiting as working with Osbourne might have been, Sarzo could not ignore the fact that he was trading a fairly secure future with heavy metal's oldest extant institution for a return to the bars. He later remarked that even if Quiet Riot had never made it, he would not have regretted his decision. Upon Sarzo's return, DuBrow decided to reinstate the Quiet Riot name, because it was felt that even without Randy, "the spirit of the old band was back."

But it seems that even then the Riot/Ozz connection was not broken. Even had Quiet Riot not re-formed, something of its sound would have been carried on by Rhoads in Osbourne's band, where he was not only the star instrumentalist, but Ozzy's chief cowriter. The similarities between some of the material on *Blizzard* and *Diary* and several early Quiet Riot tracks is uncanny, particularly on Osbourne's "Suicide Solution," written with Rhoads, who wrote its ancestral soundalike, Quiet Riot's "Force of Habit." And DuBrow, for one, feels that the resemblances are not just mere coincidence. Relations between DuBrow and Ozzy have been strained: Maybe the former still harbors a resentment over having his band stolen from under him; maybe Osbourne was not happy about losing Sarzo back to Quiet Riot. Neither singer is comfortable discussing the matter.

With everything riding on Quiet Riot's third record, there was not time to look back. If it was a success, they were prepared to go on indefinitely; if it flopped, Quiet Riot would be over for good. After nearly eight years of hard work, they were tired of being losers.

Though it started out slowly upon its release, *Metal Health* began to accrue sales over the summer, spurred partially by the group's last-minute appearance at the US Festival in San Bernardino, California. By fall, it had inched its way up to the top rungs of the charts, eventually selling four and a half million copies in the United States alone and launching "Cum On Feel the Noize." But as phenomenal as the success was, it is more difficult to pinpoint its source. For one thing, the group lacked the outrageous image that is *au courant* in metal. Even their L. A. colleagues like Motley Crue were regressing to the Kiss-influenced Spandex-and-mascara look many thought passé. Second, the group lacked a single instrumental virtuoso of Rhoads's caliber. There is, in fact, very little about the band that is original.

"Of course holding up a bottle of Jack Daniel's is pandering to the audience. But if I'm not there to pander to them, then what the hell do I get paid for? Pandering is part of my job."
—Kevin DuBrow

Though Kevin DuBrow's belief in his band has always been strong, even he concedes that the album's spectacular sales had as much to do with timing as it did with the record's actual content. He acknowledges that the fact that Van Halen was taking 1983 off and that other heavy-metal competitors, such as Scorpions, Judas Priest, and Rush, were between albums helped bolster *Metal Health*'s sales. All the same, one cannot deny that their music struck a responsive chord with its upbeat, celebratory spirit.

But in light of their stardom, Quiet Riot have found themselves having to defend their two Slade covers. DuBrow answers critics with a commercially conscious pragmatism that has long been out of vogue in rock & roll in general, and especially in heavy metal. "We don't write hit singles, and these days you need hit singles." Certainly the members of Slade were not complaining. Having been without an American record deal for several years, the venerable British group was able to make an impressive comeback in 1984, thanks largely to Quiet Riot's exposure of its work to a new audience.

Still, this reliance on outside material raised the question of whether or not Quiet Riot would be able to sustain its success, and, more importantly, establish its own musical identity. The onstage shtick of DuBrow hoisting Cavazo onto his shoulders had originated in the late Seventies with AC/DC; many of Riot's songs were too earnestly anthemic ("Party All Night," "We Were Born to Rock"), with gang-style shout-along choruses that also owe a debt to AC/DC; and the ear-shriveling scream on "Metal Health" is a direct cop from another of DuBrow's idols, the Who's Roger Daltrey (on "Won't Get Fooled Again").

"I think we do the same old thing," DuBrow concedes hesitantly, "but we do it in a new way." In that respect, the singer is correct, for as much as Quiet Riot borrows from heavy-metal traditions, it does imbue that music with several trademarks that are all its own.

For one thing, there is Banali's incessant, danceable beat—a real rarity in heavy metal, which is often characterized by its soporific rhythms. Even on the midtempo anthem "Metal Health," with its rousing exhortation to "Bang your head," Banali plays a consistent four-on-the-floor beat punctuated by his steady bass drum. And on the two Slade revivals, which in their original versions had a stuttered beat, Quiet Riot keeps it rudimentary but ultimately more effective, especially for the Eighties, a more dance-conscious decade, even for metalheads.

And Quiet Riot avoids the typical hard-rock posturing, with a tongue-in-cheekness that even DuBrow will admit probably eludes a good portion of its audience. DuBrow in particular goes against the heavy-metal grain, his stage presence significantly less macho than that of most hard-rock singers. For one thing, he wears no leather onstage, moves with a playful grace that could almost be considered effeminate, and is con-

Pandering to the audience, claims DuBrow, is part of a hard-rock frontman's job. He contends that, like all performers, he's "a professional prostitute."

stantly raking back his thatch of curly black hair in a gesture that suggests full-tilt insanity. The band members tend to grin a lot onstage, in sharp contrast to the scowling, often somber posture of other hard-rock groups. And Quiet Riot displays a playful sense of humor on record too. On *Condition Critical*'s "Party All Night," DuBrow mockingly intones an adult's warning against having fun in a deep voice reminiscent of the boss/father/politician figures on Eddie Cochran's "Summertime Blues."

As is typical of DuBrow, he is comfortable bucking a trend. "There seems to be this rule that if you're a heavy-metal band, you can't smile onstage, that heavy metal is nothing but grinding teeth and a lot of sneers. A lot of the heavy-metal singers who try to be very macho onstage turn me off; I think with a lot of them it descends from a lack of security about their masculinity to start with." Hence Quiet Riot's unusually large female-to-male ratio of fans, a pattern the group established in its earliest days.

In a relatively short time, DuBrow has perfected an onstage persona that, when he is truly being Kevin DuBrow, is original in the context of heavy metal. But, for many rock & roll musicians, those inveterate images of their own rock & roll heroes sometimes imbue themselves subconsciously. DuBrow's posture as party host can devolve into unintentional parody—as when he hoists a Jack Daniel's bottle with which to tipsily toast the crowd, and all the bottle holds is herbal tea. Isn't that unconscionably pandering to the audience?

"Of course it is," is DuBrow's frank reply.

"Holding up the bottle is a bit of shtick,'and yeah, it is pandering to the audience. But if I'm not there to pander to them, then what the hell do I get paid for? Pandering is part of my job. I'm a professional prostitute, and that, after all, is what all performers are: prostitutes."

It's this sort of candidness that has gotten the opinionated DuBrow into plenty of trouble. His controversial views on other bands—generally unfavorable—often have his fellow band members in fits, and have been known to create a feeling that is less than congenial among the competition. The long-running and accelerating feud between DuBrow and Motley Crue, for example, peaked at a hard-rock festival in Kalamazoo, Michigan, on May 27, 1984. During Quiet Riot's set, Crue drummer Tommy Lee attempted to provoke an incident by skulking onstage, which is strictly forbidden, and making faces. When DuBrow's bodyguard demanded that Lee leave, he stormed off the stage and broke a whisky bottle on a trailer. Quiet Riot finished its set, then the quartet was herded into cars, "just like the Beatles," DuBrow cracked. "I thought it was pretty cool."

Motley Crue bandleader Nikki Sixx, however, failed to see any humor. "It was very serious," he said shortly after the Michigan show. Sixx's general attitude toward criticism—including DuBrow's—is "I take my band very seriously, and I'll cut your throat to defend it." Later in the summer, a form of détente had been reached, and the incident was, if not forgotten, then at least minimized.

Even DuBrow's personal manager—his mother,

Following pages: Def Leppard (175)—Rick Allen, Phil Collen, Rick Savage, Steve Clark, and Joe Elliott—is not only one of metal's youngest bands, but one of the few cute enough to appeal to the girls. Here Elliott and Collen at London's Hammersmith Odeon (176-177). ⊂≣ Randy Rhoads (178) was metal's brightest and most acclaimed guitarist to emerge since Eddie Van Halen. An original member of Quiet Riot, he was on tour with Ozzy Osbourne when he died at age twenty-five in 1982. At the time, another Riot alumnus, Rudy Sarzo, was in the Blizzard of Ozz, but returned to Quiet Riot in time for its big break in 1983 (179). Left to right: Sarzo, Carlos Cavazo, Kevin DuBrow, and Frankie Banali. ⊂≣ Right on their heels came fellow Los Angelenos Motley Crue, perhaps the most outrageous and offensive metal band ever. Leader/founder/guitarist Nikki Sixx (180) still maintains that the violent world view he expresses in the Crue's music is not only realistic but therapeutic. Onstage, Sixx and lead singer Vince Neil (180-181), and posing (182): Sixx, Tommy Lee, Mick Mars, and Neil.

a former L.A. realtor who supervises her son's onstage wardrobe—finds his statements sometimes out of line. "She rags me for the same things as everybody else—for slagging other people in the press, for my attitude with women, screwing everything that walks," but he acknowledges, "she is probably the major force that has kept me going."

Two months after the Kalamazoo show, Quiet Riot released its second album, *Condition Critical*, and as promised, it varied not a trace from the direction set by *Metal Health*. Unlike many bands that are left breathless by a surprise smash debut album and find themselves unable to plot their next move, Quiet Riot knew exactly what to do.

Recording *Condition Critical* was no less pressure-filled than *Metal Health*. When he first began laying down the vocal tracks, DuBrow initially feared that he had lost his voice for good. Clearly the financial rewards of the first album had not made recording the second any easier. While DuBrow claimed to find the songwriting a little harder, Quiet Riot consciously resisted the temptation to cruise. Even though their earnings from the debut had made each wealthy enough to retire, they had to play and think hungry. "Everything we'd done in 1983," DuBrow said, "all the accomplishments, we had to pretend that they didn't exist."

Quiet Riot eluded the sophomore jinx, and *Condition Critical* blasted off quickly, hitting #15 in just three weeks and going platinum soon after. But it lacked its predecessor's tenacity, beginning its descent after just five weeks. For one thing, it signified little or no progression from *Metal Health*. The debut contained "Cum On Feel the Noize," and so *Condition Critical* had "Mama Weer All Crazee Now," given a flat, slowed-down treatment that lacked the firepower of both Slade's original and Quiet Riot's first Slade cover.

In general, the band seemed to be aiming its songs too carefully—too many attempts at anthems ("Party All Night," "Stomp Your Hands, Clap Your Feet," its title taken from a Slade LP, and "Scream and Shout") that came off sounding more patronizing than rallying. Perhaps the "street-sense radar" that DuBrow bragged the band possessed in abundance on "Sign of the Times" had gone awry.

The best songs here rely on more personal subjects, applying to the band's underdog-to-overdog journey, while still remaining general enough not to be taken for conceit. On "Winners Take All," Quiet Riot addresses the dangers inherent to stardom, or any kind of success, by stressing the importance of retaining one's principles. And the chorus is apparently intended to apply to the band's fans as much as the four members themselves: "Together we stand / We won't take no fall / 'Cause we're winners / And winners take all."

Will Quiet Riot be in for a future shock? How long can a band that "doesn't write hit singles" exist in a market that is more 45-conscious than at any time since the Sixties? Its having to go outside its own repertoire for hit material already does not sit too well with critics; if that pattern were to continue, would fans follow suit and lose interest?

Though many of heavy metal's third-generation bands endured an arduous struggle before breaking commercially, they still often seem unprepared once they reach the top. It is possible that along with the return to shorter songs, there is also a return to shorter group lifespans, as fan loyalties wane more quickly, perhaps the result of the glut of bands whose leathery images are paraded past their eyes on rock-video channels every day. Quiet Riot was nearly hailed as the new Zeppelin around the time of *Metal Health*'s one-week reign at Number One. Does this mean the time is right for a new Quiet Riot?

Kevin DuBrow does not think so, and in fact states confidently that Quiet Riot's most creative accomplishments are yet to come, in the next four or five years. But the group's place in rock & roll history, he contends, was established with the very first American album.

"We proved that you can be silly in a very intelligent way. I don't think you have to be a moron to play heavy metal."

MOTLEY CRUE

A NAME TO LIVE UP TO

EVEN in a milieu overrun with self-proclaimed bad boys, Motley Crue can offend. Dressed in tattered clothes that look as though they'd been fed into a paper shredder, their faces flecked with war paint, and playing against a $100,000 stage set of a crumbling city, looking like it had been lifted from the film *Escape from New York*, the members of Motley Crue scream out lyrics that teem with explicit sexuality, uncamouflaged misogyny, and venal hate. In short, they are scary as hell.

Motley Crue apparently feels that it has a name to live up to, and it does. Even many music-business types hardened by years of working in what must be the most lucrative asylum in the Western World find the band too much to take. Love them or hate them, one cannot deny that Motley Crue embodies several quintessential heavy-metal characteristics, starting with their unrepressed sense of outrage. That they elicit

such vitriolic reactions from anyone past his teens seems to delight the band members, who even made sure that their official bio—the public-relations tool that most performers use to gloss over any personal facts that are less than laudatory—contained such pearls as guitarist Mick Mars relating that he is "always horny, I need mucho chicks," or about how the band members all made sure to write their initials on a teenage groupie's bottom.

Motley Crue manages to appeal to its fans on several levels and for a wide range of reasons. To begin with, its music is standard heavy-metal fare, not that much unlike any of a number of third-generation groups. But it is the larger-than-life outlaw image, the Crue's total disregard for any conventions or rules, its seemingly unrestrained expression of power through violence and sex that plays very well in a musical form that already bases part of its appeal on the promise of

vicarious living. In Motley Crue's world, regardless of how tough things are, they—that is to say you—always come out on top. For kids whose power over their own lives is nil, Motley Crue provides the perfect answers: Stand tall, be tough, don't take any shit. It is an attitude whose appeal is not restricted to heavy metal, and in a society where the survivor is the hero, the key to Motley Crue's success is anything but a mystery.

On a more conventional front, Motley Crue glorifies youth and the sort of live-fast, die-young philosophy that has fascinated teens since the days of James Dean. And at least in the case of bandleader/bassist Nikki Sixx, who writes the band's visceral lyrics and most of its music, his intensely misanthropic viewpoint seems to spring from his own experiences.

Sixx is an imposing character—cock-of-the-walk tough, with jet-black hair that bursts out from his head at crazy angles. Judging from his

writing, you expect him to swing from the ceiling lights while tearing meat from the bones of a nubile female admirer and, at very best, grunt in monosyllabic responses. That he is well-spoken and deadly serious about this band is surprising, not to mention a little disconcerting.

Sixx was born in San Jose, California, but his family lived in several locales before settling in Seattle. According to his bio, he was born in 1959, and Nikki Sixx is his real name.

"I was a rowdy kid," says Sixx, whose early remembrances of his youth include the time he stole his first guitar: "I went into a store in Seattle and asked for an application for work. I had an

Even in a milieu overrun with self-proclaimed bad boys, Motley Crue can offend, with songs that teem with explicit sexuality, misogyny, and violence.

Overleaf: Motley Crue—Nikki Sixx, Vince Neil, Mick Mars, and Tommy Lee (not shown)—came together in January 1981 and recorded their first single that year.

empty guitar case I'd borrowed from my friend. And when the guy at the counter turned around to get me an application, I put a Les Paul in the case, closed it up, accepted the application, and," he says, cackling, "my music career started."

At fifteen he left Seattle for Los Angeles, where a relative had arranged for him to work in, of all places, a music store. L.A.'s streets became Sixx's home. He worked during the day and rehearsed at night with one of many bands that he put together quickly and that would crumble just as quickly. The last song from *Shout at the Devil*, "Danger," ostensibly autobiographical, describes this period of shattered rock & roll dreams: "All my best friends died. . . . It made me hate, I can't escape."

Though he claims he would probably be in jail were it not for Motley Crue, it is possible that Sixx might have ended up a writer. As repugnant as some of his lyrics are—full of graphic depictions of the seamier side of street life, with its random, mindless violence—they are powerful, highly intelligible, and technically well constructed. Sixx just might be rock & roll's answer to Jack Henry Abbott, the convicted murderer who wrote so chillingly of the harsh realities of prison life in his book *In the Belly of the Beast*. Sixx's lyrics inspire a reaction similar to that of reading Abbott's frightening work. While on the one hand the book's subject is sickeningly violent, the fact that it is related so casually is, whether most people admit it or not, fascinating. And so it satisfies that curiosity we have about that *Clockwork Orange*-esque dark side of life, where there are no laws and power changes hands from moment to moment.

In early 1981, Sixx finally found a band that would prove to be the exception to his previous, unstable units. He had been playing the L.A. club circuit with a pop-oriented group called London, just to keep musically active. Drummer Tommy Lee, then seventeen, was a native of Athens, Greece, who had moved to Southern California with his family when he was four, and was playing for another area act, Suite 19. He and Sixx left their respective bands to work together, and, after placing ads in a local music paper, came across scowling lead guitarist Mick Mars. Now a trio, they still needed a lead singer. One night Mars was prowling the local bars and saw blond-haired Hollywood native Vincent Neil Wharton, then with the band Rock Candy and using the stage name Vince Neil. Neil, in fact, knew Tommy Lee; they'd cut class together at Royal Oaks High. He joined Motley Crue on January 17, 1981.

Two weeks after they formed, Motley Crue played their first show, opening for the Oakland hard-rock group Y&T at L.A.'s Starwood. From there, the group's local popularity, buoyed by the reemergence of hard rock in the local club scene, expanded quickly, to the point where the band was the city's prime attraction just months after its inception. In June, Crue issued one thousand copies of a single, "Stick to Your Guns" b/w "The Toast of the Town," and then decided to record an album, *Too Fast for Love*, on its own Leathur Records label.

> **"If people want to think life is all peaches and cream, then they're just fooling themselves, because it's rough out there, man, and you've gotta survive."**
> **—Nikki Sixx**

The self-produced LP is overly frantic, with tinny-sounding drums and guitars and overly complex arrangements. Neil was an ineffectual singer at this point, monovoiced and without a convincing scream, who borrowed from every previous metal singer's bag of tricks. *Too Fast for Love* does succeed, however, in getting across the band's message, beginning with the cover alone: a close-up shot of Vince Neil's crotch, apparently shoe-horned into leather pants held up with several studded belts, one with handcuffs attached.

And on the back cover, individual shots of the four: Neil striking a sultry, smirking pose; Mars holding his guitar as if it were an ax about to plunge downward, perfecting his best sneer; pursed-lipped Tommy Lee, arms defiantly folded in front of his chest; and Nikki Sixx, decadent, deranged. All wear the type of stack-heeled boots that were in vogue during early-Seventies glam-rock, a movement with which Motley Crue feels more kinship than with the heavy-metal bands of the same period. The Crue definitely evoke that period's ambisexuality, with their makeup and lipstick, yet flaunt their masculinity, as if the white foundation, triangular "cheekbones," black mascara, and bizarre coloration is a mask, just dangerous camouflage. It is a tricky line to maneuver, considering hard-rock fans' revulsion at anything that hints at gender-crossing, but this band walks it like a tightrope.

"I draw more from the punkish attitude of the glitter era," contends Sixx, who cites Sweet, David Bowie, Slade, and Mott the Hoople's Ian Hunter as his favorites from that period. The two most obvious inspirations, at least in terms of image, were Alice Cooper—for his macabre combination of ambisexuality and Vincent Price ghoulishness—and Kiss, whose members were never seen in public without their greasepaint for the first ten years of their career.

But for fourteen- and fifteen-year-olds just taking their first steps on rock & roll's wilder side, the above names mean very little, and by this time, Alice Cooper had long since abandoned the ghoul routine, and Kiss had removed the makeup. Rather than feel exploited by the Motleys, who in fact opened several West Coast shows on Kiss's 1983 American tour, founders Gene Simmons and Paul Stanley have been supportive of Motley Crue. "I think they're good," says the latter. "If people like them, more power to 'em."

The strong sales of *Too Fast for Love*—35,000— and such raves as this one from the English music paper *Sounds*: "one of the most spectacular debut

**"If kids come down to see us and get their aggressions out,"
claims Sixx (left), "they leave drained, rather than getting
into fights, robbing, or overdosing on drugs."**

albums you'll ever hear," forced the major labels to consider Motley Crue, no matter how much they might have disliked the band and what it stood for. Elektra/Asylum signed Motley Crue and rereleased *Too Fast for Love*, remixed by producer Roy Thomas Baker.

No one is more aware of the corporate hypocrisy than Nikki Sixx himself, and it only serves to reinforce his negative attitude toward the conventional society he began shunning ten years ago.

"The record companies don't know what the fuck they're doing," he spits. "They sit behind their oak desks with their red-haired secretaries, snorting lines and taking Quaaludes and trying to dictate what the music industry's all about. I don't like them, because they're all brown-nosers, and I don't like that type of person at all. If you don't like me, tell me."

Many reviewers have, focusing again and again on Motley Crue's lyrics. Other heavy-metal writers hint at violence, but Motley Crue brings you into the thick of the fight, like a Sam Peckinpah movie. It is not just the graphic detail in which the

A believer in his band's "live fast" philosophy, Vince Neil was charged with manslaughter and drunk driving in the death of rock drummer Nicholas Dingley.

violence is described, but the fact that it is relentless, in song after song. Motley Crue differs greatly from other metal bands in that its violence is not reality at all, and it is what puts it beyond the pale. The message *is* one to cause concern. On *Too Fast for Love*'s opening track, "Live Wire," Sixx issues this threat: "I'll either break her face or take down her legs / Get my ways at will." And on *Devil*'s "Too Young to Fall in Love": "Well, now I'm killing you / Watch your face turning blue." You only hurt the one you love? With Motley Crue, you maim them.

"Come On and Dance," despite its seemingly innocuous title, has as its heroine a girl, "a leather tease . . . watch her suck you clean." Sixx defends songs such as this and "Looks That Kill," about a woman with similarly exceptional sexual powers, as complimentary—an unusual turnaround in the typically misogynistic view that sex always equals power *over* women. Here women, though still victims, can share in—and sometimes wield—that power.

Violence is not restricted to women alone. "Bastard," from *Shout at the Devil*, graphically depicts murder with more blood and gore than a Brian De Palma film. "Ten Seconds to Love" is about quickie sex in an elevator: "Touch my gun but don't pull my trigger," Neil warns. Kiss had already covered similar territory on 1977's "Love Gun," and Led Zeppelin called it a lemon back on "The Lemon Song," but then, a metaphor's a metaphor.

If you find his themes distasteful, argues Sixx, it is only because they are real. "If people want to think life is all peaches and cream, then they're just fooling themselves, because it's rough out there, man, and you've gotta survive." As for the stream of criticism regarding his negativity, he says, "Is it negative? I'm simply a mirror."

If so, the images he reflects are not pretty, and possibly not healthy for the band's mostly young, highly impressionable audience. Though rock & roll has always been about rebellion—and its stars have often been cast as outlaws, much like the Motleys—at its best, rock & roll has tried to channel that spirit into something constructive.

Motley Crue's world view, on the other hand, seems just plain hateful.

Nikki Sixx's defense is one typical of heavy metal—that his band and his music provide fans with a release. "If kids come down to see us and get out their aggressions and anxieties, they leave drained, rather than going out and getting into fights, or robbing, or overdosing on drugs. We'd rather have 'em at a Motley Crue concert." He flashes a demure smile. "Hey, *we're* the good guys."

Not everyone agrees. Because of their general appearance and plumes of hair, the group has been the target of harassment while on the road. "We always get these guys coming up and saying [mock drawl], 'Y'all look lahk mah sister,'" relates Neil. "We all have reputations in this band. There's a black cloud following us all the time."

**"Sometimes I don't feel we get enough musical credit. I don't think people take us seriously."
—Nikki Sixx**

By his own admission, however, Motley Crue is frequently to blame for its "bad luck." For example, one Halloween Neil was tossed in jail for allegedly punching a woman in L.A.'s Rainbow club; the band was banned from a hotel in Vancouver, Canada, even before arriving there, because word had spread of an incident in Edmonton in which the group wrecked its room at a hotel there, tossing a TV set out of the window. "They'd also heard that we'd been molesting young girls," adds Nikki Sixx, who had his own run-in with the L.A. police, in which he accidentally bashed a cop in the face with some chains during a brawl (chronicled in the song "Knock 'Em Dead, Kid" from *Shout at the Devil*).

And on December 8, 1984, Neil was charged with manslaughter and drunk driving in the death of Nicholas Dingley, a.k.a. Razzle, drummer for the Finnish band Hanoi Rocks. Neil lost control of his 1972 Pantera sports car, in which Dingley was a passenger, on a road in Redondo Beach, California. Neil's car also struck two other autos.

With the release of *Shout* in late 1983, still more controversy was raised because of the LP's suggestive title and the pentagram, a symbol that is often linked to the occult, on its cover. Sixx, who admits he has a fleeting interest in witchcraft, explains that *Shout at the Devil* merely means to defy your own personal devils. And that Mick Mars's instrumental composition "God Bless the Children of the Beast" is not in praise of Satan's followers, but a vote of sympathy and support for those having to live in an evil world with such evil *human* characters.

That may be true, but is Motley Crue's audience able to make these distinctions? How able is their audience *not* to accept the most obvious, superficial interpretation and to analyze the songs in detail? One of the negative trends of mid-Eighties metal has been the number of bands that appear to be doing little more than exploiting the controversial Satanic angle and, with it, the gullibility of their audience. There are other factors in Motley Crue's history that would make one question the sincerity of Sixx's rationalization regarding *Shout at the Devil*. If the band is so intent on spouting "the truth," why then does it indulge in the same music-biz marketing notions of creating a mystique?

"The focus should be musical, not that we're some degenerates. People write all about our tattoos, and we think, 'Great, what's that got to do with a song called "Too Young to Fall in Love"?'"
—Nikki Sixx

Nikki Sixx himself would later have some reservations about the emphasis placed on Motley Crue's image. By mid-1984, following *Shout at*

the Devil's platinum success and a hugely successful January-through-April tour opening for Ozzy Osbourne, the band seemed confident enough to begin to start downplaying the wild side it had emphasized in the beginning.

"Sometimes I don't feel we get enough musical credit," Sixx griped on the eve of a two-month European tour. "I don't think people take us seriously." Certainly the hard-rock press (no publication except the metal-mag glossies would even touch the band) did not, though it of course realized the implications of having the band grace its pages and frequently its covers. One particularly vile published story centered on the group's sexual practices involving women and wine bottles, and led to the magazine in question being pulled from a major foodstore chain's racks.

The whole irony of that, and how it somewhat backfired on Motley Crue, is that *Shout at the Devil* was, musically, a very creditable LP, this time with very strong production from Tom Werman. In the time between it and *Too Fast for Love*, Vince Neil had found a voice, suddenly all roughed up and intentionally grating, able to sing entire verses in a near-falsetto but viciously, as on "Looks That Kill," which was made into the album's first video. (Motley Crue's very first video, for "Live Wire," was rejected by MTV as being too violent and allegedly having Satanic overtones.)

The group as a whole seemed to find its sound, and "Looks" may be Motley Crue at its wicked best, with guitars that sound like electric razors, backed by a steady, driving rhythm. The LP's weakest moment is the cover version of the Beatles' "Helter Skelter." Though thematically the song should fit right into the group's gestalt, Vince Neil cannot match Paul McCartney's original maniacal, larynx-ripping vocal, and in all, the song —which mass murderer Charles Manson misinterpreted as some sort of prophecy—comes off surprisingly tame, though it remains an inspired choice.

This is not the type of musical analysis the band generally receives. Motley Crue's virulent image is what gets reported first, "and perhaps a

little bit too much," according to Sixx. "We never wanted to popularize that," he claims, "but the more popular we got, the more interviews we did, and I guess it just kind of slipped out. Because the focus should be musical, not that we're some degenerates. People write all about our tattoos, and we think, 'Great, what's that got to do with a song called "Too Young to Fall in Love"?' "

Judging from Sixx's words, the band is about to start to stress its musicality; by late 1984 it was refraining from interviews for fear of overexposure. But one has to wonder about Motley Crue's future: Will they find themselves doomed to self-destruction by their own "live-fast, die-fast" philosophy? These are the words of Sixx, who once plowed his Porsche into a wall at seventy miles an hour and then emerged from the wreck laughing. Will these outlaws one day find themselves in a shootout they can't possibly hope to win? Sixx and the rest of Motley Crue know that one day they're going to find out.

Looking almost angelic out of makeup are Tommy Lee, Neil, Sixx, and Mars. Their second release, *Shout at the Devil*, went platinum in 1984.

Chronology

Discography

Index

Credits

❧❧❧

Chronology

APRIL 28, 1958

Guitarist Link Wray's million-selling instrumental single "Rumble" debuts on the American chart. By the time it peaks at #16, the record will have earned much notoriety. *American Bandstand* host Dick Clark will introduce Wray and his record without ever actually saying the title because some people believe that the song—which was inspired by a dance-hall brawl—will provoke further acts of teenage violence. Wray's contribution to heavy metal's prehistory lies in the grooves: the deliberate creation of a fuzzy, growly guitar sound, which he achieved by piercing his guitar amplifier's speaker with a pencil. Though the song hit in 1958, Wray recorded it in 1954.

AUGUST 17, 1964

The Kinks' first British Number One single, "You Really Got Me," is released by Pye Records. The disc, which features group cofounder and lead guitarist Dave Davies's brash power-chord work and Link Wray—inspired amplifier mutilated distortion, will peak on the American chart at #7 in November. "You Really Got Me" will also be the very first hit single for Van Halen fourteen years later.

SEPTEMBER 23, 1966

The Yardbirds—whose lineup now includes lead guitarists Jeff Beck and Jimmy Page—undertake a British tour with the Rolling Stones and Ike and Tina Turner. This much-heralded version of the British blues-rock band also includes singer Keith Relf, bassist Chris Dreja, and drummer Jim McCarty, and will last only until this November, at which time Beck will leave the group to start his solo career.

JUNE 16, 1967

The first Monterey Pop Festival opens. Over the next three days, the festival—produced by such music-business figures as Lou Adler and John Phillips of the Mamas and the Papas—will present Janis Joplin, the Who, and the American debut of the Jimi Hendrix Experience, who are introduced by Rolling Stone Brian Jones. With 50,000 people in attendance, Monterey is the era's first major rock & roll festival, and for that reason, the media soon focuses on the new "underground" music and on Joplin and Hendrix in particular. Their and other artists' performances—including Hendrix's guitar-burning climax—are captured in the D. A. Pennebaker movie *Monterey Pop*.

MARCH 9, 1968

Blue Cheer's first and biggest album, *Vincebus Eruptum*, debuts on the U.S. chart. It will eventually top at #11, largely on the strength of their hit single, an amazingly crude, loud, feedback-laced cover of Eddie Cochran's 1958 hit, "Summertime Blues."

JUNE *15, 1968*

Journey to the Center of the Mind, the Amboy Dukes' second album, enters the chart. The LP's title track, a pseudo-psychedelic invitation to mind expansion that features Motor City Madman Ted Nugent's shattering lead guitar solo, will be a Top Twenty hit later this year. In 1975, Nugent will leave the Dukes—whose career has already peaked at this early date—for multiplatinum success. The Nuge's obsession with survivalist credos, fondness for hunting and guns, and loincloth stage suit, not to mention his heavy-metal guitar chops, will make him front-cover news through the mid- to late Seventies, and one of rock & roll's most often quoted eccentrics.

JUNE *22, 1968*

The Jeff Beck Group, Beck's first post-Yardbirds venture, makes its American performance debut at the Fillmore East in New York City. The quartet—Beck, vocalist Rod Stewart, bassist Ron Wood, and drummer Mickey Waller—performs, though Stewart, who experiences an extreme case of stage fright, starts off singing from behind an amplifier. The Jeff Beck Group will record two critically acclaimed LPs, *Truth* (1968) and *Beck-Ola* (1969), before disbanding in 1970. Beck will form two more versions of the band before cofounding Beck, Bogert, and Appice in 1972. Meanwhile, Stewart and Wood will have joined the Small Faces.

JULY *7, 1968*

The Yardbirds break up. Guitarist Jimmy Page forms the New Yardbirds with Robert Plant, John Bonham, and John Paul Jones. Page, allegedly on the advice of the Who's Keith Moon, will rename his band Led Zeppelin.

JULY *20, 1968*

Iron Butterfly's *In-a-Gadda-da-Vida*, complete with its seventeen-minute title track and tedious drum solo, debuts on the American charts. Before the LP fades from the collective hard-rock consciousness, it will have sold seven million copies and its single—which was written by group leader/singer/organist Doug Ingle—will have sold three million 45s.

NOVEMBER *26, 1968*

Cream gives its farewell performance at Royal Albert Hall in London. The power trio—rock & roll's first bona fide "supergroup"—had phenomenal success, having sold over 15 million records in the two years since its debut, *Fresh Cream*. But clashing egos and sundry business problems led to the group's decision to disband. The concert is filmed for the feature-length documentary *Goodbye Cream*.

JANUARY *17, 1969*

Led Zeppelin's eponymously titled debut LP is released. By mid-February the album will make its U.S. chart debut and will break into the Top Ten. Like each of the band's subsequent albums, *Led Zeppelin* will receive instant popular acceptance but little positive critical response. From here on, Zeppelin will defy convention to create what is perhaps the definitive heavy-metal oeuvre.

MARCH *8, 1969*

The MC5's first release, *Kick Out the Jams*, enters the chart. The Detroit quintet weds the radical political philosophy of the White Panther Party with relentless hard rock. The album will peak at #30.

JUNE *29, 1969*

The Jimi Hendrix Experience plays its last concert in America at the Denver Pop Festival. Only two years after its impressive U.S. debut at the Monterey Pop Festival, the Experience—Hendrix, drummer Mitch Mitchell, and bassist Noel Redding—call it quits. Though Hendrix will continue working with other groups—the Electric Sky Church and the Band of Gypsys—neither will receive the Experience's acclaim.

SEPTEMBER *15, 1969*

Deep Purple performs Jon Lord's "Concerto for Group and Orchestra" with the Royal Philharmonic Orchestra at London's Royal Albert Hall. This merging of hard rock and classical influences sounds unlikely but was a popular concept during the period, which lauded experimentation. Like most of these adventures, this one too fails. In the wake of the resulting album's (named for the piece) lack of success, lead guitarist Ritchie Blackmore will begin to exert greater control over Deep Purple's direction. Subsequent LPs—*In Rock* (1970) and *Machine Head* (1972)—and Blackmore's trademark riff from "Smoke on the Water" (1973) will be deemed heavy-metal classics.

OCTOBER *11, 1969*

Grand Funk Railroad—soon to become the most commercially successful American metal band of the Seventies—makes its album chart debut with *On Time*. Rejected by critics but loved by millions of fans, the trio—Mark Farner, Mel Schacher, and Don Brewer—will become the prototypical "people's band" with record sales of over 20 million albums and a pair of Number One singles, "We're an American Band" (1973) and a cover of Little Eva's "The Loco-motion" (1974).

JULY 25, 1970

Five months after its formation, Cactus places its first album on the U.S. chart. *Cactus*, which peaks at #54, will prove their best-selling record. The quartet—Tim Bogert and Carmine Appice, late of Vanilla Fudge, Rusty Day, and Jim McCarty (not of the Yardbirds)—will record three more albums, none particularly successful. In addition, the line-up will shift until Bogert and Appice finally call it quits in 1972 and join Jeff Beck in Beck, Bogert, and Appice.

AUGUST 26, 1970

The Isle of Wight Festival opens in England. Among the stars performing for the quarter-million-strong crowd are Bob Dylan, Richie Havens, Joni Mitchell, Joan Baez, and Jimi Hendrix, in the last concert appearance of his life.

AUGUST 29, 1970

Black Sabbath's self-titled debut LP enters the U.S. chart, where it will peak at #23. The next three releases—*Paranoid*, *Master of Reality*, and *Volume 4*—will all crack the Top Twenty, making Black Sabbath one of the biggest-selling heavy-metal acts of the era.

SEPTEMBER 16, 1970

For the first time in seven years, the Beatles have been displaced from their position as England's top band. The new kings: Led Zeppelin.

SEPTEMBER 18, 1970

Jimi Hendrix dies in London after choking to death on his own vomit while under the influence of barbiturates. He was twenty-seven years of age. Despite some controversy regarding whether Hendrix's death was indeed accidental or, as some—most notably singer Eric Burdon—claim, a suicide, the coroner finds insufficient evidence to support the latter conclusion. Hendrix's body will be returned to his hometown of Seattle, Washington, for burial.

OCTOBER 3, 1970

Less than a year after its formation, the British hard-rock band Uriah Heep makes its U.S. chart debut with *Uriah Heep*. The quartet, named after a Charles Dickens character, will be moderately successful throughout the mid-Seventies, by which time personal and business problems will provoke sweeping personnel changes, a 1978 break-up, and a 1982 re-formation.

MAY 26, 1971

Nantucket Sleighride, Mountain's last hit LP, is certified gold. The quartet—Leslie West, Felix Pappalardi, Corky Laing, and Steve Knight—whose previous two releases attracted a wide audience, would begin a commercial decline with their next album, *Flowers of Evil*.

JUNE 5, 1971

Over 21,000 fans show up at the Shea Stadium box office in New York City to purchase tickets to see Grand Funk Railroad in concert. The show—which sells out in seventy-two hours and nets the group over $300,000—beats the Beatles' record for single-concert sales.

SEPTEMBER 11, 1971

Wishbone Ash, an English group that boasts one of the earliest dual-lead-guitar lineups in hard rock (Andy Powell and Ted Turner), makes its American chart debut with its second album, *Pilgrimage*.

FEBRUARY 23, 1972

Humble Pie's fourth LP, *Performance—Rockin' the Fillmore*—is certified gold. Led by ex–Small Face Steve Marriott, Humble Pie strikes it big with a bluesy boogie style captured here during a May 1971 show at New York City's Fillmore East. Also of note is the fact that this is founding member/lead guitarist Peter Frampton's last album with the group; he will pursue a phenomenally successful solo career. And drummer Jerry Shirley will resurface in 1983 as a member of Fastway.

MAY 6, 1972

ZZ Top's second album, *Rio Grande Mud*, enters the LP chart; it will eventually make an unimpressive showing at #104. Subsequent LPs will climb into the Top Forty, but the trio—Dusty Hill, Frank Beard, and Billy Gibbons—will find their greatest success over a decade from now when four videos from their 1983 album *Eliminator*—"Gimme All Your Lovin'," "Sharp Dressed Man," "TV Dinners," and "Legs"—are hits. Until then, ZZ Top amasses respectable album sales and concert grosses with constant touring and an uncompromised, lean hard-rock style.

JULY 10, 1972

Alice Cooper's fifth album, *School's Out*, is certified gold. The album's title track, a true rock/metal anthem, will peak at #7 and further solidify Cooper (born Vincent Furnier) as one of the fathers of metal, or at least metal's image. Cooper's hard-rock sound, however, is just part of the story. A stage act that includes live boa constrictors, macabre makeup, tattered costumes, a simulated decapitation, and the mutilation of dolls, will earn Cooper the title King of Shock Rock. Despite the hoopla, within three years Cooper's shtick will be deemed so unrevolutionary that he will star in a prime-time television special, *Alice Cooper—the Nightmare*, and have a hit ballad, "Only Women Bleed."

NOVEMBER 6, 1972

Deep Purple, named the loudest band in the world by *The Guinness Book of World Records*, receives a gold album for *Machine Head*.

MAY 12, 1973

Ex-Procol Harum lead guitarist Robin Trower's first LP enters the U.S. chart. It will reach #107, but greater success will come with next year's Top Ten hit, *Bridge of Sighs*. Trower's style, which is clearly influenced by Jimi Hendrix, finds favor in both the United States and his native England. In 1981, after a series of commercially successful solo releases, Trower will team up with ex-Cream bassist and singer Jack Bruce and drummer Bill Lordan to form BLT.

OCTOBER 13, 1973

Aerosmith's eponymously titled debut album enters the LP chart. Its showing—at #166—is less than impressive, but the group, fronted by singer Steve Tyler and guitarist Joe Perry, will emerge as one of the most successful and popular hard-rock acts in America. In 1976, a song from this album, "Dream On," will become a Top Ten hit, and Aerosmith will have received three platinum albums, one each for the debut, *Get Your Wings* (1974), and *Toys in the Attic* (1975).

MAY 11, 1974

Ex-session guitarist Ronnie Montrose's self-named band debuts with a self-named LP, *Montrose*. Montrose, who had played with Van Morrison, Boz Scaggs, and others, will lead this California-based quartet through two albums before lead singer Sammy Hagar departs for a solo career. By 1978, the two other original Montrosites—Bill Church and Denny Carmassi—will have joined the Red Rocker.

AUGUST 24, 1974

Child of the Novelty, Mahagony Rush's second LP, becomes its first to hit the charts. It will scrape into the Top Seventy and, like all of the group's later releases, fail to be a substantial hit. But its music is not necessarily what makes Mahagony Rush interesting. Though accounts differ on the details, group founder Frank Marino—who had never played an instrument in his life—claims that he awoke in the hospital after an accident, picked up a guitar, and discovered he could play just like Jimi Hendrix. Marino's explanation: he had been visited by the spirit of Hendrix.

SEPTEMBER 28, 1974

Barely six months after making their performance debut in Newcastle, England, Bad Company has a Number One album, *Bad Company*. The album's hit single, "Can't Get Enough," which features the hard-rock vocals of ex-Free member Paul Rodgers, will hit #5 next month. Bad Company will enjoy solid commercial success throughout its career. In 1984, Rodgers will team with Jimmy Page to form the Firm.

MARCH 29, 1975

For the first time in history, one group has six albums on the chart at once. The group is Led Zeppelin, and the albums are *Physical Graffiti* (Number One), *Led Zeppelin IV*, *Houses of the Holy*, *Led Zeppelin II*, *Led Zeppelin*, and *Led Zeppelin III*.

APRIL 7, 1975

Deep Purple lead guitarist Ritchie Blackmore plays his last concert with the group, at the Paris Olympia Theatre, before leaving for a solo career.

AUGUST 9, 1975

British heavy-metal veterans UFO make their first appearance on the American chart with their fifth LP, *Force It*. The group, which despite being in its sixth lineup since its formation in 1969, still contains three founding members—Pete Way, Phil Mogg, and Andy Parker—and since June 1973 includes ex-Scorpions lead guitarist Michael Schenker.

SEPTEMBER 6, 1975

Ritchie Blackmore's group Rainbow debuts on the American album chart with their first, an eponymously titled release. The group, which Blackmore founded earlier this year, will go through countless personnel changes—and at points include vocalists Ronnie James Dio, Graham Bonnet, and Joe Lynn Turner, drummers Cozy Powell and Bobby Rondinelli, bassists Jimmy Bain and Roger Glover, and numerous keyboardists—before Blackmore disbands it to rejoin Deep Purple in 1984. In 1982 Rainbow—with Turner—will have its biggest hit single, "Stone Cold."

DECEMBER 20, 1975

Angel's self-titled debut album enters the chart. The quintet—whose blown-dry shags, all-white and tight wardrobe, and laser-and-fog-ridden stage show, were designed to appeal to the teenybopper metalheads—becomes the source of much fun. The group's plastic "pod" stage entrance will turn up in the parody film *This Is Spinal Tap* and even Frank Zappa will satirize lead singer Punky Meadows in his song "Punky's Whips." Despite aggressive promotion, Angel will never achieve the grand success of their Casablanca Records stablemates Kiss. After four more albums, the group will disband. Keyboardist Greg Giuffria will reemerge in 1984 with his band Giuffria.

MARCH *19, 1976*

Paul Kossoff, former lead guitarist of Free and founder of Back Street Crawler, dies of a heart ailment on an airplane en route from London to New York. Kossoff had left Free in 1972 and formed his own Back Street Crawler (later known as Crawler) with whom he recorded *The Band Plays On* and *Second Street*. The group will record two more LPs under the Crawler name before disbanding. Kossoff was twenty-five years old.

APRIL *8, 1976*

The Scottish quartet Nazareth receives a gold single for its Top Ten cover of the old Everly Brothers hit, "Love Hurts." The single is notable for being one of several incongruous cover versions Nazareth will essay during its long career. Others include Joni Mitchell's "This Flight Tonight" and Bob Dylan's "The Ballad of Hollis Brown."

APRIL *17, 1976*

Irish hard-rockers Thin Lizzy make their first U.S. chart appearance with their sixth release, *Jailbreak*. Led by black Irishman singer/bassist Phil Lynott, the group, which was formed around 1970, will continue through numerous changes. *Jailbreak*, which features the hit single "The Boys Are Back in Town," will be Lizzy's biggest claim to fame stateside. Thin Lizzy is another of the few groups of this era to feature two lead guitarists; in this case, Scott Gorham and Snowy White.

MAY *14, 1976*

Keith Relf, former lead singer and cofounder of the Yardbirds, dies after being electrocuted in his London home. He was thirty-three.

DECEMBER *4, 1976*

Former Deep Purple lead guitarist Tommy Bolin dies in a Miami hotel room of a multiple drug overdose at age twenty-five. Bolin had replaced Ritchie Blackmore and appears on *Come Taste the Band* (1976), *Last Concert in Japan* (1977), and *When We Rock We Rock* (1978). Before joining Deep Purple, Bolin had been a member of Zephyr and the James Gang, and had recorded a pair of solo albums, *Teaser* (1975) and *Private Eye* (1976).

JUNE *17, 1977*

UFO lead guitarist Michael Schenker disappears after a show in Leeds, England. Schenker will resurface in his native West Germany six months later and return to UFO, with whom he will continue to work until 1978, when he will briefly rejoin his brother Rudy's band, Scorpions.

JUNE *30, 1977*

Marvel Comics, publisher of Spider Man and other superhero comic books, publishes the first of two comic books starring the masked marauders of Kiss. The red ink allegedly contains a small bit of real blood from the group members.

AUGUST *13, 1977*

AC/DC makes its U.S. chart debut with *Let There Be Rock*, its second release. This time out, AC/DC will top out at #154, but in two more years it will fully consolidate its stateside following with *Highway to Hell*.

FEBRUARY *23, 1978*

Whitesnake—David Coverdale, Bernie Marsden, Pete Solley, Mick Moody, Neil Murray, and David Dowle—play their first show at the Sky Bird Club in Nottingham, England.

MARCH *11, 1978*

Van Halen's self-titled debut album enters the chart, where it will remain for fifty-four weeks, peaking at #19. Over the next six years, this album, which contains the group's hit cover of the Kinks' "You Really Got Me," will sell five million copies. Within two months, it will be certified gold.

APRIL *8, 1978*

Judas Priest's fourth LP, *Stained Class*, becomes its first to chart in the United States. In its three brief weeks in the Top 200, the album will reach only #173.

SEPTEMBER *7, 1978*

Keith Moon, drummer for the Who, dies after overdosing on Heminevrin, a drug prescribed to help alleviate symptoms of alcohol withdrawl. Moon, who was thirty-one, died in his London apartment.

OCTOBER *10, 1978*

Aerosmith singer Steve Tyler and guitarist Joe Perry are injured in Philadelphia after a fan tosses a cherry bomb onto the stage. Thereafter the band will perform from behind a cyclone fence that is erected before each show.

MARCH *16, 1979*

Four years before they will be signed to a U.S. record deal, longtime local favorite Twisted Sister becomes the first unsigned band to headline at New York City's 3,000-seat Palladium.

MAY *5, 1979*

Canadian trio Triumph hits the U.S. chart with its second album, *Just a Game*. The group, Mike Levine, Gil Moore, and Rik Emmett, formed in 1975.

SEPTEMBER *7, 1979*

In through the Out Door, Led Zeppelin's last studio album, enters the English album chart at Number One. Next week, the LP will begin a seven-week run at Number One on the American chart as well.

FEBRUARY *19, 1980*

Bon Scott, lead singer of the Australian heavy-metal band AC/DC, dies in London after choking to death on his own vomit following a night of drinking. He was thirty-four.

APRIL *19, 1980*

It is announced by AC/DC that Brian Johnson, former lead singer for the group Geordie, will replace the late Bon Scott.

MAY *3, 1980*

Def Leppard makes its American debut with *On through the Night*. The LP—which in England was preceded by their highly successful, independently produced EP *Getcha Rocks Off*—will peak at #51 and win the young quintet instant acclaim.

SEPTEMBER *25, 1980*

Led Zeppelin drummer John Bonham dies in Jimmy Page's home after choking to death on his own vomit. Bonham, who knew Robert Plant from their days together in the Birmingham, England, group, the Band of Joy, joined the New Yardbirds in 1968. Bonham was thirty-two.

OCTOBER *13, 1980*

Back in Black, AC/DC's first album with Brian Johnson, is certified platinum. It will eventually hit #4 and be one of the group's most popular releases.

DECEMBER *4, 1980*

Jimmy Page, Robert Plant, and John Paul Jones officially announce that they will not re-form Led Zeppelin or replace the late John Bonham.

DECEMBER *26, 1981*

AC/DC have the Number One album in the United States: *For Those about to Rock We Salute You.*

JANUARY *20, 1982*

Ozzy Osbourne inadvertently chews the head off of a live bat a fan has tossed to him during a performance. Osbourne, who by now has become notorious for his tasteless publicity stunts, pleads ignorance. He says that he truly believed that the bat was plastic. At the end of the show, Ozzy is rushed to a Des Moines hospital to begin receiving a series of unpleasant rabies and tetanus shots.

MARCH *19, 1982*

Twenty-five-year-old lead guitarist Randy Rhoads dies in Leesburg, Florida, after the small plane in which he is riding crashes into a house. Rhoads, an original member of Quiet Riot, is on tour with Ozzy Osbourne's Blizzard of Ozz.

APRIL *17, 1982*

Iron Maiden's *The Number of the Beast* debuts on the U.K. chart at Number One. This, their fourth release, will prompt a new wave of anti-Satanist backlash. The number of the beast refers to the mark of Satan, the numerals 666.

MAY *22, 1982*

British heavy-metal trio Motorhead makes a belated debut on the U.S. chart with *Iron Fist*. Though the album will peak at #174, the group—founded and led by Lemmy Kilminster—will find a core of devoted fans.

The all-female British heavy-metal quartet Girlschool makes its U.S. chart debut with its second LP, *Hit and Run*. In its original form, the album had hit the Top Five in England. But the American version (which also includes tracks from the debut album, *Demolition*) fails to break into the Top 100.

FEBRUARY *12, 1983*

Ozzy Osbourne is forced to cancel a concert at the Catholic Youth Center in Scranton, Pennsylvania, because the center's director, the Reverend Richard Czachor, objects to what he calls Osbourne's "Satanical worship, desecration of a monument [a reference to Ozzy's urinating at the Alamo] and cruelty to animals."

APRIL *17, 1983*

Felix Pappalardi dies in New York City after his wife, Gail Collins, shoots him. He was forty-three years old. In the fall, Collins, who cowrote several songs with her husband, will be convicted of criminally negligent homicide.

MAY 28, 1983

Fastway's eponymously titled debut album enters the U.S. chart; it will peak at #31. The group, which includes guitarist Fast Eddie Clarke (formerly of Motorhead) and drummer Jerry Shirley (of Humble Pie), features the driving single "Say You Will," a blues-rock hit in the vein of Humble Pie's mid-Seventies records.

MAY 29, 1983

Heavy Metal Day at the US Festival in San Bernardino, California, features performances by Quiet Riot, Motley Crue, Ozzy Osbourne, Judas Priest, Scorpions, Triumph, and headliners Van Halen.

SEPTEMBER 10, 1983

Y&T, a Bay Area heavy-metal band that has been around since 1974, makes its chart debut with its fifth album, *Mean Streak*. Over the next few weeks, it will just graze the Top 100, stalling at #103.

SEPTEMBER 18, 1983

Kiss appear in public for the first time in their decade-long career without their makeup. The unveiling takes place on MTV, receives much publicity, and regenerates some interest in a band whose star has been on the wane. Says cofounder Paul Stanley, "Taking off the makeup doesn't change the way we feel." Nor does it change much of anything else about the group. Next month *Lick It Up* will debut on the charts, and in 1984 the group will return to platinum with *Animalize*, full of the kind of stomp-and-shout paeans to sex Kiss launched its career with ten years ago. Of the quartet, only two—Stanley and bassist Gene Simmons—are original members.

NOVEMBER 26, 1983

Quiet Riot's *Metal Health* hits Number One. Though the group's American debut will hold the top position for only a week, the showing still gives Quiet Riot the distinction of having the highest-charting heavy-metal debut in history.

DECEMBER 27, 1983

Van Halen releases "Jump" from their sixth LP, *1984*. The song will become the band's first Number One single.

APRIL 30, 1984

Scorpions' *Love at First Sting* becomes the group's first album to be certified platinum. The original cover—a Helmut Newton photograph of a man tattooing a woman—will be replaced by a picture of the band.

JULY 16, 1984

Lead guitarist Yngwie (Ing-vay) Malmsteen leaves Alcatrazz, a group formed by ex-Rainbow vocalist Graham Bonnet, to found his own band, Rising Sun. Malmsteen, who is widely regarded as one of the most promising young guitarists, will be replaced by Steve Vai, an alumnus of Frank Zappa's band.

AUGUST 6, 1984

Ratt's *Out of the Cellar* is certified platinum. This Los Angeles–based quintet features a dual-guitar lineup—Warren DeMartini (who had earlier replaced Jake E. Lee) and Robbin Crosby—and broke onto MTV with "Round and Round," a clip that costarred their manager's uncle, comedian Milton Berle.

AUGUST 9, 1984

Iron Maiden begins its tour behind the Iron Curtain. The group's show in Poland is filmed for release as a home video that will be premiered on MTV later this year.

SEPTEMBER 12, 1984

Holy Diver (1983) and *The Last in Line* (1984), Ronnie James Dio's first solo albums since he left Black Sabbath in 1982, are certified gold.

OCTOBER 3, 1984

Stay Hungry, Twisted Sister's second U.S. LP, is certified platinum. With the help of rock video, this decade-old New York–based club band gets a new lease on life.

DECEMBER 9, 1984

Motley Crue lead singer Vince Neil is booked on a charge of manslaughter after the car he was driving collides with another auto, leaving three people injured and Neil's passenger, Nicholas Dingley, a.k.a. Razzle, the drummer for the Finnish hard-rock band Hanoi Rocks, dead. The accident, which occurred near Neil's hometown of Redondo Beach, California, makes headlines all over the country.

DECEMBER 31, 1984

Rick Allen, on vacation from the recording of Def Leppard's fourth album, loses his left arm in an auto accident in Sheffield, England. The arm is reattached during ten hours of surgery and there is initially hope that it will be saved. However, when surgeons operate several days later, they discover massive infection, and the arm is amputated. Allen is twenty-one years old.

Discography
⫸⫸⫸

BLACK SABBATH

1970 *Black Sabbath* **(Warner Bros.)**
SIDE ONE: "Black Sabbath," "The Wizard," "Wasp," "Behind the Wall of Sleep," "Bassically," "N.I.B."
SIDE TWO: "Wicked World," "A Bit of Finger," "Sleeping Village," "Warning."

1971 *Paranoid* **(Warner Bros.)**
SIDE ONE: "War Pigs," "Paranoid," "Planet Caravan," "Iron Man."
SIDE TWO: "Electric Funeral," "Hand of Doom," "Rat Salad," "Fairies Wear Boots."

1971 *Master of Reality* **(Warner Bros.)**
SIDE ONE: "Sweet Leaf," "After Forever," "Embryo," "Children of the Grave."
SIDE TWO: "Orchid," "Lord of This World," "Solitude," "Into the Void."

1972 *Black Sabbath—Volume 4* **(Warner Bros.)**
SIDE ONE: "Wheels of Confusion," "Tomorrow's Dream," "Changes," "FX," "Supernaut."
SIDE TWO: "Snowblind," "Cornucopia," "Laguna Sunrise," "St. Vitus' Dance," "Under the Sun."

1973 *Sabbath, Bloody Sabbath* **(Warner Bros.)**
SIDE ONE: "Sabbath, Bloody Sabbath," "A National Acrobat," "Fluff," "Sabbra Cadabra."
SIDE TWO: "Killing Yourself to Live," "Who Are You," "Looking for Today," "Spiral Architect."

1975 *Sabotage* **(Warner Bros.)**
SIDE ONE: "Hole in the Sky," "Don't Start (Too Late)," "Symptom of the Universe," "Megalomania."
SIDE TWO: "Thrill of It All," "Supertzar," "Am I Going Insane (Radio)," "The Writ."

1976 *We Sold Our Soul for Rock 'n' Roll*
      (Warner Bros.)
SIDE ONE: "Black Sabbath," "The Wizard," "Warning."
SIDE TWO: "Paranoid," "War Pigs," "Iron Man."
SIDE THREE: "Tomorrow's Dream," "Fairies Wear Boots," "Changes," "Sweet Leaf," "Children of the Grave."
SIDE FOUR: "Sabbath, Bloody Sabbath," "Am I Going Insane (Radio)," "Laguna Sunrise," "Snowblind," "N.I.B."

1976 *Technical Ecstasy* **(Warner Bros.)**
SIDE ONE: "Back Street Kids," "You Won't Change Me," "It's Alright," "Gypsy."
SIDE TWO: "All Moving Parts (Stand Still)," "Rock 'n' Roll Doctor," "She's Gone," "Dirty Women."

1978 *Never Say Die!* **(Warner Bros.)**
SIDE ONE: "Never Say Die," "Johnny Blade," "Junior's Eyes," "A Hard Road."
SIDE TWO: "Shock Wave," "Air Dance," "Over to You," "Breakout," "Swinging the Chain."

1980 *Heaven and Hell* **(Warner Bros.)**
SIDE ONE: "Neon Knights," "Walk Away," "Heaven and Hell," "Die Young."
SIDE TWO: "Children of the Sea," "Lonely Is the Word," "Wishing Well," "Lady Evil."

1981 *Mob Rules* **(Warner Bros.)**
SIDE ONE: "Turn Up the Night," "Voodoo," "The Sign of the Southern Cross," "E5150," "The Mob Rules."
SIDE TWO: "Country Girl," "Slipping Away," "Falling off the Edge of the World," "Over and Over."

1983 *Live Evil* **(Warner Bros.)**
SIDE ONE: "E5150," "Neon Knights," "N.I.B.," "Children of the Sea," "Voodoo."
SIDE TWO: "Black Sabbath," "War Pigs," "Iron Man."
SIDE THREE: "The Mob Rules," "Heaven and Hell."
SIDE FOUR: "The Sign of the Southern Cross," "Heaven and Hell (Continued)," "Paranoid," "Children of the Grave," "Fluff."

1983 *Born Again* **(Warner Bros.)**
SIDE ONE: "Trashed," "Stonehenge," "Disturbing the Priest," "The Dark," "Zero the Hero."
SIDE TWO: "Digital Bitch," "Born Again," "Hot Line," "Keep It Warm."

OZZY OSBOURNE

1981 *Blizzard of Ozz* **(Jet)**
SIDE ONE: "I Don't Know," "Crazy Train," "Goodbye to Romance," "Dee," "Suicide Solution."
SIDE TWO: "Mr. Crowley," "No Bone Movies," "Revelation (Mother Earth)," "Steal Away (the Night)."

1981 *Diary of a Madman* **(Jet)**
SIDE ONE: "Over the Mountain," "Fly High Again," "You Can't Kill Rock & Roll."
SIDE TWO: "Believer," "Little Dolls S.A.T.O.," "Diary of a Madman."

1982 *Speak of the Devil* **(Jet)**
SIDE ONE: "Symptom of the Universe," "Snowblind," "Black Sabbath."
SIDE TWO: "Fairies Wear Boots," "War Pigs," "The Wizard."

SIDE THREE: "N.I.B.," "Sweet Leaf," "Never Say Die."
SIDE FOUR: "Sabbath, Bloody Sabbath," "Iron Man / Children of the Grave," "Paranoid."

1983 *Bark at the Moon* **(Jet)**
SIDE ONE: "Bark at the Moon," "You're No Different," "Now You See It (Now You Don't)," "Rock 'N' Roll Rebel."
SIDE TWO: "Centre of Eternity," "So Tired," "Slow Down," "Waiting for Darkness."

JUDAS PRIEST

1974 *Rocka Rolla* **(Gull, U. K.)**
SIDE ONE: "One for the Road," "Rocka Rolla," "Winter," "Deep Freeze," "Winter Retreat," "Cheater."
SIDE TWO: "Never Satisfied," "Run of the Mill," "Dying to Meet You," "Caviar & Meths."

1976 *Sad Wings of Destiny* **(Janus)**
SIDE ONE: "Prelude," "Tyrant," "Genocide," "Epitaph," "Island of Domination."
SIDE TWO: "Victim of Changes," "Ripper," "Dreamer Deceiver," "Deceiver."

1977 *Sin after Sin* **(Columbia)**
SIDE ONE: "Sinner," "Diamonds and Rust," "Starbreaker," "Last Rose of Summer."
SIDE TWO: "Let Us Prey," "Call for the Priest / Raw Deal," "Here Come the Tears," "Dissident Aggressor."

1978 *Stained Class* **(Columbia)**
SIDE ONE: "Exciter," "White Heat, Red Hot," "Better by You Better than Me," "Stained Class," "Invader."
SIDE TWO: "Saints in Hell," "Savage," "Beyond the Realms of Death," "Heroes End."

1979 *Hell Bent for Leather* **(Columbia)**
SIDE ONE: "Delivering the Goods," "Rock Forever," "Evening Star," "Hell Bent for Leather," "Take On the World."
SIDE TWO: "Burnin' Up," "The Green Manalishi (with the Two-Pronged Crown)," "Killing Machine," "Running Wild," "Before the Dawn," "Evil Fantasies."

1979 *Unleashed in the East (Live in Japan)* **(Columbia)**
SIDE ONE: "Exciter," "Running Wild," "Sinner," "Ripper," "The Green Manalishi (with the Two-Pronged Crown)."
SIDE TWO: "Diamonds and Rust," "Victim of Changes," "Genocide," "Tyrant."

1980 *British Steel* **(Columbia)**
SIDE ONE: "Breaking the Law," "Rapid Fire," "Metal Gods," "Grinder," "United."
SIDE TWO: "Living after Midnight," "Don't Have to Be Old to Be Wise," "The Rage," "Steeler."

1981 *Point of Entry* **(Columbia)**
SIDE ONE: "Heading out to the Highway," "Don't Go," "Hot Rockin'," "Turning Circles," "Desert Plains."
SIDE TWO: "Solar Angels," "You Say Yes," "All the Way," "Troubleshooter," "On the Run."

1982 *Screaming for Vengeance* **(Columbia)**
SIDE ONE: "The Hellion," "Electric Eye," "Riding on the Wind," "Bloodstone," "(Take These) Chains," "Pain and Pleasure."
SIDE TWO: "Screaming for Vengeance," "You've Got Another Thing Comin'," "Fever," "Devil's Child."

1984 *Defenders of the Faith* **(Columbia)**
SIDE ONE: "Freewheel Burning," "Jawbreaker," "Rock Hard Ride Free," "The Sentinel."
SIDE TWO: "Love Bites," "Eat Me Alive," "Some Heads Are Gonna Roll," "Night Comes Down," "Heavy Duty," "Defenders of the Faith."

SCORPIONS

1972 *Lonesome Crow* **(Brain, West Germany; released in the United States by RCA, 1976)**
SIDE ONE: "I'm Going Mad," "It All Depends," "Leave Me," "In Search of the Peace of Mind."
SIDE TWO: "Inheritance," "Action," "Lonesome Crow."

1974 *Fly to the Rainbow* **(RCA)**
SIDE ONE: "Speedy's Coming," "They Need a Million," "Drifting Sun," "Fly People Fly."
SIDE TWO: "This Is My Song," "Far Away," "Fly to the Rainbow."

1975 *In Trance* **(RCA)**
SIDE ONE: "Dark Lady," "In Trance," "Life's like a River," "Top of the Bill," "Living and Dying."
SIDE TWO: "Robot Man," "Evening Wind," "Sun in My Hand," "Longing for Fire," "Night Lights."

1976 *Virgin Killer* **(RCA)**
SIDE ONE: "Pictured Life," "Catch Your Train," "In Your Park," "Backstage Queen," "Virgin Killer."
SIDE TWO: "Hell-Cat," "Crying Days," "Polar Nights," "Yellow Raven."

1977 *Taken by Force* **(RCA)**
SIDE ONE: "Steamrock Fever," "We'll Burn the Sky," "I've Got to Be Free," "The Riot of Your Time."
SIDE TWO: "The Sails of Charon," "Your Light," "He's a Woman—She's a Man," "Born to Touch Your Feelings."

1978 *Tokyo Tapes* **(RCA)**
SIDE ONE: "All Night Long," "Pictured Life," "Backstage Queen," "Polar Nights," "In Trance."
SIDE TWO: "We'll Burn the Sky," "Suspender Love," "In Search of the Peace of Mind," "Fly to the Rainbow."
SIDE THREE: "He's a Woman—She's a Man," "Speedy's Coming," "Top of the Bill," "Hound Dog," "Long Tall Sally."
SIDE FOUR: "Steamrock Fever," "Dark Lady," "Kojo No Tsuki," "Robot Man."

1979 *Lovedrive* **(Mercury)**
SIDE ONE: "Loving You Sunday Morning," "Another Piece of Meat," "Always Somewhere," "Coast to Coast."
SIDE TWO: "Can't Get Enough," "Is There Anybody There?" "Lovedrive," "Holiday."

1979 *Best of Scorpions* **(RCA)**
SIDE ONE: "Steamrock Fever," "Pictured Life," "Robot Man," "Backstage Queen," "Speedy's Coming," "Hell Cat."
SIDE TWO: "He's a Woman—She's a Man," "In Trance," "Dark Lady," "The Sails of Charon," "Virgin Killer."

1980 *Animal Magnetism* **(Mercury)**
SIDE ONE: "Make It Real," "Don't Make No Promises (Your Body Can't Keep)," "Hold Me Tight," "Twentieth Century Man," "Lady Starlight."
SIDE TWO: "Falling in Love," "Only a Man," "The Zoo," "Animal Magnetism."

1982 *Blackout* **(Mercury)**
SIDE ONE: "Blackout," "Can't Live without You," "No One like You," "You Give Me All I Need," "Now!"
SIDE TWO: "Dynamite," "Arizona," "China White," "When the Smoke Is Going Down."

1984 *Love at First Sting* **(Mercury)**
SIDE ONE: "Bad Boys Running Wild," "Rock You like a Hurricane," "I'm Leaving You," "Coming Home," "The Same Thrill."
SIDE TWO: "Big City Nights," "As Soon as the Good Times Roll," "Crossfire," "Still Loving You."

1984 *Best of Scorpions, Vol. 2* **(RCA)**
SIDE ONE: "Top of the Bill," "They Need a Million," "Longing for Fire," "Catch Your Train," "Speedy's Coming (Live)," "Crying Days."
SIDE TWO: "All Night Long (Live)," "This Is My Song," "Sun in My Hand," "We'll Burn the Sky (Live)."

RUSH

1974 *Rush* (Moon/Mercury)
SIDE ONE: "Finding My Way," "Need Some Love," "Take a Friend," "Here Again."
SIDE TWO: "What You're Doing," "In the Mood," "Before and After," "Working Man."

1975 *Fly by Night* (Mercury)
SIDE ONE: "Anthem," "Best I Can," "Beneath, Between, & Behind," "By-Tor & the Snow Dog (I. At the Tobes of Hades; II. Across the Styx; III. Of the Battle; IV. Epilogue)."
SIDE TWO: "Fly by Night," "Making Memories," "Rivendell," "In the End."

1975 *Caress of Steel* (Mercury)
SIDE ONE: "Bastille Day," "I Think I'm Going Bald," "Lakeside Park," "The Necromancer."
SIDE TWO: "In the Valley," "Didacts and Narpets," "No One at the Bridge," "Panacea," "Bacchus Plateau," "The Fountain."

1976 *2112* (Mercury)
SIDE ONE: "2112 (I. Overture; II. The Temples of Syrinx; III. Discovery; IV. Presentation; V. Oracle: The Dream; VI. Soliloquy; VII. Grand Finale)."
SIDE TWO: "A Passage to Bangkok," "The Twilight Zone," "Lessons," "Tears," "Something for Nothing."

1976 *All the World's a Stage* (Mercury)
SIDE ONE: "Bastille Day," "Anthem," "Fly by Night," "In the Mood," "Something for Nothing."
SIDE TWO: "Lakeside Park," "2112 (Overture; The Temples of Syrinx; Presentation; Soliloquy; Grand Finale)."
SIDE THREE: "By-Tor & the Snow Dog," "In the End."
SIDE FOUR: "Working Man," "Finding My Way," "What You're Doing."

1977 *A Farewell to Kings* (Mercury)
SIDE ONE: "A Farewell to Kings," "Xanadu."
SIDE TWO: "Closer to the Heart," "Cinderella Man," "Madrigal," "Cygnus X-1."

1978 *Archives* (Mercury)
SIDE ONE: "Finding My Way," "Need Some Love," "Take a Friend," "Here Again."
SIDE TWO: "What You're Doing," "In the Mood," "Before and After," "Working Man."
SIDE THREE: "Anthem," "Best I Can," "Beneath, Between & Behind," "By-Tor & the Snow Dog."
SIDE FOUR: "Fly by Night," "Making Memories," "Rivendell," "In the End."
SIDE FIVE: "Bastille Day," "I Think I'm Going Bald," "Lakeside Park," "The Necromancer."
SIDE SIX: "In the Valley," "Didacts and Narpets," "No One at the Bridge," "Panacea," "Bacchus Plateau," "The Fountain."

1978 *Hemispheres* (Mercury)
SIDE ONE: "Cygnus X-1 Book II," "Hemispheres (I. Prelude; II. Apollo, Bringer of Wisdom; III. Dionysus, Bringer of Love; IV. Armageddon, the Battle of the Heart and Mind; V. Cygnus, Bringer of Balance; VI. The Sphere, a Kind of Dream)."
SIDE TWO: "Circumstances," "The Trees," "La Villa Strangiato."

1980 *Permanent Waves* (Mercury)
SIDE ONE: "The Spirit of Radio," "Freewill," "Jacob's Ladder."
SIDE TWO: "Entre Nous," "Different Strings," "Natural Science."

1981 *Moving Pictures* (Mercury)
SIDE ONE: "Tom Sawyer," "Red Barchetta," "YYZ," "Limelight."
SIDE TWO: "The Camera Eye," "Witch Hunt," "Vital Signs."

1981 *Exit . . . Stage Left* (Mercury)
SIDE ONE: "The Spirit of Radio," "Red Barchetta," "YYZ."
SIDE TWO: "A Passage to Bangkok," "Closer to the Heart," "Beneath, Between, & Behind," "Jacob's Ladder."
SIDE THREE: "Broon's Bane," "The Trees," "Xanadu."
SIDE FOUR: "Freewill," "Tom Sawyer," "La Villa Strangiato."

1982 *Signals* (Mercury)
SIDE ONE: "Subdivisions," "The Analog Kid," "Chemistry," "Digital Man."
SIDE TWO: "The Weapon," "New World Man," "Losing It," "Countdown."

1984 *Grace under Pressure* (Mercury)
SIDE ONE: "Distant Early Warning," "Afterimage," "Red Sector A," "The Enemy Within."
SIDE TWO: "The Body Electric," "Kid Gloves," "Red Lenses," "Between the Wheels."

AC/DC

1976 *High Voltage* (Atlantic)
SIDE ONE: "It's a Long Way to the Top (If You Wanna Rock 'n' Roll)," "Rock 'n' Roll Singer," "The Jack," "Live Wire."
SIDE TWO: "T.N.T," "Can I Sit Next to You Girl," "Little Lover," "She's Got Balls," "High Voltage."

1977 *Let There Be Rock* **(Atlantic)**
SIDE ONE: "Go Down," "Dog Eat Dog," "Let There Be Rock," "Bad Boy Boogie."
SIDE TWO: "Overdose," "Crabsody in Blue," "Hell Ain't a Bad Place to Be," "Whole Lotta Rosie."

1978 *Powerage* **(Atlantic)**
SIDE ONE: "Gimme a Bullet," "Down Payment Blues," "Gone Shootin'," "Riff Raff."
SIDE TWO: "Sin City," "Up to My Neck in You," "What's Next to the Moon," "Cold Hearted Man," "Kicked in the Teeth."

1978 *If You Want Blood You've Got It* **(Atlantic)**
SIDE ONE: "Riff Raff," "Hell Ain't a Bad Place to Be," "Bad Boy Boogie," "The Jack," "Problem Child."
SIDE TWO: "Whole Lotta Rosie," "Rock 'n' Roll Damnation," "High Voltage," "Let There Be Rock," "Rocker."

1979 *Highway to Hell* **(Atlantic)**
SIDE ONE: "Highway to Hell," "Girls Got Rhythm," "Walk All over You," "Touch Too Much," "Beating around the Bush."
SIDE TWO: "Shot Down in Flames," "Get It Hot," "If You Want Blood (You've Got It)," "Love Hungry Man," "Night Prowler."

1980 *Back in Black* **(Atlantic)**
SIDE ONE: "Hells Bells," "Shoot to Thrill," "What Do You Do for Money Honey," "Given the Dog a Bone," "Let Me Put My Love into You."
SIDE TWO: "Back in Black," "You Shook Me All Night Long," "Have a Drink on Me," "Shake a Leg," "Rock and Roll Ain't Noise Pollution."

1981 *Dirty Deeds Done Dirt Cheap* **(Atlantic; originally released in Australia in 1976)**
SIDE ONE: "Dirty Deeds Done Dirt Cheap," "Love at First Feel," "Big Balls," "Rocker," "Problem Child."
SIDE TWO: "There's Gonna Be Some Rockin'," "Ain't No Fun (Waiting round to Be a Millionaire)," "Ride On," "Squealer."

1981 *For Those About to Rock We Salute You* **(Atlantic)**
SIDE ONE: "For Those About to Rock (We Salute You)," "Put the Finger on You," "Let's Get It Up," "Inject the Venom," "Snowballed."
SIDE TWO: "Evil Walks," "C.O.D.," "Breaking the Rules," "Night of the Long Knives," "Spellbound."

1983 *Flick of the Switch* **(Atlantic)**
SIDE ONE: "Rising Power," "The House Is on Fire," "Flick of the Switch," "Nervous Shakedown," "Landslide."
SIDE TWO: "Guns for Hire," "Deep in the Hole," "Bedlam in Belgium," "Badlands," "Brain Shake."

1984 *'74 Jailbreak* **(EP) (Atlantic)**
SIDE ONE: "Jailbreak," "You Ain't Got a Hold on Me," "Show Business."
SIDE TWO: "Soul Stripper," "Baby, Please Don't Go."

VAN HALEN

1978 *Van Halen* **(Warner Bros.)**
SIDE ONE: "Runnin' with the Devil," "Eruption," "You Really Got Me," "Ain't Talkin' 'bout Love," "I'm the One."
SIDE TWO: "Jamie's Cryin'," "Atomic Punk," "Feel Your Love Tonight," "Little Dreamer," "Ice Cream Man," "On Fire."

1979 *Van Halen II* **(Warner Bros.)**
SIDE ONE: "You're No Good," "Dance the Night Away," "Somebody Get Me a Doctor," "Bottoms Up!," "Outta Love Again."
SIDE TWO: "Light Up the Sky," "Spanish Fly," "D.O.A.," "Women in Love," "Beautiful Girls."

1980 *Women and Children First* **(Warner Bros.)**
SIDE ONE: "And the Cradle Will Rock," "Everybody Wants Some," "Fools," "Romeo Delight."
SIDE TWO: "Tora! Tora!," "Loss of Control," "Take Your Whiskey Home," "Could This Be Magic?," "In a Simple Rhyme."

1981 *Fair Warning* **(Warner Bros.)**
SIDE ONE: "Mean Street," "'Dirty Movies'," "Sinner's Swing," "Hear about It Later."
SIDE TWO: "Unchained," "Push Comes to Shove," "So This Is Love?," "Sunday Afternoon in the Park," "One Foot out the Door."

1982 *Diver Down* **(Warner Bros.)**
SIDE ONE: "Where Have All the Good Times Gone!," "Hang 'em High Cathedral," "Secrets," "Intruder," "(Oh) Pretty Woman."
SIDE TWO: "Dancing in the Street," "Little Guitars (Intro)," "Little Guitars," "Big Bad Bill (Is Sweet William Now)," "The Full Bug," "Happy Trails."

1984 *1984* **(Warner Bros.)**
SIDE ONE: "1984," "Jump," "Panama," "Top Jimmy," "Drop Dead Legs."
SIDE TWO: "Hot for Teacher," "I'll Wait," "Girl Gone Bad," "House of Pain."

IRON MAIDEN

1980 *Iron Maiden* (Capitol)
SIDE ONE: "Prowler," "Remember Tomorrow," "Running Free," "Phantom of the Opera."
SIDE TWO: "Transylvania," "Strange World," "Sanctuary," "Charlotte the Harlot," "Iron Maiden."

1981 *Killers* (Capitol)
SIDE ONE: "The Ides of March," "Wrathchild," "Murders in the Rue Morgue," "Another Life," "Genghis Khan," "Innocent Exile."
SIDE TWO: "Killers," "Twilight Zone," "Prodigal Son," "Purgatory," "Drifter."

1981 *Maiden Japan* (EP) (Capitol)
SIDE ONE: "Running Free," "Remember Tomorrow."
SIDE TWO: "Wrathchild," "Killers," "Innocent Exile."

1982 *The Number of the Beast* (Capitol)
SIDE ONE: "Invaders," "Children of the Damned," "The Prisoner," "22 Acacia Avenue."
SIDE TWO: "The Number of the Beast," "Run to the Hills," "Gangland," "Hallowed Be Thy Name."

1983 *Piece of Mind* (Capitol)
SIDE ONE: "Where Eagles Dare," "Revelations," "Flight of Icarus," "Die with Your Boots On."
SIDE TWO: "The Trooper," "Still Life," "Quest for Fire," "Sun and Steel," "To Tame a Land."

1984 *Powerslave* (Capitol)
SIDE ONE: "Aces High," "2 Minutes to Midnight," "Losfer Words (Big 'Orra)," "Flash of the Blade," "The Duellists."
SIDE TWO: "Back in the Village," "Powerslave," "Rime of the Ancient Mariner."

DEF LEPPARD

1980 *On through the Night* (Mercury)
SIDE ONE: "Rock Brigade," "Hello America," "Sorrow Is a Woman," "It Could Be You," "Satellite," "When the Walls Came Tumbling Down."
SIDE TWO: "Wasted," "Rocks Off," "It Don't Matter," "Answer to the Master," "Overture."

1981 *High 'N' Dry* (Mercury)
SIDE ONE: "Let It Go," "Another Hit and Run," "High 'N' Dry (Saturday Night)," "Bringin' On the Heartbreak," "Switch," "Me & My Wine."

SIDE TWO: "Bringin' On the Heartbreak (Remix)," "You Got Me Runnin'," "Lady Strange," "On through the Night," "Mirror, Mirror (Look into My Eyes)," "No No No."

1983 *Pyromania* (Polygram)
SIDE ONE: "Rock! Rock! (till You Drop)," "Photograph," "Stagefright," "Too Late for Love," "Die Hard the Hunter."
SIDE TWO: "Foolin'," "Rock of Ages," "Comin' under Fire," "Action! Not Words," "Billy's Got a Gun."

QUIET RIOT

1983 *Metal Health* (Pasha)
SIDE ONE: "Metal Health," "Cum On Feel the Noize," "Don't Wanna Let You Go," "Slick Black Cadillac," "Love's a Bitch."
SIDE TWO: "Breathless," "Run for Cover," "Battleaxe," "Let's Get Crazy," "Thunderbird."

1984 *Condition Critical* (Pasha)
SIDE ONE: "Sign of the Times," "Mama Weer All Crazee Now," "Party All Night," "Stomp Your Hands, Clap Your Feet," "Winners Take All."
SIDE TWO: "Condition Critical," "Scream and Shout," "Red Alert," "Bad Boy," "(We Were) Born to Rock."

MOTLEY CRUE

1982 *Too Fast for Love* (Elektra; originally released in 1981 on Leathur Records)
SIDE ONE: "Live Wire," "Come On and Dance," "Public Enemy #1," "Merry-Go-Round," "Take Me to the Top."
SIDE TWO: "Piece of Your Action," "Starry Eyes," "Too Fast for Love," "On with the Show."

1983 *Shout at the Devil* (Elektra)
SIDE ONE: "In the Beginning," "Shout at the Devil," "Looks That Kill," "Bastard," "God Bless the Children of the Beast," "Helter Skelter."
SIDE TWO: "Red Hot," "Too Young to Fall in Love," "Knock 'Em Dead, Kid," "Ten Seconds to Love," "Danger."

Index

Move, 37, 49
Murray, Dave, 53, 54, 141, 142, 150
Mushrooms, 74
Mythology, 37

Nazareth, 25
Neil, Vince, 188, 191-192
Nena, 70
Newton, Helmut, 130
Newton-John, Olivia, 97
New Yardbirds, 18, 20
New York Dolls, 35
Nicholas, Andy, 154
Night Ranger, 48
Noone, Frank, 154
Nugent, Ted, 26, 76, 100, 156

Ohio Players, 110
Orbison, Roy, 134
Orwell, George, 43
Osbourne, Ozzy, 29, 34, 36-49, 68, 159, 163, 164, 170-171, 192
Osbourne, Thelma, 43, 46, 48
Ostin, Mo, 127

Page, Jimmy, 17-18, 20, 22, 23, 24, 28, 84, 101, 154
Paice, Ian, 26
Pappalardi, Felix, 23
Parson, Tony, 142
Pat Travers Band, 44, 150, 156
Peart, Neil, 82, 85-86, 88, 89-92
Peebles, Andy, 154
Perry, Joe, 7, 28
Peterson, Dickie, 20
Phillips, Simon, 52
Pink Floyd, 86, 88, 93
Piper, 33
Plank, Conny, 75
Plant, Robert, 18, 20, 23, 28, 30, 84, 145
Plimsouls, 167
Poe, Edgar Allan, 140, 146
Police, 91
Pop, 167
Presley, Elvis, 6, 12, 49, 74-75, 95
Pretty Things, 74, 141
Proffer, Spencer, 162-163

Queen, 27, 28, 136
Queensryche, 71
Quiet Riot, 9, 34, 35, 44, 162-183

Ralphs, Mick, 26
Ramones, 29
Rand, Ayn, 82, 85
Rarebell, Herman, 71, 76, 81
Rare Breed, 37
Ratt, 35, 48, 170
Rattles, 71
Redding, Noel, 14
Redding, Otis, 23
Reddy, Helen, 97
Reed, Lou, 28
Relf, Keith, 18, 23
REO Speedwagon, 33
Rhoads, Randy, 44, 46, 48, 163, 164, 166-167, 170-171
Richard, Cliff, 17
Richards, Keith, 12-13, 28, 30
Rock Candy, 188
Rock Goddess, 30

Rodgers, Paul, 20, 26
Rolling Stones, 12-13, 17, 20, 28, 95, 100, 101, 103, 134
Rondinelli, Bobby, 81
Ronstadt, Linda, 128
Rosenthal, Jurgen, 75
Rose Tattoo, 35
Roth, David Lee, 24, 108-110, 127, 128, 130-131, 134, 136-137, 139
Roth, Johann, 76
Roth, Ulrich, 75, 76, 81
Rotten, Johnny, 101
Roxy Music, 52
Rudd, Phil, 97, 101, 107
Runaways, 30
Rush, 52, 82-93, 171
Russell, Ken, 140
Rutsey, John, 82, 85

Samson, 29, 143
Samson, Doug, 142
Samwell-Smith, Paul, 17
Santana, 110
Sarzo, Rudy, 44, 46, 48, 163-164, 166-167, 170-171
Savage , Rick, 152, 154
Savoy Brown, 141
Saxon, 29, 35
Schenker, Michael, 74, 75, 76-77, 80-81
Schenker, Rudolf, 70-71, 72, 74, 75-77, 80-81
Scorpions, 12, 29-30, 34, 44, 52, 54, 70-72, 74-81, 171
Scott, Bon, 97, 100-101, 103-104, 106
Searchers, 71
Sex Pistols, 29, 101
Seymour, Phil, 167
Shirley, Jerry, 35
Sidewinders, 33
Simmons, Gene, 27, 28, 127, 146, 189
Simon, Paul, 89
Sir Lord Baltimore, 25
Sixx, Nikki, 146, 174, 185, 188-193
Slade, 150, 162, 164, 171-172, 183, 189
Slick, Grace, 30
Smiler, 141
Smith, Adrian, 53, 54, 142, 146, 150
Smith, Bessie, 30
Snider, Dee, 9
Snow, 167, 170
South, Joe, 26
Sparks, 110
Spector, Phil, 30
Squier, Billy, 33, 159, 160
Stanley, Paul, 9, 28, 146, 189
Starr, Ringo, 13
Starz, 142
Steinman, Jim, 160
Stephens, Leigh, 20
Steppenwolf, 4
Stewart, Rod, 17, 23, 163-164
Stockhausen, Karlheinz, 74
Stratton, Dennis, 142
Streetwalkers, 150
Suite 19, 188
Summers, Andy, 91
Sweet, 189

Tangerine Dream, 74
Taylor, James, 21
Taylor, Roger, 28
Templeman, Ted, 127, 128

Ten Years After, 20
Thin Lizzy, 154
Tipton, Glenn, 50, 52, 53-54, 63, 66-67
Torme, Bernie, 48
Townshend, Pete, 11, 13-14, 52, 134
Trapeze, 54
T. Rex, 154
Triumph, 7, 30, 34
Trust, 150
20/20, 167
Twisted Sister, 9, 34, 35
Tygers of Pan Tang, 29
Tyler, Bonnie, 160
Tyler, Steve, 7, 28

UFO, 75, 76-77, 80, 110
Ultravox, 91
Urchin, 142
Uriah Heep, 44, 156

Valentine, Kathy, 30
Vanda, Harry, 104, 107
Van Halen, 9, 13, 24, 29, 34, 43, 44, 63, 108, 127-139, 162, 167, 171
Van Halen, Alex, 108, 110, 128, 134, 139
Van Halen, Eddie, 17, 108, 110, 127-128, 131, 134, 136-137, 139
Van Halen, Jan, 110

Wagner, Richard, 72
Walker, Dave, 43
Walsh, Joe, 154
Ward, Bill, 37, 38, 40, 41, 43-44, 49
Warhol, Andy, 53
Wasp, 35
Waters, Muddy, 12-13, 16
Webster, Max, 30
Wenner, Jann, 23
Werman, Tom, 192
West, Leslie, 22-23
Whaley, Paul, 20
Whitesnake, 29
Whitford, Brad, 28
Who, 10, 13-14, 16, 17, 20, 52, 172
Wilcox, Dennis, 142
Williams, Cliff, 103
Williams, Jake, 48
Williams, Joe, 100
Willis, Pete, 53, 154, 156, 157-158
Wilson, Ann, 30
Wilson, Nancy, 30
Wishbone Ash, 141
Wood, Ron, 17
Wozniak, Steve, 34
Wray, Link, 12, 13
Wright, Chuck, 170
Wright, Simon, 107

Y&T, 35, 188
Yardbirds, 11, 16, 17-18, 23, 28, 38, 74, 75, 95-96
Yes, 85, 86
Young, Angus, 94-97, 101, 103, 104, 106, 107, 154
Young, George, 95, 104, 107
Young, Malcolm, 95-97, 101, 104
Young, Neil, 83
Youngblood, Rachel, 46, 48

Zappa, Frank, 26, 88
Zebra, 35

Credits

⊂⊃ ⊂⊃ ⊂⊃

LYRIC CREDITS

"Anthem" by Neil Peart, Geddy Lee, and Alex Lifeson, Copyright © 1975 Core Music Publishing.

"Baby, Please Don't Go" by Joe Williams, Copyright © 1944, 1963 MCA Music.

"Back in Black" by Malcolm Young, Angus Young, and Brian Johnson, Copyright © 1980 J. Albert Ltd./Marks Music.

"Bad Boys Running Wild" by Klaus Meine, Herman Rarebell, and Rudolf Schenker, Copyright © 1984 Summer Breeze Music.

"Beneath, Between, & Behind" by Neil Peart, Geddy Lee, and Alex Lifeson, Copyright © 1975 Core Music Publishing.

"Big Balls" by Malcolm Young, Angus Young, and Bon Scott, Copyright © 1976 J. Albert & Sons Ltd.

"Children of the Grave" by F. Iommi, W. Ward, T. Butler, and J. Osbourne, Copyright © 1972 TRO-Essex Music International, Inc.

"Come On and Dance" by Nikki Sixx, Copyright © 1981 Warner-Tamerlane Publishing Corp./Motley Crue Publishing.

"Danger" by Nikki Sixx, Mick Mars, and Vince Neil, Copyright © 1983 Warner-Tamerlane Publishing Corp./Motley Crue Music.

"Eat Me Alive" by Glenn Tipton, Rob Halford, and K. K. Downing, Copyright © 1984 April Music, Inc., Crewglen Ltd., Ebonytree Ltd., and Geargate Ltd.

"Hallowed Be Thy Name" by Steve Harris, Copyright © 1982 Zomba Music Publishers Ltd.

"Have a Drink on Me" by Malcolm Young, Angus Young, and Brian Johnson, Copyright © 1980 J. Albert Ltd./Marks Music.

"Heavy Duty" by Glenn Tipton, Rob Halford, and K. K. Downing, Copyright © 1984 April Music, Inc., Crewglen Ltd., Ebonytree Ltd., and Geargate Ltd.

"Let There Be Rock" by Malcolm Young, Angus Young, and Bon Scott, Copyright © 1977 J. Albert & Sons Ltd.

"Limelight" by Neil Peart, Geddy Lee, and Alex Lifeson, Copyright © 1981 Core Music Publishing.

"Live Wire" by Nikki Sixx, Copyright © 1981 Warner-Tamerlane Publishing Corp./Motley Crue Publishing.

"Me & My Wine" by Rick Savage, Steve Clark, and Joe Elliott, Copyright © 1981 Zomba Enterprises, Inc.

"My Generation" by Peter Townshend, Copyright © 1965 Fabulous Music Ltd., Seven Musics, Inc.

"The Number of the Beast" by Steve Harris, Copyright © 1982 Zomba Music Publishers Ltd.

"Rock Hard, Ride Free" by Glenn Tipton, Rob Halford, and K. K. Downing, Copyright © 1984 April Music, Inc., Crewglen Ltd., Ebonytree Ltd., and Geargate Ltd.

"Rock 'N' Roll Rebel" by Ozzy Osbourne, Copyright © 1983 Nymph Music, Inc.

"Rock 'N' Roll Singer" by Malcolm Young, Angus Young, and Bon Scott, Copyright © 1976 J. Albert & Sons Ltd.

"Rock of Ages" by Steve Clark, Robert John "Mutt" Lange, and Joe Elliott, Copyright © 1983 Zomba Enterprises, Inc.

"She's Got Balls" by Malcolm Young, Angus Young, and Bon Scott, Copyright © 1976 J. Albert & Sons Ltd.

"Show Business" by Malcolm Young, Angus Young, and Bon Scott, Copyright © 1975 J. Albert & Sons.

"Some Heads Are Gonna Roll" by Bob Halligan, Jr., Copyright © 1983 Screen Gems-EMI Music, Inc.

"The Spirit of Radio" by Neil Peart, Geddy Lee, and Alex Lifeson, Copyright © 1980 Core Music Publishing.

"Stairway to Heaven" by Jimmy Page and Robert Plant, Copyright © 1971 Superhype Music, Inc.

"Subdivisions" by Neil Peart, Geddy Lee, and Alex Lifeson, Copyright © 1982 Core Music Publishing.

"Ten Seconds to Love" by Nikki Sixx and Vince Neil, Copyright © 1983 Warner-Tamerlane Publishing Corp./Motley Crue Music.

"Too Young to Fall in Love" by Nikki Sixx, Copyright © 1983 Warner-Tamerlane Publishing Corp./Motley Crue Music.

"The Trooper" by Steve Harris, Copyright © 1983 Zomba Music Publishers Ltd.

"2 Minutes to Midnight" by Adrian Smith and Bruce Dickinson, Copyright © 1984 Iron Maiden Publishing Ltd. and Zomba Enterprises, Inc.

"2112" by Neil Peart, Geddy Lee, and Alex Lifeson, Copyright © 1976 Core Music Publishing.

"War Pigs" by F. Iommi, W. Ward, T. Butler, and J. Osbourne, Copyright © 1970 TRO-Andover Music, Inc.

"Wasted" by Steve Clark and Joe Elliott, Copyright © 1980 Def Lepp/Marksman Music Ltd.

"Whole Lotta Rosie" by Malcolm Young, Angus Young, and Bon Scott, Copyright © 1977 J. Albert & Sons, Ltd.

"Winners Take All" by Kevin DuBrow, Copyright © 1984 The Grand Pasha Publisher.

"The Wizard" by F. Iommi, W. Ward, T. Butler, and J. Osbourne, Copyright © 1970 TRO-Andover Music, Inc.

PHOTO CREDITS

(ii-iii, vi, viii, 3) Copyright © 1984 Ross Marino; (5) Copyright © 1980 M. Snake/LGI; (10) Copyright © 1985 Paul Natkin/Photo Reserve; (15) Michael Ochs Archives; (16) Copyright © 1983 Chris Walter/Retna Ltd.; (18-19) Copyright © 1985 Neal Preston; (21) Michael Ochs Archives; (22) Michael Ochs Archives; (25) Michael Ochs Archives; (27) Copyright © 1980 Lynn Goldsmith/LGI; (31) Copyright © 1985 Paul Natkin/Photo Reserve; (32-33) Copyright © 1984 Mark Weiss; (37) Copyright © 1985 LFI/Retna Ltd.; (39) Copyright © 1984 Ross Marino; (41) Copyright © 1983 Ebet Roberts; (42) Copyright © 1981 M. Snake/LGI; (45) Copyright © 1985 Paul Natkin/Photo Reserve; (47) Copyright © 1985 Paul Natkin/Photo Reserve; (51) Copyright © 1984 Ebet Roberts; (53) Copyright © 1985 Chris Walter/Retna Ltd.; (55) Copyright © 1984 Mark Weiss; (56-57) Copyright © 1985 Mark Weiss; (57) Copyright © 1985 John Bellissimo/Retna Ltd.; (58-59) Copyright © 1984 Mark Weiss; (60) Copyright © 1984 Mark Weiss; (61) Copyright © 1984 Mark Weiss; (62) Copyright © 1984 Ebet Roberts; (64-65) Copyright © 1982 Ross Marino; (67) Copyright © 1982 Laurie Paladino; (68-69) Copyright © 1981 Lynn Goldsmith/LGI; (71) Copyright © 1985 LFI/Retna Ltd.; (72-73) Copyright © 1984 Ross Marino; (77) Copyright © 1982 Ebet Roberts; (78-79) Copyright © 1984 Ross Marino; (83) Mercury/Polygram Records; (84) Copyright © 1985 Fin Costello/Retna Ltd.; (87) Copyright © 1985 Paul Natkin/Photo Reserve; (90) Copyright © 1983 Debra Trebitz/LGI; (93) Copyright © 1984 Gary Gershoff/Retna Ltd.; (95) Copyright © 1984 Ross Marino; (96) Copyright © 1977 Ebet Roberts; (98-99) Atlantic Records; (102-103) Copyright © 1985 Paul Natkin/Photo Reserve; (105) Copyright © 1983 Tami Langan/LGI; (109) Copyright © 1985 Paul Canty/Retna Ltd.; (111) Copyright © 1984 Mark Weiss; (112-113) Copyright © 1985 Gary Gershoff/Retna Ltd.; (113) Copyright © 1984 Mark Weiss; (114-115) Copyright © 1984 Patrick Harbron/LGI; (116) Copyright © 1983 Mark Weiss; (116-117) Copyright © 1983 Ross Marino; (118) Copyright © 1981 Mark Weiss; (119) Copyright © 1984 Ebet Roberts; (120-121) Copyright © 1984 Laurie Paladino; (122-123) Copyright © 1984 Michael D'Adamo/Retna Ltd.; (124-125) Copyright © 1984 Mark Weiss; (125) Copyright © 1981 Mark Weiss; (126) Copyright © 1983 Laurie Paladino; (129) Copyright © 1984 Ross Marino; (130) Copyright © 1981 Lynn Goldsmith/LGI; (132-133) Copyright © 1984 Ross Marino; (135) Copyright © 1984 Mark Weiss; (137) Copyright © 1984 Ross Marino; (138) Copyright © 1985 Lynn Goldsmith/LGI; (141) Copyright © 1985 Simon Fowler/LFI/Retna Ltd.; (143) Copyright © 1981 Ebet Roberts; (147) Copyright © 1983 Laurie Paladino; (148-149) Copyright © 1984 Ross Marino; (153) Copyright © 1985 Chris Walter/Retna Ltd.; (155) Copyright © 1985 Adrian Boot/Retna Ltd.; (158) Copyright © 1983 Laurie Paladino; (161) Copyright © 1983 Laurie Paladino; (163) Copyright © 1983 Laurie Paladino; (165) Copyright © 1983 Ron Wolfson/LGI; (166) Copyright © 1983 Laurie Paladino; (168-169) Copyright © 1985 Paul Natkin/Photo Reserve; (172-173) Copyright © 1983 Laurie Paladino; (175) Copyright © 1984 Ross Marino; (176-177) Copyright © 1983 Laurie Paladino; (178) Copyright © 1985 Paul Cox/Retna; (179) Copyright © 1983 Mark Weiss; (180) Copyright © 1984 Laurie Paladino; (180-181) Copyright © 1984 Mark Weiss; (182) Copyright © 1984 Ebet Roberts; (185) Copyright © 1984 Ebet Roberts; (186-187) Copyright © 1984 Laurie Paladino; (189) Copyright © 1984 Ebet Roberts; (190) Copyright © 1984 Ross Marino; (193) Copyright © Ann Summa/Retna Ltd.

cacaca

PHILIP BASHE is currently the managing editor of *International Musician and Recording World*. Previous to that, he held senior editing positions with *Circus*, *Good Times*, and *Focus*, and published his own magazine, *Foxtrot*. His work has appeared in *Trouser Press*, *On Your Own*, and the *Buffalo Evening News*, and he was a contributor to *The Rolling Stone Rock Almanac*. In addition to his career as a writer, he has worked as an FM radio announcer, television news director, and leader of the ill-fated pop band the Pathetics.

ROB HALFORD is the lead singer of Judas Priest.

Heavy Metal Thunder was produced by Sarah Lazin Books. It was designed and its production overseen by Kathleen Westray and Ed Sturmer of Printing Productions, New York City. The text was set in Bodoni Book with display type in Poster Bodoni and Bodoni Bold by Mackenzie-Harris Corp., San Francisco.

Front cover photograph of Marcel LaFleur of Smashed Gladys Copyright © 1985 Mark Weiss.

Studio assistance and lighting, Harry Barone; makeup and costume, Sally Cato.

Special thanks to Randy Cullers of Gibson Guitars for the Gibson Flying V.